D1490887

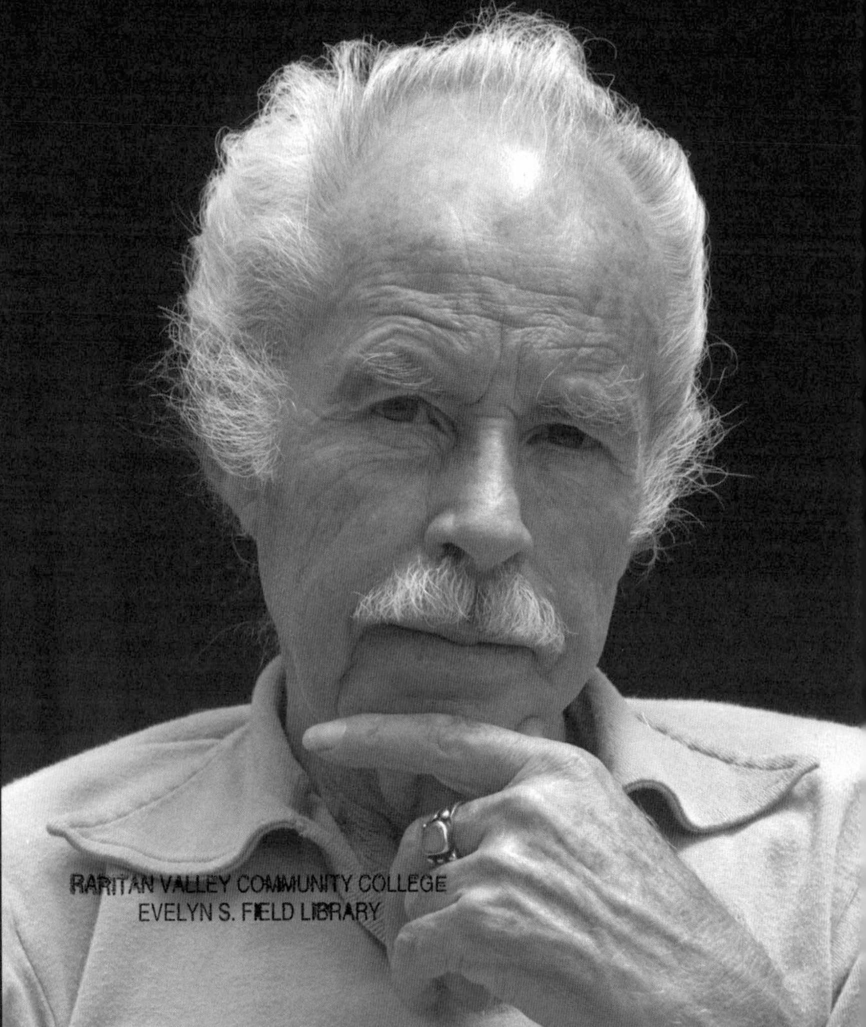

Wright Morris Territory

A TREASURY OF WORK

WRIGHT MORRIS

Edited by David Madden
with Alicia Christensen

Biographical Sketch by Joseph J. Wydeven

University of Nebraska Press ~ Lincoln and London

Source acknowledgments for previously published material appear on
pages 301–2, which constitute an
extension of the copyright page.

© 2011 by the Board of Regents of
the University of Nebraska

∞
Library of Congress
Cataloging-in-Publication
Data

Morris, Wright, 1910–1998.
Wright Morris territory: a treasury
of work / Wright Morris; edited
by David Madden with Alicia
Christensen; biographical sketch by
Joseph J. Wydeven.
p. cm.
Includes bibliographical references.
ISBN 978-0-8032-3658-5 (pbk.: alk.
paper)
I. Madden, David, 1933–
II. Christensen, Alicia, 1978–
III. Title.
PS3525.O7475A6   2011
813.52—dc22   2011014151

Set in Quadraat by Kim Essman.
Designed by R. W. Boeche.

Contents

Editor's Introduction

The American Land, Character, and Dream
in the Works of Wright Morris

DAVID MADDEN

One senses in Wright Morris's novels the abiding presence of his Nebraska childhood. But Morris is not "regionalist" in the narrow sense. He writes about Nebraska only as it represents conflicting extremes in the American land and character. Landscapes, houses, and inhabitants on the Great Plains become metaphors of the American Dream. "The emptiness of the plain generates illusions that require little moisture, and grow better, like tall stories, where the mind is dry." Standing in the wasteland of the present, dreaming of a heroic past, some men and women become blighted victims of the "poison of the Great American Myth." Bringing into focus a representative part of America, Morris seeks the meaning of the legends, myths, and realities of America as they survive and prevail today in the minds of common people.

In *The Field of Vision* the question is posed: Did one live on the plains in spite of the fact that the conditions were terrible? "No, one lived there *because* of it. Only where fools rushed in were such things as heroes bred." These conditions, says Morris, produce "the power to transform. . . . The budding hero found it more than enough." In Morris's early books the reader may perceive that the plains, despite their adverse effects, produced a breed of men both positively and negatively charged. In Lone Tree, Nebraska, the American Dream and the American East-West conflict have become fossilized. With its imagination responding to the magnet of the fabled West, the frontier that no longer exists, and its back turned toward the industrial East, Lone Tree is a perfect manifestation of an American tendency to build great technological complexities but to gaze in the direction of dreams. "There never was a people who tried so hard—and left so little behind as we do. There never was a people who traveled so light—and carried so much" (*The Inhabitants*).

In *The Territory Ahead*, a literary study, Morris focuses on what he conceives to be the major fault in American writers of genius and in their imitators: the inability to transform, through imagination, technique, and conception, the raw material of experience, with the result that the writer becomes trapped in a mythic past unable to move on to the territory ahead—the living present. In the faults of the masters whom he discusses, Morris recognizes his own: "The realization that I had to create coherence, conjure up my synthesis, rather than find it, came to me, as it does to most Americans, disturbingly late. . . . It is the territory behind that defeats our writers of genius, not America. . . . In a way my books show the development of an escape from nostalgia." In his first six novels Morris is immersed in the raw material of his past; in all the others he is moving toward the territory ahead. "Since he must live and have his being in a world of clichés, he will know it by the fact that he has not been there before. The true territory ahead is what he must imagine for himself. . . . It seems to be the nature of man to transform—himself, if possible, and then the world around him—and the technique of this transformation is what we call art. . . . Both talent and imagination are of little value" without the conception that transforms.

A central, recurring theme in Morris's novels, around which many other themes revolve and through which his vision is often focused, is the relationship between the hero and his witness. The hero is the character with whose effect on the other characters most of the novels are concerned; usually he is not the main character in the ordinary sense and his is not the dominant point of view. The witnesses are those characters who become in some way transformed as a result of their relationship with the hero, whose powers derive from audacity and improvisation. He or she makes the act of transformation possible, but before that act can occur, the witnesses must achieve imagination and compassion.

My Uncle Dudley (1942), Morris's first novel, is a wryly humorous chronicle of an odyssey The Kid—the unnamed adolescent narrator—and his Uncle Dudley make across country in an old Marmon touring car with seven men who share expenses. The car is a gasoline raft afloat on an asphalt river. In the wagon treks West, survival of the fittest was physically determined, but this spiritual journey of The Kid and Dudley is primarily a matter of moral survival. For The Kid, the campfire and the jail offer two views of the American Land and Character. Having discovered the land and few of its heroes, The Kid can then set out alone in search of one of its products: himself.

In *The Man Who Was There* (1945), Morris offers three views of Agee Ward (perhaps The Kid as a young man). The first is Agee's view as he returns to the home place. A painter passionately in search of a myth, Agee tries to escape captivity in the nostalgia of the past by processing the past, transmuting it as myth into the formal, conceptual realm of art. Two witnesses resurrect the hero through visions invoked by psychological ordeals that their memories and intuitions of Agee inspires.

If "an epic is how you feel about something," the episodes, names, and dates in Morris's books are part of one great epic, the epic of the American consciousness: the only wide-open spaces we have left. Like The Kid and Agee Ward, Morris attempts to discover America first, to enter into the "collective memories of the pioneer American past." Morris asks Crevecoeur's "disquieting and perennial question": What is American? For Morris the answer lies somewhere on the farms and in the small towns of the Midwest, roots of American strength that flower in the East. In *The Inhabitants* (1946) an experimental use of photographs with texts, the emphasis is on the land and on the artifacts used by the inhabitants; in *The Home Place* (1949), on the inhabitants themselves; and in *The World in the Attic* (1948), on what the land and the people signify to one man: Clyde Muncy (alias The Kid and Agee Ward), writer and self-exiled Nebraskan, who is nearing middle age—the returning Creative Native.

In *The Home Place*, as in the other two books, Morris is concerned with America's "appalling and visible freedom to be blighted." Although the rural way of life is narrow, it seems to win, at least, on its own ground, represented by the old folks. Before the old rural way is lost, Americans need to *look* at it, to assimilate the best of it. The Muncys represent the urban way in which "the new is obsolete on its appearance." Morris insists that Americans need to go home again, and that, in order for Americans to come of age, they must. Drawn back by nostalgia, the promise of the past, Muncy reacts with nausea, the present failure of the dream.

In *The World in the Attic* Muncy feels he lacks connection with the town, Junction. It has broken for him mainly at those points where it has broken for the town itself. The novel is a recollection and a recognition, a requiem. Nostalgia-nausea and the death of a way of life are linked themes that are conveyed to Muncy in "The World" and conceptualized in "The Attic." In Grandfather's will, "divided among his children, were the splintered fragments of three frontiers—Paradise won, Paradise lost, but never regained." The irony is that Americans strive to erase the very conditions which made them great, while sustaining many of the conditions which contribute to failure. When the town's promise was young, there seemed to be an "unseen force" like a magnet around which they all arranged themselves "in an orderly manner." Unique and exciting, Caddy Hibbard once personified that force. Caddy, like the dream, led a man "to think and to feel what he might not have been led to think or to feel at all."

At the end of "The World" Muncy ponders what he has observed: Junction is "a house divided, the old town facing the west . . . but the once up-and-coming part of town facing the east. For the east was . . . the way to leave." Since morning Muncy's wife, Peg, has sarcastically interrogated Muncy as to the connection between the past and present, the old and the new. That night she answers herself: "Maybe you're the connection." Artifacts, rituals, and gestures have been a means of connecting with the past.

In *The Works of Love* (1952) the American Dream proves real but hollow. In the Great American Desert, the American Dream of Success both flowered and withered: "In the dry places, men begin to dream. Where the rivers run sand, there is something in man that begins to flow." Men like Will Brady, who thrive on dreams, often welcome ready-made ones. In one view of the American Dream, anything and everything is possible for every man. But since the Nebraskan and the American past are both mythic and real, the concept of the American Dream, based on the clichés of the past, conflicts with the often nightmarish realities of American life. Contrary to reality, Will succeeds as easily as the myth promises. But Morris shows that, once translated into reality, the dream becomes like the "giant brooding" statue of Abraham Lincoln himself in Chicago—soft green with corrosion. Will does not witness the real heroism out of which the storybook idea of success was fabricated, an idea that is worshipped by men who seek compensation for their own emotional and spiritual lacks.

In Will Brady, Morris has created an archetypal character who symbolizes the American myth of the dream of success, an outgrowth of the myth of the pioneer spirit. He exemplifies the

American character and spirit as it has failed; but, in the manner of its failing, it has somehow succeeded in emotional works of love (even though Will Brady as a father, lover, and husband fails) and in mystical works of love, from "The Wilderness" of the Great Plains to "The Wasteland" of the great city. His tragipathetic need for love and permanence could be satiated only in the Chicago canal, symbol of the decay of the American spirit and of the breakdown of the American Dream.

In suburban Philadelphia the microcosm of family and home is the focus for two close observations on middle-class manners on the American scene. Mrs. Ormsby and Mrs. Porter of *Man and Boy* (1951) and *The Deep Sleep* (1953) are the first of Morris's female forces to be observed in direct action. Archetypal mothers, they reject the defunct male West and "make do" in the East. In the house, run by Mrs. Ormsby's and Mrs. Porter's principles, the wilderness and the wasteland meet.

In *Man and Boy* the house is overtly ruled by a "momarchy." A feature editorial recently proclaimed that "mother had, single-handed, saved a good part of the nation for the quail." Her son, Virgil, missing in action, "had been missing, some people would say, for a good many years." It is Mother who christens the ship named after her son, a national hero. Mother is a bewitcher who creates public ceremonies in which transformations are possible; her husband's imagination and compassion achieve private transformations in impersonal love and in a vision of permanence.

In *The Deep Sleep* revelations produce resurrections. For Webb, the artist intent upon getting the well-composed picture, the Porter house "brought the conflicting forces together and gave them shape. It added up to more than the sum of the separate lives." When he first came to the large but modest house in "the historic, haunted, big-name country" near Valley Forge and saw the image of the house gathered in the lens of a mirror, it "seemed to Webb, right at that moment, that he had gone abroad not to find himself, or other such prattle, but in order to return to this room and rediscover America." Fifteen years later Webb is still faced with the challenge of making sense of the lives of the inhabitants of this house. By the end of the day—the day of the preparations for the funeral of his father-in-law, the Judge, whom he loved and respected—Webb achieves compassion for his mother-in-law, who had seemed, characteristically, to lack feeling.

The urban novels deal, away from the plains, with the problematic question: How does one escape captivity in the mythic past to live in the everyday present? In these novels the author develops attitudes and techniques for confronting the persistent enigma of his Nebraska background. Produced by the Midwest, Lawrence, the hero of *The Huge Season* (1954), represents the American Dream and Character. The audacity and tenacity of his grandfather, who built an empire in the barbed-wire business, come out, in future generations, only in Lawrence, champion tennis player and bull-fighter. Perhaps his failure to achieve physical and spiritual conquest over himself symbolizes both the failure of the mythic West and the failure of the 1920s. Foley, his main witness, wonders: "Did they lack conviction? No, they had conviction. What they lacked was intention." Because the hero lived so bewitchingly in the present and killed himself when he saw he had no future as a perfect hero, the witnesses—a gallery of fossils in the present—are captive in the past, unable to light out for the territory ahead. "The shot that killed Lawrence had crippled all of them." With its youthful rites of vitality, the 1920s promised more than the individuals, even Charles Lindbergh, could deliver, at least consistently. But in Foley's imagination, it is "a permanent scene, made up of frail impermanent things." Foley does achieve this moment of truth and begins to bury the past.

Some of the best conditions under which one may learn the impersonal wisdom of the body and connect with the immediate living present are those which prevail in travel. One crosses interior and exterior frontiers; new scenes arouse the impulse to "make it new!" The lovers in *Love Among the Cannibals* (1957) and *What a Way to Go* (1962) do not go beyond the cannibalistic sexual level where, Morris suggests, everything else begins. Sex is the new frontier, and the Greek and Cynthia are a new species of audacious female; they persuade the male that, on the sexual frontier, where one may start from scratch, "the real McCoy" is still possible.

Morris has observed that one of the most obvious traits of the American character is the ability or the impulse to improvise: "the passion, sometimes the mania to *make it new*." As a massive culture, America is unique in history, remaining "as a *process*, changing its shape and its nature daily, before the world's eyes." For the artist, improvisation becomes experimentation. "If you live in a world of clichés, as I do," says Horter, middle-aged writer of popular song lyrics in *Love Among the Cannibals*, "some of them of the type you coined yourself, you may not realize how powerful they can be." But Mac, who writes the music that goes with the lyrics, points out that the phony is all one has, it *is*, as opposed to what was or is yet to be; and one must make it real. The American impulse to "make it new" is an effort to reshape reality to the heart's desire. Horter attempts to transform, to make new the fluctuating clichés of American life.

Professor Soby, in *What a Way to Go*, is encumbered by his past; in her spontaneous response to the wisdom of the body, Cynthia teaches Soby that sex is one means of living contentedly in the immediate present. On ancient ground (Venice and Greece) wise-cracking Cynthia is the nerve center of the lively present; as she helps him get to the simplicity of the Greeks, Soby brings the dead mythic past alive again in his imaginative field of vision. In the midst of the Old World clichés, Soby observes life imitating art, fact and fiction merging ambiguously. He learns to transform imaginatively his environments and his relationships with the people he meets by chance. If the process is successful, "the new element forged" is oneself.

Warren Howe, middle-aged television script-writer in *Cause for Wonder* (1963), deliberately re-experiences his own past. He returns to a castle in Austria where a madman of his youth still audaciously improvises upon moments in the lives of his guests to cause perceptions and transformations. This novel demonstrates the simultaneity of past and present in skull time-and-space; past and present in both America and Europe are the ambience of self-discovery. Even forgotten moments of the past are preserved in the creative memory that reconstructs as it resurrects. Howe contemplates as he experiences it the human nature of time-and-space, which are coexistent dimensions of each other. "If you live in the present," he discovers, "you can't help but be ahead of your time." The usable past is "the here and now." Morris shows how the moment of individual creative vision synthesizes memory and immediate perception, time and space.

Boyd and McKee, as hero and witness in *The Field of Vision* (1956) and *Ceremony in Lone Tree* (1960), represent two opposed sides of the American Dream. There comes a point when this relationship must end; the witness must wake from the spell and the hero must free himself of dependence on his witness. Severance begins in *Field* at a Mexican bullring, and is accomplished, for better or worse, in *Ceremony*. The break must occur on native ground, the sanded navel of the world.

None of Morris's characters are capable of achieving the ideal state through all three ways of self-transcendence: love, imagination, and the heroic. "The heroic," says Wayne C. Booth, "can never be an end in itself; it is only a means to the imaginative transformations it can effect, the moments of truth it can yield. . . . The insight itself is what is important." *The Field of Vision* develops the theme that the hero-witness relationship may result both in transforming and in transfixing the hero as well as the witness. Boyd's trouble is that his acts always give off more heat than light, and what has beguiled his witnesses is their hope that the hero will someday make the light they feel hopelessly incapable of making for themselves. When the witnesses realize that, because of the hero's acts, they are, like Scanlon, trapped in the past and unable to function, they back out of his magnetic field. The world may love a fool but to remain bewitched by him can mean paralysis; the past may be alive, but the present is dead. The present reality, offering only what one can know, without glorious promises, is all one has to work with.

Morris's chief purpose in *Ceremony in Lone Tree* is to free his characters from the past in the midst of an actual conflict between past and present, under the threat or promise of the future. *Ceremony* conveys a sense of past and present in weird coexistence; living and dead "fossils" on the scene parallel immediate things. Lacking a mythic past or a folk tradition that sustains rather than cripples them, and lacking the creative hero that should follow an era of raw experience, the witnesses (and the defunct hero) are caught up in a complex problem of identity that is especially acute in *Ceremony*. Aware that something is ending in Lone Tree, the characters wildly improvise on new selves.

Like Agee and Muncy, Boyd, the audacious amateur, can almost transform the American Land and Dream into art; he can impose upon the past a semblance of order and meaning. But his shaping imagination is stunned by the senseless fragmentation of the present. The motherly owner of the motel near the atomic proving grounds, eager for Boyd to see the great show, writes WAKE BEFORE BOMB beside his name. Boyd wonders, "How did one do it? Was it even advisable?" Since neither past nor present is creatively alive, what is lost if one doesn't wake? In the world man has remade, is it best to sleep in the past or be awake in the present, to let one's emotions sleep or to rouse them? When the bomb of the past explodes, its light may reveal the extent to which Boyd (and the American Dream expressed in him) has failed. Daughter, the wise-cracking beatnik who travels with him, suggests that he has always been scared of the present; should the past explode now, it might scare him to sleep. "The past, whether one liked it or not, was all that one actually possessed. . . . The present was the moment of exchange—when all might be lost."

In *One Day* (1965) Morris makes public and private events impinge significantly upon each other in the immediate present on the American scene; he parallels the trivial events of every day with a single, enormous historical event (the assassination of President Kennedy) of a single day. Each character is so stimulated by a frightening present to immerse, if not immolate himself, in memories of a haunting, distant past that the events of the day, even the assassination, pale. Veterinarian Cowie, the Morris voice, wonders: "Who could say when this day had begun, or would ever end?" Morris suggests an answer in the way he restructures time and space in his characters' various fields of vision. Never before has Morris's technique of using one day as a time and point of view device had such complex thematic significance. The conceptual power that distinguishes him from many of his contemporaries finds its consummation and justification in that day. Consistent with his increasing interest in the immediate American scene, Morris relates various manifestations of the fluctuating American character to that still point where the trigger found the center of vision and the dance stopped for a moment. X marks the spot where the American character revealed itself to itself and to all the world. Confronted with a senseless human act, Americans immediately attempt to understand the perpetrator. Morris depicts the blighted hero of the American Dream surrounded by beguiled witnesses. To excite on almost every page a laughter that turns to acid in the mouth is a near miracle of creation. *One Day* burns with a demonic vision that would be tragic were Morris's comic impulse not so responsive, his humanity not so embracive. It is a cross-eyed vision that looks in one direction with a Sophoclean glance and in another with an Aristophanean glance. At the intersection between the two flash such images as Americans see in their nightmares. *One Day* raises the question: After such knowledge, how does Morris manage the compassion that forgives?

In *Orbit* (1967), like most of Morris's novels, examines the human nature of time. Morris contemplates volatile images of the present as they presage the future. Instead of describing artifacts that are imbued metaphysically with the past, Morris sets in orbit objects that exist only for the present. As in most of his novels, the time span is one day, but here Morris intermingles everyday events with a natural and a public human event that affects only one representative American small-town cosmos. The task of imaginative synthesis is mainly the reader's.

The structure of this short novel visibly expresses the theme. Each chapter, except the last, opens with a brief scene in which Jubal, a wandering motorcyclist, encounters one of the other characters. Morris evokes the pathos of the isolation from each other of similar minds by showing how separate lives plug into a common current of feeling and perception unaware. Tableaux and events are even funnier from the reader's complex viewpoint. The comedy in Morris is, at times, rather broad, but in every image Morris has a black comic vision that sometimes sees things with a cross-eyed folksiness. Morris wants the reader to end with the "disturbingly personal" and timeless vision.

In this new variation of the hero-witness relationship, the weird behavior of the witnesses, whose gestures Jubal misinterprets, sets off impulses in him. We see here more clearly than in Morris's earlier novels, the ways in which suppressed but wild people affect the hero. The witnesses have an inner disposition to produce then respond to the hero. Morris shows the beneficial effects of losing one's mind now and then. It is the mind that is most important. Morris is determined to subordinate the action of events to psychological epiphanies. Psychological effects on the characters are more violent than the actual encounters. Compared with all his witnesses, Jubal, Morris suggests, is stable.

In Orbit shows the interaction of sexual, psychological, intellectual, mechanical, and natural forces. Their paths crisscross by chance and finally converge in a tornado. The controlling energy is Morris's conceptual power, which compresses chaos into a pattern and gives these forces life as well as symbolic value. Morris opens and closes the novel with a catalytic poetic image of Jubal riding his motorcycle. Jubal responds to the immediate moment spontaneously with speed, and the spectacle of his response affects the "ordinary people who encounter him. The image of the motorcyclist expresses the nature of the contemporary American character and scene: most of our experiences are moments in motion, seeming to have no relevant past. The natural and the anti-natural are the opposing forces Morris depicts. Morris often stresses the irony of the American's persistent suppression of the natural desire to expose oneself to risk. The motorcycle and the twister as complementary forces are juxtaposed. The motorcyclist and the twister are supernatural and natural forces which happen on Pickett "as luck would have it." More than any other Morris novel, *In Orbit* illustrates the concept of a novel as a tissue of images over which lingers a single image. In his selection and controlled condensation and juxtaposition of images, Morris achieves the dynamism of the dance.

In *The Fork River Space Project* (1977), Dahlberg, a house painter and one-time writer of semi-science fiction, and Harry Lorbeer, a plumber and proprietor of The Fork River Space Project, change the lives of Kelcey, an aging writer of "humorous fantasy-type pieces," and his young second wife, Alice. This short novel is Kelcey's witty and lyrical meditation on a constellation of images that revolve around two mysterious and suspenseful questions: Did the population of Fork River, Kansas, vanish in a twister or a space ship? Are Dahlberg and Harry planning a space trip, and will Alice go with them? In different ways Harry and Dahlberg become heroes to Kelcey and Alice, their witnesses. Alice's response is to become Dahlberg's lover; Kelcey's is to transform himself through his imagination.

Two major motifs that characterize the American experience throughout history are the "great expectations" aroused by the landscape and its prospects for spiritual and physical development and the long "ceremony of waiting" for those expectations to come to pass. Ultimately, space is the territory ahead that Huck Finn set out for at the end of Twain's classic. In each of his novels, Morris has been heading for that space, where imagination, mystery, and awe make everything possible. The novel is told in the first person, a point of view perfectly suited to a book that demonstrates the power of the imagination leavened with lucid intelligence, abundantly and complexly image-laden, thought provoking, and poetically suggestive. Through his imagination, expressed in a witty, paradoxical, punning style, Kelcey ponders the nature of human perception and experiences intuition in rarefied moments that Morris embodies in charged images. Kelcey meditates on people, situations, concepts, images. The reader's active participation as collaborator is built into the structures of Morris's style.

Two of Morris's novels are brief meditations of old age. Floyd Warner, an old man who has no real future, experiences the past in *Fire Sermon* (1971) and his own last moments in the present in *A Life* (1973). Morris makes his eleventh trip back to the home place—a ritualistic compulsion to re-experience the past while capturing the spirit of the immediate present. The old man wants to go home to the house his favorite sister's death has left vacant. But he also wants his orphaned eleven-year-old nephew, born and raised in California, to know where he came from. While the old man's life is full but stagnating, the boy's is empty. The reader and the characters feel the presence of people who are dead or distant.

Warner drives an old Maxwell coupe pulling a bullet-shaped trailer in which two hitch-hikers, Joy, a radical groupie, and Stanley, a Weatherman, demonstrate the latest works of love before the bugged eyes of the boy. We see events through the mingled visions of the boy and his uncle. The highway dead-ends in the future, with a brief fire stop in Chapman, Nebraska, parched navel of the world. As the house burns, the boy runs away with Joy and Stanley. In *A Life*, Warner journeys alone to visit a farm of his early childhood. He dies, almost willingly, at the hands of another hitch-hiker, a modern Indian. Both novels have a static quality that not even Morris's dynamic style can activate consistently.

Morris's style is at its meditative best, though, in *Plains Song: For Female Voices* (1980), which deals with three generations of women (and their men) on the home place, once again. It is a quietly lyrical celebration and an excruciatingly poignant lamentation. Morris makes us feel that up from the flat windy American plains rises everybody's song—a plain song, a plaintive song, at moments almost unbearable but absolutely unforgettable. In singing of the unfulfilled promises of the Great Plains experience, Morris fulfills his own promise as an American writer.

Wright Morris's achievement is that he has been able to project upon the literary firmament a many-faceted, serio-comic view of the American Dream, Landscape, and Character. In vision and content he is, I believe, the most thoroughly American contemporary writer. Although he has nominal affinities with a number of American writers past and present, Morris has little in common with the raw material, themes, styles, or techniques of his immediate contemporaries. He alone, it seems, has maintained a constant though always refocusing view of his characters and of the world they inhabit throughout a large body of work over a relatively short period of creativity.

Although thus far this piece has been a survey of themes that characterize Morris's novels, the scope of the present volume is much broader. Included are some of his finest short stories, photographs, interviews, letters, and essays—personal, literary, autobiographical—that offer examples of the same elements outlined earlier. Furthermore, this book is a distinct treasure, reprinting sections from Morris's novels as they were first published in magazines or literary journals. Many of these original printings are difficult to track down, but often differ from the novel version in important and interesting ways.

Wright Morris Territory is not arranged chronologically nor labeled thematically. Such organizational strategies are less helpful for reading Morris's work than relying on a design that moves the reader through a series of unannounced groupings that consist of pieces that are chosen to be juxtaposed to each other, somewhat as in a movie when two images that are not literally related to each other are juxtaposed to create a montage that by comparison and contrast elicit responses, conscious or unconscious, that the viewer would not experience in a literal organization. Morris himself often employed such an organizational technique in his fiction and in his books of short prose opposite photographs.

A look at Morris's variable use of narrative voice in the first eight selections may provide a guide through the rest of Morris territory as charted here. First, the photographer-narrator from *The Inhabitants* is juxtaposed with "A Man of Caliber," which features Will Brady, one of Morris's most memorable Nebraska characters. In sharp contrast is the young man's voice in the selection from *My Uncle Dudley*, one of Morris's few first-person narrated novels. That rarity is paired to an "authentic" first-person narrative, a section from Morris's memoir of his own childhood, *Will's Boy*. "Our Endless Plains" is focused on a grandmother archetype and regional native, while "The Rites of Spring," a short story set on the Texas plains, is from a boy's youthful perspective. The view broadens with "Origin of a Species," an essay in which Morris writes about his early novels and thus employs a critical, authorial voice. Finally, the first-person narrator in a selection from *Love Among the Cannibals* sounds like an older version of the boy in *My Uncle Dudley*.

This organizational design welcomes the reader who chooses to dip in and out of the book, selecting pieces at random. But for the reader who moves from start to finish, the design of the book may kindle a fresh perspective on Wright Morris's work.

Biographical Sketch of Wright Morris

No Place to Hide

BY JOSEPH J. WYDEVEN

Wright Morris was born in Central City, Nebraska, on January 6, 1910, the son of Will and Grace Osborn Morris. Six days later one of the most important events in his life occurred: his mother died, leaving Morris "half an orphan."[1] Morris's father was a wanderer who frequently left his son in the care of neighbors, but he also took Morris on his first extended trips by car, at least once to California. Will Morris was not an ideal father; even as an adult, Morris was unable to be consistent about his feelings toward his father. Although Morris disapproved of his father's behavior with women, he admired Will Morris's manner of carrying himself as a successful man. Morris's sympathies for his father were mostly retrospective, for over time they drifted apart; Morris seems not to have known of his father's death until some time after it occurred. Nevertheless, the powers of attraction-repulsion were hard at work, and his father's life is embedded in *The Works of Love* and *Will's Boy*.

Morris spent much of his childhood in various towns in Nebraska, perhaps inevitably in Omaha, where he moved in 1919 with his father and his new stepmother, Gertrude, a woman closer in age to the son than to the father. Wright Morris lived in Omaha from 1919 to 1924, part of the time with the Mulligan family, who saw the advantages of son Joe's having a "brother" who was like a twin to him.[2] During this time Morris acquired one of Babe Ruth's back pockets, an episode occurring when Morris, Joey Mulligan, and their fathers attended a barnstorming event. Mulligan Sr. caught Ruth's foul ball and sent Morris onto the field to have it autographed. By the time Morris got to the Babe he was rounding third base and a number of other boys had decided to join him. Before Ruth escaped to the dugout, Morris had latched on to his pocket and torn it away.[3] This event shows up frequently in Morris's fiction (sometimes with Ty Cobb substituting for Babe Ruth).

Sometime during Morris's residence in Omaha, he spent part of a summer on his Uncle Harry and Aunt Clara's farm near Norfolk, Nebraska. This was an important place for Morris's imagination: first during his summer there, then during a visit in 1942, and later, in 1947, when he returned to take the photographs for The Home Place. Uncle Harry appears occasionally as a character in Morris's writing—usually with his own name—as does his aunt Clara, appearing variously as Clara, Aunt Sarah, or Cora but usually with the real Aunt Clara's glass eye. Lacking a full-time father, Morris relished his relationships with uncles and aunts, often deliberately seeking them out. "In the family of American character I consider aunts and uncles my peculiar province—I take them in, like umbrellas, and after a few repairs put them back into service."[4]

Morris and his father moved to Chicago in 1924, perhaps arriving there with fourteen-year-old Morris at the wheel.[5] He lived in Chicago, part of the time with his father, from 1924 to 1927, including time out for a car trip to California that became the basis for Morris's first novel. Life with his father was not easy, and he describes how he came upon the man having sex on the bed they both slept in. Morris "arrived on the scene too late; the machine would not stop. Coins dropped from the man's pockets to roll about on the floor. No, it was not a good scene. It considerably widened the widening gap." About his own proclivities, he added, "the boy was a great one for Sir Gawain, the Green Knight, and feared disease from stool seats and unclean thoughts."[6] Perhaps as a result, Morris spent a good deal of time at the Larrabee YMCA, a site of much significance to his fiction.

In 1930 Morris briefly attended the Adventist-run Pacific Union College in California, courtesy of his God-fearing grandfather; in relation to that experience he met some of his extended family, including two of his mother's sisters, Winona and Violet. The meeting provided him with "an image of human goodness that I had been lacking" (WB, 161). Morris was particularly impressed with Winona, making her a belated mother surrogate, seeing her physical presence "the time-stopped dazzle of Vermeer's paintings."[7]

Finding Pacific Union College stifling, and upon being asked to leave because of his disruptive influence on other students (nothing personal, the dean assured him, he just "lacked an Adventist upbringing" [WB, 166]), Morris went to Texas to work for his uncle Dwight. His time with Dwight epitomized futility, for it was necessary to plow the "dustbowl" around the clock and hope for the rain that never came. Though the experience was depressing, it was laden with images that penetrated Morris's imagination: Dwight showed up forty years later in *Cause for Wonder* and as the basis for the character of Floyd Warner in *Fire Sermon* and *A Life*. Other events from Texas include Morris's shooting a hog by getting in the pen with the animal and luring it with an ear of corn stuck in his fly, then shooting it between the eyes with a Winchester. This event haunts McKee's memory when he searches for parallels to the bullfight in *The Field of Vision*.

The following September, Morris entered Pomona College in California, a place he likened to the Garden of Eden. One of his professors there was Leon Howard, who became Morris's friend; later Howard wrote a monograph on Morris's work. Among Morris's readings was Spengler's *The Decline of the West*, which he underlined with a passion; this tome, read at a crucial period of his life, stuck in his mind and perhaps influenced his later pessimism about the decline of American culture. Morris wrote to Spengler "to question his assumption that the West had declined west of the Missouri River," adding that Spengler's failure to reply indicated "perhaps he needed more time to think it over."[8]

Morris remained at Pomona until 1933, when he left, without completing his degree, for his *Wanderjahr* to Europe. This trip was momentous, and its impact so great that he dedicated an entire volume of memoir and much of the novel *Cause for Wonder* to describing it. Morris is vague about what impelled him, at age twenty-three, to such a measure, but apparently he required of himself the European experiences of the generation of American writers preceding him.[9] For economic reasons, however, Morris found himself at first not in the expatriates' Paris but in Vienna, spending the winter in Schloss Ranna castle and contemplating the mysteries of time: "[I]t seemed to me that time, as I used to live it, had stopped. That what I saw before me was a snippet of time, cut from the moving reel, a specimen with more of a past than a future, a crack in time's door that I had my eye to, where no bird flew, no snow fell, no child played on the pond ice and no dog barked. To be out of this world was to be out of time. One day I liked it. The next day I thought I might go nuts" (*Solo*, 77–78). Occasionally he linked his own experiences to those depicted in old paintings, especially those of Breughel.

Other memories included a "blind Garten" in Vienna, where only blind people walked, providing for Morris "a visual metaphor that I found exciting. What I had seen from the window would prove—over the next fifty years—to be inexhaustible each time I looked" (*Solo*, 37). A bicycle tour of Italy included detainment "as a threat to Mussolini" in a prison in Grossetto and his unlikely rescue by the native Italian grandfather of two boys he had befriended in Chicago.[10] Finally Morris managed to spend the summer in Paris, where he read French writers and "found time to ponder what I was up to, . . . to reflect on the separate lives I had lived as a boy" (Cloak, 10). One day he found his pocket picked and his money gone, and so his sojourn came to a close.

Morris returned from Europe in 1934, fully conscious of his stock of raw material and ready to begin his creative life. He married Mary Ellen Finfrock that same year and lived with her in Claremont, California. Morris has given several different accounts of this period, but apparently by the mid-1930s he was photographing seriously and experimenting with the combination of photographs and short prose passages. He had a part-time job with the Works Progress Administration and worked on drafts of several novels. In 1938 his wife took a teaching job in Middlebury, Connecticut, and she and Morris moved east.

During this time he was experimenting with a variety of cameras, among them a Zeiss Kolibri purchased in Austria, a Rolleiflex, a Japanese view camera, a 3¼x4¼ (and, later, a ¼) Graphic View camera with a wide-angle Schnieder Angulon lens (Cloak, 38).[11] He set up a darkroom with an enlarger. That winter he spent a few months living in a cabin on Quassapaug Pond, writing a novel, and reading Thoreau (P&W, 18). In 1940 his first photo-text work was published as "The Inhabitants," and he had his first photo-text show at the New School for Social Research. A review of that exhibition praised his writing and described him as "[o]ne of this country's distinctive camera artists."[12]

His successes led him to contemplate an expansive project on American cultural objects and structures. He intended a "photo-safari" through parts of the South, Midwest, and West, and spent a winter writing in California before returning east. This trip involved fifteen thousand miles by car—and an escape from domestic responsibilities. His artistic motives were, as usual, dual: on one hand, to photograph American icons; on the other, to preserve the past. As he put it later, he aimed "to celebrate the eloquence of structures so plainly dedicated to human use and to salvage those that were on the edge of dissolution" (P&W, 32). Thinking of attaching himself somehow to the Farm Security Administration photography unit, Morris looked up Roy Stryker in Washington DC, but Stryker was puzzled by the lack of people in Morris's photographs and unsympathetic to his motives.

The photo-safari went much as planned. It was the unplanned events that proved the most memorable—such as Morris's arrest in Greenville, South Carolina, "as a vagrant and . . . possible spy" (P&W, 26). In jail he met a "local desperado" named Furman, who would furnish the conclusion to My Uncle Dudley. While photographing in Alabama, Morris was warned off by a shotgun blast, an experience he used a decade later to begin an essay on the problematic relations between privacy and photography. In Mississippi he met Eudora Welty but hesitated to intrude on William Faulkner. Instead, he located Faulkner's friend Phil Stone, with whom he discussed Southern relationships between black and white (and who allowed Morris to spend the night in his driveway!). In Kansas he found the huge Gano grain elevator, the subject of perhaps his best-known photograph. Arriving in Los Angeles, Morris began work on what became his first published novel.

With the publication of My Uncle Dudley in 1942, Morris's career as a novelist had begun, but he still relished the photo-text medium and was determined to pursue it, most immediately through a Guggenheim Fellowship. With the award he and his wife returned to California, stopping in Nebraska on the way. His father having died in 1941, Morris desired to revisit his childhood—including his first return to "the home place" of Uncle Harry and Aunt Clara, where, "drugged by feelings that both moved and disturbed me," Morris took no photographs but resolved to return. He also met the barber Eddie Cahow and took photos in Cahow's shop. This return to Nebraska was the key to Morris's "pact with the bygone": "By the time we left, . . .

the setting sun burning on the windshield, I was committed to the recovery of a past I had only dimly sensed that I possessed" (P&W, 40–41).

In Claremont, Morris wearied of waiting to be drafted, so he tried to enlist in the navy and the army but was rejected by both because of a heart murmur. Morris was thus "home free," as he put it (Cloak, 108), to pursue his work. When Morris's wife got a job teaching piano in Bryn Mawr, Pennsylvania, they again moved east. In Haverford the Morrises met Loren and Mabel Eiseley, and so began a long friendship, including book-hunting forays into Philadelphia and long conversations about the mysteries of nature and Darwin's theories. Morris playfully included Mabel Eiseley's name among Virgil Ormsby's newspaper staff in Man and Boy.

When The Man Who Was There was published in 1945, Morris's career was well on its way, though he still had not decided which artistic medium to give precedence. The following year Charles Scribner's Sons published the photo-text The Inhabitants after Morris convinced Max Perkins to take a chance on the book. In 1947, armed with his second Guggenheim grant, Morris was back at Uncle Harry and Aunt Clara's farm, taking the photographs that formed the basis for The Home Place. He also intended to incorporate photographs into the next novel, but the publisher demurred. The decision not to print photographs in The World in the Attic may have been a factor in pressing Morris further toward narrative, though he did not abandon his photographic practice entirely until the early 1950s.

Morris was a provocative participant at a 1950 symposium called What Is Modern Photography? held at the Museum of Modern Art in New York. According to John Szarkowski, Morris took on the talent in the room (all well-known photographers) by defending the idea of privacy from photographers who would snoop into people's personal lives. The argument "was offensive both to the Left, who felt that only the rich could afford privacy, and to the Right, who owned the magazines," but it was central to Morris's concerns as an American image maker.[13]

Between 1948 and 1960 Morris wrote most of the major works that established his reputation, among them *Man and Boy*, *The Works of Love*, *The Deep Sleep*, *The Huge Season*, *The Field of Vision*, *Love Among the Cannibals*, the impressionistic study of American writers *The Territory Ahead*, and *Ceremony in Lone Tree*. Mass appeal threatened briefly with a paperback reprint contract for *Love Among the Cannibals*. Meanwhile, Morris's marriage had grown increasingly shaky, and he continued to make "welcome escapes" from domesticity, indulging what he called "my familiar flight pattern" (*Cloak*, 229). During a long stay in Mexico in 1954 when he was armed with his third Guggenheim, he went to the bullfights, which focused his thinking for *The Field of Vision*. On another Mexico trip he began *Ceremony in Lone Tree*. He took several trips to Europe, including one in 1959 when he "bolted" to Venice with Josephine Kantor, whom he had met the year before and married a year later, upon divorce from his first wife. In 1962 *Critique* published a special issue on Morris's work; in the same year he became professor of creative writing at California State University in San Francisco State College (now University), a position he retained until 1975.

For fully twenty years after *Ceremony in Lone Tree* was published Morris turned away from writing about his Nebraska origins: *Cause for Wonder* and *What a Way to Go* are set in Europe; *One Day in California*; *In Orbit* in Indiana. In the 1970s *Fire Sermon*, *A Life*, and *The Fork River Space Project* are set once again in the American West, but these books are focused on other than regional concerns, such as the changes in perspective and perception experienced in old age. He collected his acerbic critical essays in *A Bill of Rites, A Bill of Wrongs, A Bill of Goods*.

In 1971 Morris's friendship with Granville Hicks led Hicks to edit *Wright Morris: A Reader*, perhaps thinking (erroneously) that publication would lead to rediscovery of Morris as a major American talent. There were already signs that Morris was thinking about the end of his career. The books that followed the ambitious *One Day* tended to be short novels or collections—of photographs taken in Venice, of short stories, or of essays, as in *About Fiction* and *Earthly Delights, Unearthly Adornments*. In 1975 he was novelist-in-residence at the University of Nebraska and the subject of the Montgomery Lectures (texts and interview published as *Conversations with Wright Morris*); a retrospective of his photography was exhibited at the University's Sheldon Art Museum.

In 1980, Morris's final novel, *Plains Song for Female Voices*, returned him to the Nebraska plains for his subject matter. *Plains Song* was an appropriate work with which to conclude his career as a novelist, for it allowed him to revisit the settings that had first nurtured him. The novel won the American Book Award. Morris must have known it was his final novel, for his activities in the decade that followed suggest a deliberate tidying up of his career. He composed three volumes of memoirs (the third, *A Cloak of Light*, carried his life from the end of *Solo* to 1960); wrote short stories; and compiled retrospective collections of his photographs and critical essays on photography.

Morris's renewed attention to photography at this time was dramatic. *Photographs and Words* offers the best reproductions of Morris's photographs and his first extensive account of his adventures with photography. The editor, Jim Alinder, had been intimately involved in the Morris *Structures and Artifacts* show, and he collaborated with Morris on *Picture America*, for which Morris wrote the words accompanying Alinder's photographs. Continued interest in Morris's photographs was evidenced by two shows of national prominence: the first at the Corcoran Gallery in Washington DC in 1983, and the second, perhaps the most significant Morris event in the 1990s—one Morris privately hailed as his "last hurrah"—a retrospective at the San Francisco Museum of Modern Art in 1992. Perhaps the most important Morris book of the decade, *Time Pieces: Photographs, Writing, and Memory*, included almost all the essays he wrote on photography and "photographic" perception throughout his career.

Among Morris's many awards are the Mari Sandoz Award, the Robert Kirsch Award, the Mark Twain Award, the Life Achievement Award from the National Endowment for the Arts, the Whiting Award, and the Commonwealth Award for Distinguished Service in Literature.

In his last days Wright Morris lived at the Redwoods Retirement Center in Mill Valley, California, not far from where he and his wife had lived together at 341 Laurel Way in Mill Valley. There he continued to have visitors and at least twice he gave extended interviews to scholars of his work. He died on April 25, 1998, and was buried next to his mother in the Chapman, Nebraska, cemetery. His wife, Josephine Kantor Morris, always protective of her husband's work, died four years later.

The Lone Tree Literary Society in Morris's home town of Central City, Nebraska, has been diligent in overseeing properties associated with him. This group is largely responsible for preserving as National Register of Historic Places sites the Wright Morris Boyhood Home, built in 1893 (and Morris's home from 1910 to 1919), and Eddie Cahow's barbershop, built in 1889, in nearby Chapman (made famous by Morris in The Home Place and other works),. Eddie Cahow's barber chair is now in the Merrick County Historical Museum in Central City. The Lone Tree Literary Society was also largely responsible for having The Home Place chosen as the official 2010 One Book, One Nebraska selection and for sponsoring the Wright Morris Centennial Year Conference in Central City in October 2010. Two sites associated with The Home Place—Uncle Harry and Aunt Clara's house and Ed's Place—are still to be seen near Norfolk, Nebraska. At several points during his late life Morris said the home place house had been torn down, but in truth it was simply moved down the road.

Since the deaths of Wright and Jo Morris, Morris's works have had to fend for themselves. As the Suggested Works section at the end of this volume may indicate, in the last decade much more critical attention has been given to Morris's photographs and photo-texts than to his novels. Nevertheless, critical inquiry continues and many of the research materials are available for fresh scholarship. Many of Morris's papers and manuscripts are held in the Bancroft Library in Berkeley, California, and books and papers from Morris's home were bequeathed by Jo Morris to the University of Nebraska library in Lincoln. As for Morris's photographs, copyright is now owned by the Center for Creative Photography in Tucson, Arizona.

Notes

1. Wright Morris, *Will's Boy: A Memoir* (New York: Harper & Row, 1981), 35; hereafter cited as *WB*.

2. Wright Morris, "How I Met Joseph Mulligan, Jr.," *Harper's Magazine* (February 1970): 83.

3. Wright Morris, "Babe Ruth's Pocket," *Ford Times* (September 1972): 50–54.

4. Wright Morris, "Made in U.S.A.," *American Scholar* 29 (Autumn 1960): 486.

5. Wright Morris, "The Cars in My Life," *Holiday* 24 (December 1958): 47.

6. Wright Morris, *God's Country and My People* (New York: Harper & Row, 1968), n.p.

7. Wright Morris, "Real Losses, Imaginary Gains," in *Real Losses, Imaginary Gains* (New York: Harper & Row, 1976), 6.

8. Wright Morris, *Solo: An American Dreamer in Europe, 1933–1934* (New York: Harper & Row, 1983), 1; hereafter cited as *Solo*.

9. Wright Morris and Jim Alinder, "Interview," in *Structures and Artifacts: Photographs, 1933–1954* (Lincoln NE: Sheldon Memorial Art Gallery, 1975), 115.

10. Wright Morris, *Photographs and Words* (Carmel CA: The Friends of Photography, 1982), 27; hereafter cited as *P&W*.

11. Morris, *Structures and Artifacts*, 122.

12. Howard Devree, "A Reviewer's NoteBook: Brief Comment on Some of the Recently Opened Group and One-Man Shows," *New York Times*, October 26 1941, sec. 9, p. 10.

13. John Szarkowski, "Wright Morris the Photographer," in *Wright Morris: Origin of a Species* (San Francisco: Museum of Modern Art, 1992), 13.

Wright Morris Territory

Houses on Incline, Virginia City, Nevada, 1941. Photograph by Wright Morris. Collections Center for Creative Photography, University of Arizona. © Arizona Board of Regents.

Excerpt from *The Inhabitants*

I said a look is what a man gets when he is inhabited by something.

In the mirror he could see the slab of the wall and the small table with the Bible—a Gideon Bible with the raw red stain on the leaves. There was a path from the table to where he sat on the bed. He raised his feet and the rug beneath was worn to strands of burlap, the loose strings caulking the cracks in the floor. Did they come here to sleep—those who came here—or to walk between the bed and the table, between the bed and the Book with the raw red stain on the leaves? As if they wondered what the Book was for. As if there was something about a Hotel room and a Gideon Bible—as if the connection, some kind of connection, wasn't clear. As if a long distance call had something very vague about it, the message garbled, but ringing one number all night long. As if the connection had to be made by waiting, waiting and walking—walking the carpet between the front and the back of the mind. For there was something about a bedroom, a carpet and a Gideon Bible, when the connection, the answer, was up to him.

White House, Cape Cod, 1939. Photograph by Wright Morris. Collections Center for Creative Photography, University of Arizona. © Arizona Board of Regents.

You can see for yourself—

Revolution? Seems to me that's where we come in. I guess some people think that's where we go out. Seems to me we all like to think that what was done was done forever, the revolution leaving us free to do pretty much as we like. Putting last things first is what we like. We're pretty good now at laying the wreath, holding the flag, raising the mortgage, swearing allegiance and saying the last shall be first. We're so good that I just don't know—I don't know how to tell you, how to tell anybody, what it is that really comes first. Even the revolution doesn't come first. Before the flag and before the mortgage, before the allegiance and laying the wreath—before all that a man named Columbus has to come first. For the revolution is to discover America.

Logwall, rural Ohio, ca. 1940. Photograph by Wright Morris. Collections
Center for Creative Photography, University of Arizona. © Arizona Board
of Regents.

What it is to be an American.

There's no one thing to cover the people, no one sky. There's no one dream to sleep with the people, no one prayer. There's no one hope to rise with the people, no one way or one word for the people, no one sun or one moon for the people, and no one star. For these people are the people and this is their land. And there's no need to cover such people—they cover themselves.

A Man of Caliber

This story, originally published in the Kenyon Review in 1949, is an early version of the novel The Works of Love.

On summer nights, the window open, he could lie there and hear the hum of the wires, or the click when the semaphore changed from red to green. Then he would roll on his side, put up his head, and watch the Flyer go through. The streaming coaches made a band of yellow light on the plains. It would be a little while before the night was quiet again.

South of the tracks was the cattle loader, strong with the smell of fermenting manure, and down the spur to the west, past the sawmill, the house of a man named Schultz. This man lived alone on a ten-acre farm. In his bedroom, along toward morning, a lamp chimney could be seen smoking, and now and then his shadow moved about the room. This man Schultz was something of an eccentric, and many years before—so it was said—he had loved a city girl with soft white hands. But after one night and day in his house she had run away. Nobody blamed her. No, nobody blamed her for that.

A little after the Flyer went by, stirring up the night air, rustling in the trees, the eastbound local came up from North Platte. It stirred nothing up. It was hardly a train at all. Will Brady would hear the chug of the motor, or maybe the long honk of the whistle, while he stood in the kitchen, the pancake flapper in his hand. But as this local brought men in, and sometimes took men away, a man like Will Brady, who ran the Merchants Hotel, had to be there. Now and then pretty important people came to Callaway. Once a month, for example, T. P. Luckett, a big man in every respect, who had charge of the Union Pacific Commissary in Omaha. Mr. Luckett had his breakfast in the Hotel, and while sitting in the lobby, smoking his cigar, he seemed to feel like talking to someone. At that time in the morning Will Brady was the only man there. In T. P. Luckett's opinion, that of a man who spoke frankly, Callaway was dead and didn't know it—a one-horse town with the horse ready for pasture, as he put it. Nebraska, he said, had spread itself too thin, the western land was not particularly good, and what future there was—for men of caliber—lay in the east. The whole state was tipped, T. P. Luckett said, low in the east, high in the west, and the best of everything had pretty well run off of it, like a roof. The good land was along the Missouri, near Omaha. The good men, as well, and in T. P. Luckett's opinion it was high time a young fellow like Will Brady gave it serious thought. Saw which way the wind was blowing, that is, and got off the dime. Callaway might always need, he said, a jerkwater hotel to meet the local, but a jerkwater man, not Will Brady, should take care of it.

Will Brady had never thought of himself in terms like that. Whether he was an up-and-coming man, and ought to be up and coming with the east, or whether what he was doing, or not doing, was wasting his time. He just did it. That was the end of it. But it doesn't take a man long to acquire a taste for the better things—all he needs are these things. The taste comes naturally.

For example, when you're married and settled down, and have stopped, in a way, thinking about women, you find you have the time, now and then, to sit and think about something else. Eggs, for instance. A man like T. P. Luckett thought about eggs all the time.

He thought about eggs because fresh eggs were one of the big dining car problems, and T. P. Luckett was the top dining car man. This problem kept a man like Luckett awake half the night. Wondering how and where he could just put his hands on a real fresh egg. Eggs were always on his mind, and perhaps it was natural that Will Brady, with nothing on his mind to speak of, would get around to thinking about them. He made T. P. Luckett's problem his own. Take those eggs he had for breakfast, for instance. At one time he would have eaten them, that was all, but now he looked at the shell and marked the weight of each egg in his hand. He broke them into a saucer to peer at the yolks, examine them for small rings. He considered the color of the egg, and one morning he made the observation that the whites of some eggs held their shape in the pan. Other eggs, perhaps old ones, had whites like milky water, the yolk poorly centered and slipping off to one side. T. P. Luckett thought that very interesting. But his particular problem—T. P. Luckett said, looking at him in a friendly manner—was to determine something like that with the egg in the shell. Then he laughed, but he went on to say that any man who could study like that—his own eggs, for instance—might well discover anything. He put his hand on Will Brady's shoulder, looked him straight in the eye, and forgot himself to the extent of offering him a good cigar. Will Brady had to remind him that he neither drank nor smoked.

Then a week or two later, toward morning, a time that Will Brady did most of his thinking, the solution to T. P. Luckett's problem occurred to him. The way to get fresh eggs was to lay them, on the spot. Get the chickens, the spot, and let the eggs be laid right there. Day-old eggs, which was about as fresh as an egg might be. All this fellow Luckett needed was a man to raise as many chickens as it took to lay the required number of eggs. That might be quite a few. But that's all that he would need.

This egg should be white, as the white egg looked the best in the carton, just as the rich yellow yolk looked best in the pan. And what chicken laid an egg like that? White Leghorns. It just so happened that white chickens laid the whitest egg.

T. P. Luckett, a patient man, listened to all this without a word. A baldheaded man, he took off his straw, wiped the sweat off the top of his head, then stuffed the handkerchief into the pocket of his coat.

"All right, Will—" he said, "you're the man."

"I'm what man?" he said.

"I've got five thousand dollars," T. P. Luckett said, "five thousand simoleons that says you're the man. That'll buy a lot of chickens. That'll even buy you some nice hens." Will Brady didn't have an answer to that. "Tell you what I'll do," T. P. Luckett said, "I'll throw in ten acres I've got near Murdock. Murdock is a lot better chicken country anyhow."

"Mr. Luckett," Will Brady said, "I've got a wife and two kids to think of. I've got this hotel, several pieces of property here in town."

"You think it over," T. P. Luckett said, and wiped his head with the back of his sleeve. "You think it over—right now you could sell all this stuff for what you got in it. Twenty years from now you couldn't give it away."

"In a way," Will Brady said, "I like it here."

"Tell you what you do," T. P. Luckett said. "You put the little woman in the buggy and some fine day you drive her over to Murdock, show her around. Leave it up to her if she wouldn't rather live in the east."

"I'll see what she says," Will Brady said.

"I'm not thinking of eggs. I'm thinking," T. P. Luckett said, "of a man like yourself. A man of your caliber sitting around in the lobby of a jerkwater hotel."

As a man could marry only one woman, Will Brady had once brooded over such matters as the several thousand women that he—and most men—would have to do without. As no woman had everything, in the broadest sense of the term, the problem narrowed down to whatever it was, in the long run, that is, that the ideal woman ought to have. As he had thought about women, now he thought about eggs. Something always complicated the problem of women, but there was no earthly reason why a man couldn't pick—and have, that is—the finest thing in eggs.

So much for the egg—but what about the chicken laying it? Did it take two, maybe three of them, to lay one egg? Did they quit after a while, die over the winter, or, out of spite, lay eggs with chickens in them? To determine these matters he bought three dozen hens, several roosters. He kept a ledger in which he entered, every morning, the number of eggs, the amount of grain eaten, and the proportion of large eggs to the case. Every morning he cracked two eggs, peered at the yolks, then fried them in creamery butter, or he boiled them and served them in an official dining car egg cup. He had never been of much use with his hands, he hit himself with hammers, cut himself with knives, but it seemed that he could handle an egg with the best of them. He could take five in each hand, right out of the case, or he could take two of them, crack the shells, and fry them with one hand. There were people who would like to have seen that. He studied eggs, just as a matter of course, and walked across the wet cement floor in the creamery, soaking his feet, just to see what an egg candler looked like. With his own hands, from a Karo can, he made himself one. As all of his own eggs were fresh and didn't need to be candled, he had a case of cold storage eggs shipped out from Omaha. He mixed them up with his own eggs, then sorted them out. It took him quite a while, but he learned—without anyone around to tell him—how a fresh egg *looked*, and about how old a storage egg was.

If an egg was fresh nothing much showed if he held it to the light, twirled it, and the air space at one end of the egg would be pretty small. If it wasn't fresh, this space would be large.

Shrinkage—from sitting in a cold storage room somewhere. There were quite a few things to learn about eggs when you start from scratch, with the chicken, such as the fact that a normal looking egg might blow up. Not only that, but the lighter the egg, the harder the punch. If the egg was warm to the hand, and struck you as a little lighter than a real egg should be, don't put it down or stand around thinking about it. Go bury it. People who talked a good deal about skunks were either just born storytellers, or they were people who knew nothing at all about eggs. A skunk was a skunk, but an egg could go off right there in your hand.

And yet he liked this feel of eggs in his hands, for he came home early, just to sort them, and he kept a milk-white egg, made of glass, in the drawer of his desk. Some days he carried this egg around with him. More than likely he had something on his mind as a man doesn't live with eggs for nothing, or spend most of his time, his face more or less vacant, thinking about them. T. P. Luckett was not the only person to notice this. He was the only man to speak of it, however, and it strengthened the general impression that this fellow Brady, among other things, was too big for the town. He was one of these men they would more than likely hear from—later, that is.

In April he took a Sunday off to drive his wife over to Murdock, a town of several thousand people, some nice homes, and big shady trees. Just east of town was a two-way drive with a strip of grass right down the middle, lamps on concrete posts, and one side of this street was paved. This road itself went to the east, there was no such street on the west side of town, which was a sign of how things were going for those who needed it. T. P. Luckett's ten acres of land were just north of town, a nice flat piece of land between the road and the high banked curve of the C. B. & Q. There was plenty of room for several thousand chickens, maybe more. They drove around it, then they came back and had dinner in the Japanese restaurant, where there were paintings on the walls, and a violin played throughout the meal. There was no such entertainment in Callaway. One sat in booths, with a light on the table, and though his wife had seen many fine things, and had been in St. Louis, it was clear that she had seen nothing like this. The violin was at the front of the restaurant, in a glass case, with a slot for your coin, and when the coin dropped the violin would begin to play. One hand held the bow, the other plucked the strings. As his wife was fond of music he walked forward twice and played it for her.

At the end of this meal he told her what he had in mind. He described, pretty much in detail, what T. P. Luckett had told him, and how Callaway, inside of twenty years, would be a dead town. A man of his caliber, he said—quoting T. P. Luckett—had no business wasting his life in a jerkwater hotel. He had meant to say small, not jerkwater, but when he got there the word came out, and he saw that it made quite an impression on her. She had never seen the hotel, nor the town, in that light before. He asked for another pot of tea, which was what they served in Japanese restaurants, and while she sipped it he played the violin once more. One of the songs, she said, was about a yellow tulip and a red, red rose.

In May he went over to find a house, and several weeks later he drove his family, his wife and two boys, over to look at it. He had tried to find something like the home she had. Something with a yard full of trees, which he thought the boys would like, and a large bay window with diamond-shaped panes of colored glass. What he found was the cottage type, with a yard taking up the corner, shady elms out in front, and several white birch trees near the house. Right down the street was the Methodist church, and that spring day there were boys on the hitchbar and one of them hung, with his head swinging, his hair sweeping the grass. This boy thumbed his nose with both hands as they went past. Somehow Will Brady, many years later, remembered that. A man of caliber, he had an eye for important details.

But that day, as his wife turned for a last look at the house she said, "You're going to have chickens, Will?"

He nodded; he looked back at the house himself.

"Well, I suppose if we're going to have eggs we might as well have chickens too."

Had she said *we*? Indeed she had.

"Yes, Ethel," he replied, "I thought we might as well."

Excerpt from *My Uncle Dudley*

When it was cold we walked around. When it was morning the pigeons came and looked but when nothing happened walked away. When it was warm we sat in the sun. Cars came down Sunset and when the light was red we could see the good-looking women inside. When it was hot the pigeons left the square. They made a great noise and spilled shadows everywhere, on my Uncle Dudley looking up at them. He looked off where they would come back just as they did. He waited till the last one came down, then he looked at me.

"You had enough milk and honey?" he said.

"I guess I've had enough," I said.

We got up and walked across the street. A boy selling papers held one out and my Uncle Dudley stopped to read. A fellow named Young had just won twenty-five thousand bucks. He'd swum all the way from Wrigley's island to a place right on the coast. There was a picture of him still covered with lard.

"You chew gum?" said Uncle Dudley.

"Sure," the boy said.

"Look what you've done," said Uncle Dudley, "look what you've done—ain't you ashamed?" We all looked at the fellow still covered with lard. Yesterday, it said, he hadn't a cent. Now he had twenty-five thousand bucks.

"Paper?" said the boy.

"No," Uncle Dudley said. We walked through the pigeons and crossed the square. We walked up Main street past the City Hall. The hock shops were just putting out their signs—Buck Jones was at the Hippodrome. Uncle Dudley looked in a mirror on a door. When he was in shape he was like an avocado, when he wasn't he was like a pear. Now he was mostly like a pear. We walked on down to a corner in the sun. "If I could lay my own eggs—" said my Uncle Dudley very loud, "if I could lay my own eggs I'd like it here!"

"Ain't it the goddam truth," said a man. My Uncle Dudley looked at him. The man looked back and Uncle Dudley smiled and felt where he kept his cigars. Then the light changed and the man walked away.

We crossed to be on the shady side. A fellow with tattooed arms was making hot cakes in a window, a row of bacon sizzled on the side. On one arm he had a man and on the other arm a woman—where the woman was his arm was shaved. Except her head and other places women have hair. She was a red-headed woman and had two diamond rings.

A man chewing a toothpick stopped to look at her too. He took the toothpick out and pressed his face to the glass. Bubbles were showing in the dough and the smell of bacon came out in the street—the fellow turned the cakes and they were the tough kind. He stacked them on a plate and set them aside. He poured three more on the griddle and wiped his hands. Then he picked up the plate and walked to the end of the counter, unrolling his sleeves before he sat down. He buttoned the one on the red-headed woman and began to eat.

"If I could lay my own eggs—" said Uncle Dudley, and he looked at the man as if he could. But the one with the toothpick didn't seem to hear. He kept looking inside at the new cakes on the griddle. The fellow at the counter began to eat very fast.

We crossed back to the sunny side. Near the corner there was a crowd looking at a doughnut machine; a woman was working it and wearing rubber gloves. The doughnuts went by on little trays and she sugared them. When she got ahead of the machine she held up two cards—one said 2 for 5, the other one said GOOD FOR YOU. "A wonderful thing!" my Uncle Dudley said. The door was open and the woman looked at him. She put down the cards and leaned on the doughnut machine. "If I was a machine," went on Uncle Dudley, "if I was a doughnut or nickel machine—" He looked around and everybody looked at him. The man with the toothpick came in close and chewed on it. "If I could just lay my own—doughnuts," Uncle Dudley said.

"Ain't it the goddam truth," said the same man.

"Harry—" said Uncle Dudley, cuffing the man on the arm, "come have one on the Kid and me—a little farewell. We've leavin this wonderful land—this sunshine. We're goin home."

"Bygod," said the man. "I sure wish I was too." He was a tall man and used to wearing overalls. His thumbs kept feeling for the straps, scratching his chin.

"And now that we're leavin," said Uncle Dudley, "we never felt better in our life. We never felt better—did we, Kid?"

"Never!" I said.

"Mister—" said the man with the toothpick, "you sound like an Eastern man?"

"Right!" said Uncle Dudley. "Chicago's our home. . . ."

"Good old Chi?"

"Good old Chi!"

"I'm a Chicago man too," he said.

"My friend," said Uncle Dudley, "—that I knew."

"Not right in Chicago—more like Oak Park. Used to drive in Sundays to Lincoln Park—"

"Lincoln Park! Spring in Lincoln Park. No green in the world like Lincoln Park—boats on the lagoon—"

"Not on the lagoon—"

"Harry," said Uncle Dudley, "permit me—in my time—"

"Lived in Oak Park ten years—"

"Boats—" said Uncle Dudley, "on the old lagoon. No green in the world like the green in that park. And that's the green on the back of a bill. What I seen out here all that green's back there too."

"When you leavin, Mister?"

"Tomorrow," Uncle Dudley said. "Kid and I just now on our way to the *Times*. Put in a little ad—driving back, have big car. Too big for us, glad to share it with few friends. Share gas and oil—help us all some that way. Must be plenty men here like to get back to old Chi. Only trouble is Kid and I won't have room. How much room, Kid?" he said. "How much room we got?"

"Well—" I said.

"Not much—maybe two—three. Want it to be nice—southern route all the way. Be in New Orleans in time for Mardi Graw. Any you men been to the Mardi Graw?"

"Thought about goin," said the Oak Park man, "—one fall."

"The Mardi Graw," said Uncle Dudley, "is not in the fall."

"How much?" said a man.

"The Mardi Graw?"

"Good old Chi—"

"That—" said Uncle Dudley, "Kid and I'd like your opinion on. Kid and I think twenty-five—twenty-five do the trick. Not tryin to make any money. Just gas—gas an oil."

"What kinda car?"

"Big car—but easy on gas. Very easy on gas. What we been gettin, Kid—?"

"Eighteen and twenty," I said.

"Time I come out," said a man, "didn't get any more than ten. Goddam car was like a long leak on the road. We was 'fraid to get outa town . . . "

"Ring job—need the carbon out. When was it, Kid, we had the carbon out?"

"Last week," I said.

"Well—" said Uncle Dudley, "got to get on with that ad. Want to get out of town by noon. Since you men think twenty-five O.K.—twenty-five goes in the ad. First come first served. Too bad can't—"

"Twen-fife dolls?"

"To Chicago—all the way."

"Dee-troit?"

"Right next door. Fine town—right next door."

"Twen-fife dolls?" Uncle Dudley looked at him. He was a big man in a brand new suit. He stood very straight like it fit pretty tight.

"Detroit," said Uncle Dudley, "—maybe five dollars more."

"More?"

"More."

The big man looked at him. Then his mouth was open and his eyes half closed—he finished counting and looked out again. "Twen-fife dolls?"

"Chicago—" Uncle Dudley said. The big man smiled and reached down in his pants. It pulled the buttons open and he had to stop and button up, then reach down in his pants again. He had a small roll of brand new tens. He counted off three into Uncle Dudley's hand.

"Right negs door?" he said. Uncle Dudley nodded and smoothed the bills. They were so new they all made a frying sound.

"You can never tell," said my Uncle Dudley, "—bygod you can never tell." He was just talking to himself like no one was around. "Old as I am," he said, "I still can't tell." The big man took off his hat and grinned. Something made him blush and the color showed through his hair, it went clear back where his head started down again. "Glad to meet you, Harry," Uncle Dudley said. "My name's Osborn—Dudley Osborn."

"Hansen—" said Mr. Hansen, and put on his hat.

"You're a lucky man," said Uncle Dudley, "—a very lucky man." And he shook Mr. Hansen's hand and slapped his arm.

Mr. Hansen was wearing a pin and it fell off. It said, Visit Minnesota—Land O' Lakes. Mr. Hansen had more in his pocket and he gave me one, Uncle Dudley one. The man from Oak Park wanted one but Mr. Hansen just looked back. Uncle Dudley took out his fountain pen and one of his T. Dudley Osborn cards and we all moved back so he could write on the glass. He put the card right where the woman was looking out. Under Dudley Osborn he wrote Biltmore Hotel, and on the back Mr. Hansen's receipt. "And now," said Uncle Dudley, "—twenty-five from thirty, right?"

"—negs door," Mr. Hansen said.

"Hmmm—" said Uncle Dudley, and walked in by the doughnut machine. He bought a half dozen doughnuts just plain and then three with the powdered sugar; the woman got red and put on more sugar than she should. Then he bought two White Owls and came outside with the change. Mr. Hansen took off his hat and put it on again. "Well—" said Uncle Dudley, handing him five, "come by early—want to get away early." Mr. Hansen gave me another button and patted my head. "Well—" said Uncle Dudley. Mr. Hansen grinned and walked away. Uncle Dudley didn't wait to see where but turned, and we walked away too. We stopped once and looked at shoes, once we looked at boys' hats. We stopped once where a movie was showing and looked at the signs. We crossed the street and then we stopped and looked back. Uncle Dudley stood on the curb and rocked at the knees. When he saw one that was really all right he rocked at the knees. I looked up and down for her and then I saw her on the corner; she was looking back our way but not at me.

"Should we buy a car now—or should we eat?" said Uncle Dudley.

"Let's eat first," I said.

"O.K.," he said. "Let's eat."

Excerpts from *Will's Boy: A Memoir*

I was born on the sixth of January, 1910, in the Platte Valley of Nebraska, just south of the 41st parallel, just west of the 98th meridian, just to the north, or south, or a bit to the east of where it sometimes rained, but more than likely it didn't, less than a mile from what had once been the Lone Tree station of the Pony Express on the Overland Trail.

My father had come west from Ohio to begin a new life with the Union Pacific Railroad in Chapman, Nebraska. My mother had been born on the bluffs south of the Platte in a house with the cupola facing the view to the west. They met in the barber shop of Eddie Cahow, who had come up from Texas on the Chisholm Trail, but found that he preferred barbering to a life in the saddle. The open range had been closed by strips of barbed wire, and the plow, for both better and worse, had replaced the six-shooter and the man on horseback, a change predicted when the town called Lone Tree at its founding was changed to Central City before I was born. Early settlers felt, and with reason, that a Lone Tree might encourage maverick, wandering males, but discourage most marriageable females. My childhood impressions wee not of the big sky, and the endless vistas, but of the blaze of light where the trees ended, the sheltered grove from where I peered at the wagons of the gypsies camped at its edge.

Six days after my birth my mother died. Having stated this bald fact, I ponder its meaning. In the wings of my mind I hear voices, I am attentive to the presence of invisible relations, I see the ghosts of people without faces. Almost twenty years will pass before I set knowing eyes on my mother's people. Her father, a farmer and preacher of the Seventh-Day Adventist gospel, shortly after her death would gather up his family and move to a new Adventist settlement near Boise, Idaho. My life begins, and will have its ending, in this abiding chronicle of real losses and imaginary gains.

My father, William Henry Morris, born on a farm near Zanesville, Ohio, was one of fourteen children, all of whom grew to maturity. In the early 1890s, with his older brother, Harry, he came west to the treeless plains of Nebraska. To my knowledge no one ever referred to my father as Bill. Both friends and relations called him Will. The housekeeper, Anna, brought up from Aurora to take care of a house, a widower, and a motherless child, pronounced this word as in whippoorwilllll, the sound tailing off like the bird's song, greatly enhancing my impression of the man who often took his meals with his hat on. He was a busy father; the bicycle he rode to and from his work often lay on its side, the front wheel still spinning.

On weekends in Chapman the farmers parked their buggies at the hitch bar in front of Cahow's barber shop. This provided free bleacher seat views, for those in the buggies, of the man being clipped or shaved in the chair. If the chair was pumped up, and the occupant erect rather than horizontal, he was able to exchange glances with those peering over the half curtain. In this manner, according to Eddie Cahow, my father first set eyes on my mother, leaping from the chair, the cloth dangling from his collar, to help her down from the buggy. That is the story, and who am I to change it? She was the youngest, and most favored, of the four Osborn girls. Her name was Grace. Her sisters, Winona, Violet and Marion. Grace Osborn and Will Morris were soon married, and used his recently acquired railroad pass to spend their honeymoon in San Francisco, from where he wired the bank to send him another fifty dollars. A son, Fayette Mitchell, born in 1904, lived for only a few days. Six years will pass before I am born, and a few days later Grace Osborn Morris is dead, having given her life that I might live.

On her death a debate arose as to who should raise me, my father or my mother's married sister, Violet. More than sixty years later my Aunt Winona wrote me:

When your mother died my sister Violet wanted to take you, but your father would not consent to it. He said, "He is all I have left of Grace." O dear boy, you were the center of so much suffering so many losses you will never realize, know or feel . . .

This decision would be crucial to the child who played no part in it. Much of my life would be spent in an effort to recover the losses I never knew, realized or felt, the past that shaped yet continued to elude me. Had Grace Osborn lived, my compass would have been set on a different course, and my sails full of more than the winds of fiction. Am I to register that as a child's loss, or a man's gain?

The small creatures of this world, and not a few of the large ones, are only at their ease under something. The cat crawls under the culvert, the infant under the table, screened off by the cloth that hangs like a curtain . . . in the Platte Valley of Nebraska, street culverts, piano boxes, the seats of wagons and buggies, railroad trestles, low bridges, the dark caves under front porches were all favored places of concealment. With Br'er Fox I shared the instinct to lie low. Seated in dust as fine as talcum, my lap and hands overlaid with a pattern of shadows, I peered out at the world through the holes between the slats.*

In a room of lampglow, where the shadows waver on a low ceiling, I lie full of longing at the side of a woman whose bosom heaves, but she is faceless. Would this be my father's second wife, in a marriage soon ended? Not knowing the nature of the longing I felt, would it persist and reappear as a poignant yearning for what it is in the past that eludes me?

I have another memory of lampglow and shadow. A figure looms above me, swaying like smoke, and against the flickering lamplight I see her fingers unbraid her hair. I hear the lisp of the comb, and the rasp of the brush. This will prove to be Anna, a friend of my mother's sisters, who has been hired to take care of me. Heavily, her arms resting on the bed, she kneels to pray. Her hushed whispering voice fills me with awe. To test the height of the wick's flame she stretches one of her gray hairs across the top of the chimney. Did I see it glow, like the filament of a light bulb, or is that something I have imagined, a luminous fiber in my mind, rather than the lamp? My child's soul is enlarged by this nightly ceremony of light and shadow, and the voice of the prayer. It is appropriate to this emotion that the details are vague. Later, gripping her hand in the church pew, I feel the throb of her voice before I hear it, and share her passion with fear and trembling.

One reason I see it all so clearly is that I have so often put it into writing. Perhaps it is the writing I remember, the vibrant image I have made of the memory impression. A memory for just such details is thought to be characteristic of the writer, but the fiction is already at work in what he remembers. No deception is intended, but he wants to see clearly what is invariably, intrinsically vague. So he imagines. Image-making is indivisibly a part of remembering.*

In this same house, in my sleepers with the "feet," I hurry to stand on the hot-air floor radiator while I am dressed. In the kitchen my eyes are below the level of the table where raw sugar cookies are being rolled for baking. I reach and clutch some of the dough: I love its sweet, raw taste.

In the large room at the front, where I lie with pneumonia, the panels of colored glass in the window make a bright pattern on the bedclothes. With my warm breath, and the sleeve of my elbow, I rub a hole in the frosted window and peer out. The world is white. I am able to see the white birches in the yard against the black, twisted buggy lanes in the road. Gifts are placed on the bed. The flames of candles glitter on the Christmas tree tinsel. A huge bearlike man, with a booming voice, comes in with the winter trapped in his coat. He is Dr. Brown. I am puzzled why the fur of his coat is on the inside. For reasons that are not clear he comes to see me only when I am sick.

If I attempt to distinguish between fiction and memory, and press my nose to memory's glass to see more clearly, the remembered image grows more illusive, like the details in a Pointillist painting. I recognize it, more than I see it. This recognition is a fabric of emotion as immaterial as music. In this defect of memory do we have the emergence of imagination? . . . Precisely where memory is frail and emotion is strong, imagination takes fire.*

Mr. and Mrs. Riddlemosher live in the house on the corner, facing the railroad tracks. It sits flat on the ground. Spars of grass grow between the loose boards on the front porch. In the barrel under the rain spout bugs skitter on the water and polliwogs cast shadows on the slimy bottom. The white hairs of a mare's tail, put into the barrel, will turn to garter snakes.

I sit on the side porch of the house building an airplane with rubber bands and matches. Mrs. Riddlemosher, wearing a sunbonnet, picks gooseberries in her garden. The tinfoil I collect from gum and candy wrappers I sell to Mr. Riddlemosher for seven cents a pound. In the summer dusk, from the dark of the alley, I watch my father in the porch off the kitchen crumble cornbread into a tall glass, pour Carnation milk from a can on it, and squish it up and down with the handle of his spoon before he eats it.

I see my father, against the wind-rocked streetlight, standing in his underwear at the open front window. Bells are ringing, whistles are blowing. My father scratches himself as he listens. Thinking it must be the end of the world, I wait for it to end.

I am given a drum for Christmas, and I am aware as I beat it of the power that it gives me to annoy others.

At school I sit in a circle of chairs with my classmates. When my turn comes I go to the blackboard and spell out a word that is my name. I write this word on a piece of lined paper and bring it home—a gift of myself to Anna, who is full of praise. Although largely unobserved, I instinctively take shelter beneath a buggy, a culvert, a porch, or a table, from which I peer out.

When did I thieve and strike a box of kitchen matches, sucking the charcoal tips for the flavor of the sulphur? I hear the abrasive scratch of the match, but it does not light up the darkness around me.

Gerald Cole and Dean Cole are my friends. Dean Cole is small and thin-faced, like a witch, but Gerald Cole is big and round-faced, like a pumpkin, or Happy Hooligan without a can on his head. We run shrieking across the pasture to where the airplane that has done the loop-the-loops limps along like a crippled bird.

So much for my impressions of my friends—what of theirs of me? Was I a sniveler, a tattletale, a crybaby? A snot-nosed little fart, or a slack-jawed snorfler? In all my childhood no mirror or window returns a reflection I remember.

Is it a fact that Gerald Cole, with my collaboration, dipped my head into a barrel of soft roofing tar, then clipped the curls from my head with his father's sheep sheers? That is written somewhere. Is it the writing I remember? Sixty-five years later, in a photograph of children gathered in the open for their picture, I recognize myself as the plump-faced open-mouthed child with the adenoids in the first row. My scalp cleams where my hair is parted. On my right, surely, is the witch-faced, apprehensive Dean Cole, wetting his pants. On my left, a bow in her hair, the girl who hid the eggs in our yard at Easter. Not a child in this assembly smiles at the birdie. We are sober, worried, expectant and fearful. Such incidents as I remember are uniformly free of the impression, if any, I made on my companions. I am a camera, but who it is that clicks the shutter I do not know.

The long, long thoughts of childhood approximate dreaming in the way they hover between waking and sleeping. The voice the child attends to is the one that speaks without the need of an answer—the voice of fire, of thunder, of wind, rain and silence.

§

Until my father found a house for us, we lived in a hotel near 18th and Farnam. From the fourth-floor window, my legs held by Gertrude, I peered to see the buglike people in the street. During the day, while my father was at his business, Gertrude and I sat in the lobby. Between the plants growing in wooden tubs at the front there were oak rockers facing the window. All day long streetcars passed and automobiles I didn't know the names of. My father's car, a Willys Knight touring, might be parked at the curb. I was free to walk to the corner in either direction, or sit in the car and watch the people passing. In April all the kids my age were in school, and I saw only grownups.

Most people thought Gertrude was my sister. The man who worked at the desk would ask me, "And how is your sister?" and I would say fine. Behind the desk were rows of pigeonholes for keys and mail, and to the left of the desk was the cigar case. A pad of green cloth sat on top of the case, along with a leather cup for rolling dice. If you rolled the dice and won, the glass top of the case could slide back so you could help yourself to one of the cigars. If you didn't roll the dice the girl behind the counter would reach for the cigar herself and hand it to you.

What I liked was the sound of the dice in the leather cup. It puzzled me why Gertrude had given up playing and rolling the dice to marry my father, who did not even smoke. If I was on the fourth floor and leaned over the stair rail, or listened at the gate to the elevator, I could hear the dice rattle in the cup and the sound they made spilling out on the pad. I liked the tile floor of the lobby, the swinging doors, and the men's room I could go to all by myself, now that I had pants that buttoned at the front. When my father found a house we were both disappointed: we didn't want to leave.

The house was near a big park at the end of the streetcar line, the night sky lighting up when the conductor reversed the trolley. I had a bedroom to myself, and with the window open I could hear the slam-bang as he walked through the car turning back the seats. I walked through the park to get to the school, but I played hookey most of the time to hunt for lost golf balls. Five days a week the park was empty, and I wondered why they cut the grass the way they did in parts of it, but on weekends there were clumps of men wearing knickers, carrying their bags of clubs. I watched them tee off. I watched them look for the balls in the uncut grass. The balls were easy to find if I took off my shoes and walked around in the tall grass barefoot. If the balls were not dented I sold them back to the players. With this money I bought pop, candy and marbles, which I told Gertrude I had won playing "keeps." Gertrude's family lived in Omaha, but they were not people she liked to visit. Her older sister, Evelyn, worked at the cigar counter at the Paxton Hotel on 14th Street, and went to movie matinees with me and Gertrude on Saturday afternoons. After the movie we might go to a drugstore for a cherry Coke.

My father's place of business, on 11th Street, was a low dilapidated frame building with an office at the front. In the large room at the back he fed and fattened chickens, killed and plucked them, and candled eggs. Empty egg cases filled with flats and fillers were piled along the walls. The plank floor of the room was smeared with chicken blood, feathers and the laying mash he fed the chickens. My father killed chickens by clamping the birds between his knees, slicing their necks with the blade of a razor, snapping their necks, then tossing them to flap their wings and bleed in the center of the room. Sometimes they got up and walked around, like they were tipsy, and had to be cut again. When they were bled, my father dipped them into a boiler of steaming water, hung them on a hook, plucked off their feathers. My father was so good at it he could pluck two or three chickens a minute if he didn't stop for the pin feathers. It took me three or four minutes a chicken, and the smell of the wet feathers didn't help any. I preferred to candle the eggs.

My father's candling room was like a dark, narrow pantry, the only light coming from the two holes in the candler, a Karo syrup pail with a light bulb in it. If eggs were held to the holes and given a twist, you could see the orange yolks twirl and the dark or light spots on them. You could also see the shrinkage at the end of the egg and tell if it was fresh or out of cold storage. The creameries that sent my father their eggs always tried to mix cold storage eggs in with the fresh ones, and that was why they had to be sorted. I got so I could tell a really bad egg by just picking it up.

My father could candle six eggs at a time, three in each hand, and sort them into three grades of size and freshness. He could candle two cases of eggs while I candled one. On Saturday mornings, when I came along to help him, he would pay me ten cents a case for the eggs I candled, and five cents for each plucked chicken.

I hated picking chickens, but I liked to be with my father in the candling room. He worked with his coat off, his Stetson hat on, his sleeves turned back on his forearms, a sliver from one of the egg cases wagging at the corner of his mouth. While he candled eggs he would whistle or hum snatches of tunes. Right after breakfast he might talk to me about his plans to make a deal with all the state's creameries to send him their eggs. He planned to expand, with a store in Fremont, and maybe another one in Columbus. He planned to get his own truck so he wouldn't have to use the back seat of the Willys Knight for deliveries. If he got worked up he would pause in his candling to chip the dung off one of the eggs with his thumbnail. To candle eggs you lean your front against one of the cases and get excelsior and splinters in your vest and pants front. My father bought a pair of coveralls to avoid this, but they were hard to pull on over his pants, and even harder to pull off. They were also hot to wear in muggy summer weather. What we both disliked about candling was having to break the cracked and the not-so-good eggs into a big tin pail we sold to the bakeries. Some of these eggs were so rotten I had to hold my breath while I fished them out of the pail. A really bad egg gives off heat, which you can feel in your fingers, and might explode in your hand if you aren't careful with it. I buried these eggs in a hole I dug at the rear of the shop.

I was so reluctant to work for my father I might pretend to be sick. One reason was I would rather not work at all on Saturdays, when baseball games were played in the park, and the other reason was that his contracts were not binding. Having promised me ten cents a case, he wouldn't happen to have the change in his pocket, and would *owe* it to me. It soon got so he owed me so much neither of us liked to bring it up.

In the candling room, smelling of cracked eggs and excelsior, the scorched smell given off by the candler, my father was a ponderable presence, more than a voice, more than a father. The light flashed on, then off, his face. I heard the eggs drop into the fillers. In the intense beams of light from the candler the air was thick as water. Many things swam in it. Inside the egg the yolk twirled, there was an eye like a hatpin, there was a lumpish cloud soon to be a chicken, there was a visible shrinkage, indicating age, all revealed in the light beam. I was not well paid, but I was well schooled, and would not soon forget what I had learned.

*From *Earthly Delights, Unearthly Adornments* (1978).

Our Endless Plains

This piece, originally published in Holiday in 1958, includes passages used in "The Scene," the opening segment of the novel Ceremony at Lone Tree.

Come to the window. The one at the back of the Grandmother's house. There is, as she says, nothing much to see, but perhaps that is why one goes on looking. The view is to the west. There is no obstruction but the sky. It hangs there, like a shimmering curtain, in the heat of the summer like a smokeless flame, veiling, it would seem, what might prove to be intolerable. The Grandfather liked to say that on a clear day a man with eyes in his head could see the Rockies. The Grandmother neither contradicted him nor troubled to look. When she comes to the window it is merely to wash it, or dust the sill. "I get so sick and tired of this dust," she will say, not to whoever might be listening, but to a stubborn, non-tiring part of herself. Will it never end? That is what she seems to think. The window rattles like a simmering pot, and right at the level of my eye is a flaw in the pane, one that is round like an eye. With my eye to that eye there is much to see; a scud seems to blow on the sea of grass and waves rise up from the plain as if to engulf the house. Water, water, everywhere, but not a drop of it to drink. Above it towers the sky like the sky at sea; a wind blows like the wind at sea, and the waves break with a fretwork-froth like those in the Japanese prints. Like the sea it is empty, and it is lonely: like the sea it affords no shelter. Only one thing seems lacking that the sea possesses. It is dry, not wet.

Is it a flaw in the window, or in the eye, that turns a dry place into a wet one? Or is it that the plains, both dry and wet, are less a place than an environment, the controlling factor being the limited amount of rain? The plains environment, an inland sea out of which the western mountains rise like islands, laps a wave to the east as far as Lake Michigan, divides the continent in half along the 98th Meridian and crooks one narrow finger behind the Sierras to dip it into the Pacific. Bone-dry desert and humid prairie lie within its range. But the high treeless plains of the Midwest have characteristics that qualify as a region. The promise of rain is persistent. The absence of rain is considered unseasonable. It is this ambivalence that generates the grand illusions, those that require little moisture, since fiction and romance grow well in the dry places. The tall corn may flower, the grain may wave in the wind, but the plain is a metaphysical landscape, and the bumper crop is what a man sees through the flaw in the glass.

What he sees today has changed very little from what the Grandmother saw, sixty years ago, when the windows were first put into the house. The pane rattles, the blinds flap, the dust powders the sill, but there is something familiar about the view; something very up-to-date. The man accustomed to the ruins of war might feel at home. The plain surrounding the Grandmother's house resembles nothing so much as a battlefield. All about it, as at Appomattox, one can see the scars and stumble over the reminders. The bones of a steer, the shoe of an ox, houses without windows or inhabitants, and in the blowouts on the rise, as if honed by the wind, arrowheads. The plow that broke the plains is still there in the yard, but it is clear that the plains won the return engagement. And that is the story. A skirmish won. A battle lost.

That may be why the Grandmother had a small piece of the plain fenced off. She sensed the problem. She wanted to control that much of it. Out of that immense prospect, wide as the sky, she fenced off a piece that would receive her impression. She planted a hedge, she planted trees, she had a barn for her cow, a shed for her chickens, and right there near the house, where everybody could run for it, a storm cave. The hedge, the trees, the chickens and the children have gone, but the cave remains. It is the pillbox of the battlefield. It gives you the pitch. You are at the mercy, like everything else, of the elements. The door is unhinged and it gapes like a hole in the earth. It is a place to hide in or a place to be shot from; and buried in the dead grass on the cave mound, like a piece of armor, is the iron seat of the harrow. The sun nibbles at the shadow like a grass fire and the strumming wires of the clothesline seem to be plucked by clothespin fingers, the hands missing. There is little to see and even less to smell unless the skunk is passing, or a fire is smoldering in the ditch grass along the tracks. One cannot escape it. The eye beholds parallels. The gaze turns inward and the plain, both dry and wet, is a fact that recedes, like everything else, into fiction.

When the Grandmother came to the plains the barbed wire had put an end to the cattle kingdom, and nature, although still untamed, was no longer in the raw. The great herds of buffalo had been massacred, the hostile Sioux had been silenced and pushed into reservations, the first displaced persons of the brave New World. Even the grasshoppers had come and gone, leaving only tall tales and strips of chewed harness, and for lack of competition the white man had turned back to fighting white men.

Today's traveler, crossing the plains at night to avoid the heat, or the lack of something to see, may sometimes get more than just a fleeting glimpse into the tall-tale past. Looming up before him, like a hole in space through which he sees from one world into another, he may behold tremendous figures—colossal horses and cattle—straight out of the world of Paul Bunyan. The man who is dwarfed on the plain by day may come out at night and ride the open ranges of the sky. Single-handed, he rights wrongs, rescues maidens, proves to be slow of speech but quick on the trigger, asking no more of life than a good horse, a saddle, and his own shooting irons. Who, indeed, but such giants should inhabit such a world?

The buffalo and the Indian are now to be found, as any small fry will tell you, only on the nickel, but the tourist who wants the "feel" of the plains can have it at the price of a good night's sleep. Let him choose a railroad town, perhaps a junction, for his night's stop. Let him stay, if possible, at the hotel that faces the station, or in the motel down the road that backs up against the tracks. He may not sleep, but if he is both long-suffering and curious he will know, by morning, what draws some men to the plains, and what drives many women crazy.

The romance of the railroad is the romance of the plains, and the sound of the whistle, blown thin and wild on the wind, or the rocking bell of the idle switch engine, sum up, as nothing else can, the melancholy nature of plains life. The band of coach lights on the night, the receding tail lights, the distant rumble of a freight that is approaching, or leaving, and the way that life starts, after one of its interminable pauses, when the engine wheels spin and the word is passed along from car to car till silenced by the caboose. Let the traveler raise the blind, if the room has one, and gaze into the yards where the brakeman, like a figure in Dante, goes along lighting flares or signaling with his lantern to some comrade in hell.

The plain is dark but the sky is full of light, and part of the dawn is a sense of being on the roof of the world that is not conveyed by mountains. The railroad town with its sounds, its smells, its chuffing night life, and above all its function, drama-tizes the mood of space and loneliness with which the plainsman must come to terms. It is the trains that give his life drama and when they pass remind him of the empty world in which he lives and the crowded world from which they came. All her days the Grandmother hated the cinders, the way the earth shook when a freight was passing, the way her children might be killed at one of the crossings, but a day without such noise, or such danger, would be the day the world ended, and how would she know, without the Overland Express, if her clocks were right?

The Grandmother's house sits on the plain as if it had been ordered by mail and delivered; or as if the flood had receded and left it stranded, like an ark. In the winter it appears to be locked in a sea of polar ice. The view from the window has not changed much—but it has changed. On the horizon objects swim, as if on the sea's surface, cattle stand knee deep in a blur of reflections, and across the concrete road in summer waves of heat flow horizontal, like schools of fish. In this landscape the tongue is dry, but the mind is wet. A scud of cloud waters the imagination, fictions spring up. Where there is almost nothing to see, there man sees the most.

The changing and the unchanging aspects of the view from the Grandmother's window are summed up in a story, one she never tires of telling, now that the Grandfather no longer tells it himself. It is the tale of the Grandfather and the WPA. In 1935, the year of the drought, the corn and wheat were dead, the trees were dead, and the Grandfather was as good as dead himself when this fellow from Omaha came out to tell him how to farm. From the upper floor window, where he lay in bed, the Grandfather had leveled his rifle on the sill and advised the man to go back where he came from, which he wisely did.

It makes a good story, the way the Grandmother tells it, leveling her broom at the window, but her grandchildren listen to it with more than a grain of salt. Out of that window they can see that the WPA man was right. If there was one thing in the world the Grandfather needed it was advice. He sent his own sons to the state aggie college, but not—as he was soon to tell them—so they could come home and tell him how to farm. The result was that the Grandfather never learned. Neither contour plowing, hybrid corn, crop rotation nor anything else penetrated his stubborn refusal to learn. His bumper crop was ruin, with fiction as a sideline, like an old soldier camped on the battlefield.

Just a gunshot away—if he had cared to look—young men were growing tall corn and sweet-smelling alfalfa, were raising prize steers and Poland China hogs, with vacations in the Ozarks on the money they received for not growing much of anything else.

What was the world coming to? The Grandmother could tell you that it was coming to the plains. If the Grandfather hadn't died when he did some of these new goings-on would have killed him. A helicopter, whatever that was, flow over her house during the last election scaring her half to death and urging her to get out and vote. Just for that reason she didn't. If the Grandfather had been alive, he would have shot it down.

Her own granddaughters, almost grown-up girls, walked around the streets practically naked, wearing less than would have shamed the Grandmother to wear in bed. The big change, if anybody would ask her, was not out the window but inside the people—the big change was between the grandchildren and the Grandmother. She sometimes felt they were as far away from her as the moon. Farther, maybe, since the moon seemed to hang like a lantern right above the privy, and it had not changed in the sixty-five years she had been looking at it. But one day it would. If she could believe what they told her, men would shoot rockets at it and maybe go and live there. Strange as it seemed, talk like this made the moon seems unfriendly, and the sky too. The Grandfather had gazed at the sky for the weather—for the signs of the big changes he could read. But today the big change was part of the sky itself—not a sign. Airways, rather than folkways, cast the shadow of the arrow on the Grandmother's house.

The Grandmother has never seen the plains from the air, and she is not at all sure she wants to. That view from the air would dispel her cherished illusion that she has lived on the rim of the world, and lived there almost alone. Up there she would see that the place was crowded. Neighbors everywhere. The Grandfather had lived and died thinking there was nothing to fence him in but the weather—the only thing, both on the plain and above it, that had not changed.

If the word "sea" conveys the look and mood of the plains, the word weather suggests its character. And that has not changed. It has proved as unchanging as the Grandmother herself. Men and cattle had changed, they had grown fat and softer, but the weather was just as lean and tough as ever. Pains in her weather joints, as she called them, were the source of the Grandmother's greatest pleasure, and nothing cheered her so much as the knowledge that a norther was on its way.

No, the weather had not changed, but there were plenty of things that had, and it was from the air you could see the change the best. The old and the new, sometimes, side by side. The town that had died in the drought, half buried in the tidal sand, just down the road from the town booming with oil. Here and there the desert was still on the march, but stranger to behold from the air were the man-made lakes, smooth as gems, where the water that had once raced off in spring floods had been tamed, like a bronco, and trained to burn the lights in the Grandmother's house. The plain was still treeless—that had not changed—but man-made trees, sometimes a forest of the derricks, bred to root for oil instead of water, were all over the place with some of them smoking like a forest on fire. And cutting right across it, gleaming like a zipper, was a new four-lane highway where the cars whooshed along as if there was no place to stop. The Grandmother could tell you that all this looked like more of a change than it was. The traffic on the plains was still *through* traffic—whether it took you two hours or two months to cross them, and whether you were driving a team of oxen or a sports car.

Neither the weather nor the traffic has altered, but on the surface of the plain, as seem from the air, there are man-made objects that resemble nothing else, like the craters on the moon. On closer inspection they turn out to be football stadiums. They symbolize change, visible and invisible, that has come to the plains. The surrounding campus marks the spot where changes are both tested and manufactured, and in the crater itself something called character is said to be formed. On the evidence, which is impressive, the culture plant may thrive on the plains as it has not been free to thrive anywhere else. What it takes today is room, and room is what the plains have plenty of.

What the plainsman sees today originates on the campus: both the shape of his thought and the shape of his farm owe more to the world at large than to the small piece of plain beneath his feet. If the grain elevator, like the sail at sea, is still the characteristic landmark, the football crater marks a characteristic evolution. The sons and daughters of the pioneers no longer have to go east, or abroad, for a polish—they can acquire it, with an imported flavor, right at home.

Under the heaven-sent rain of scholarships and endowments the bumper crop of the plains may soon be culture, not unlike the same product that is turned out elsewhere, but it may run a little bigger, a little further or a little faster—as you might expect. There is no more room on the plains and more reason to do such things.

Already there are crops of young men and women who want better homes, something new in gardens, who want a very dry martini, a very crisp green salad, and espresso coffee while listening to the latest jazz on the newest hi-fi. The horizon that once ended on the sky now curves with the earth.

The Grandmother would tell you that things were different when she came out as a bride. That trip west along the Platte River valley and the country she saw form the bluffs of the Missouri left her with impressions that contradictory experience did not change. She considered grass congenial to man, needing a herd of cattle or a mowing machine to tame it, and nowhere in the world had she seen so much grass, so she knew that it rained. She had no interest in the contrary evidence—in the way the grass shortened with each day's journey, the way the thick sod gave way to short tufts. She didn't pull up a handful and read the facts in the roots: more of the plant was below the earth than above. That also proved to be true of both oil and water, which would determine life on the plains in the future. In her future, she was absolutely certain it would rain. However, in the last few years the climate had been unpredictable.

On that point there was no argument. Of all men who talk about the weather perhaps the plainsman has the most to talk about. There is no small weather. So all of his talk is big.

The heat can be terrific, the cold worse, it might shift from one to the other in hours, and it was not for nothing that the deep hole in the yard was called a storm cave. These funnel-shaped twisters that evoked a twinge of terror even in the man who had never seen nor heard one were as native to the plains as the sunflower and the tumbleweed. At the beginning or the end of an unseasonable winter, at any moment—always when least expected—came one of those blizzards that set the standard for the world. A hurricanelike wind, its freight of snow parallel to the plain, sweeping it like a spray, might bury in a few hours the puny ornaments of man. Wires down, poles down, roads and whistle stops obliterated, cattle frozen upright in the fields and families frozen in their stalled cars.

In other parts of the nation storms like that belong mostly to the good old days, but on the plains they occur frequently. The Grandmother's grandchildren know as much about it as she does. That blizzard of '88—would anyone say it was worse than the blizzard of 1957? Not the Grandmother, and she had seen both.

The drift that hid the house in 1917, so that the children used their sleds from the upstairs windows, left snow in the yard till Memorial Day. The Grandfather used it to cool the picnic lemonade they took that day to the cemetery, where the grass was thick and green, thanks to the storm. As the Grandmother liked to say, if you were going to have it fat you first had to have it lean.

Seated at her front window the Grandmother observed, among other things, the turn of the century. She watched the children of the men who had come west turn, like the century, and go east. Her own, of course, did the same. The girls who departed wanted neighbors; the boys wanted rain. At one time or another, as their letters told her, they all had a try at what they wanted. But generally they ended up on the plain.

The maverick in the family, the one who went east to fish, hunt, oil his guns and marry a girl with money, was not much of a letter writer, and the Grandmother didn't hear from him for several years. When she heard, the letter didn't come from the timbered east, where it was raining, but from the treeless Texas panhandle, where it was not. He had married a Kansas girl without money and they had found a piece of land the plow had not broken. They lived in a shack brought in on a trailer and, working in shifts, the tractor never stopping, they plowed the land, planted wheat and looked forward to being rich.

In the wake of the plows the dust trailed off like a plume of smoke. It came up through the floor and came down through the shingles, it settled on the food before they could eat it, it banked like post-dirt around the roots of their teeth.

If it had rained they would have made a fortune and gone east to fish, hunt, loaf and raise a family—but it didn't rain. Most of what they plowed rose into the air, and some of it obscured the sun as far away as New York. Some of it powdered the sills of the Grandmother's house where, with her usual comment, she dusted it off.

In the letters she gets from her far-flung children it is what they talk about. There is one in Colorado, and the dust blows there; another writes from Idaho that it blows out there; and where it isn't blowing, back in Indiana, they still inquire about it. Of her seven children only one, in finding what he wanted, got away from the plains. It is this one who speaks the most of it. He always wants to know what the weather is like, and why the Grandmother goes on putting up with it.

She is apt to write and say, "Now wouldn't a man ask something like that?" Not that she doesn't wonder, but she considers it her own private business, not his.

The Grandmother likes to say that I'm the only one of her many grandchildren with any horse sense. She means that when I left, I stayed away. In a sense that is true—I live in the suburbs, in timbered country, surrounded by neighbors, about as far as a native can get from the empty plains. On the other hand I have spent most of my life puzzling over the lines on the map of my childhood. In what sense, it might be asked, have I been away? The high plain lies within me. It is something I no longer try to escape. If I stand at the window where the Grandfather stood, I see what he saw. The dream that appealed to him still appeals to me. The tall corn still flowers, the golden grain still waves, skyscrapers now rise where the dust blows and the Oklahoma Sooners won forty-seven consecutive games.

But the prevailing temper, the dominant note, is not struck by these triumphs, however deserved, but by the seat of the harrow that lies buried like a shield in the storm-cave mound. The enduring mood is pathos, the smallness of man and the vanity of his passing triumphs in the face of the mindless forces of the plains. The man who prefers, like the Grandfather, failure on his own terms to success on any other, will find the plains a haven from the prevailing cult of success. There is more than room enough for a man both to find and lose himself. There is neither shelter from the passions of nature, nor the nature of man.

If her children are led to wonder why the Grandmother still lives there, and what, if anything, she sees through the window, she will admit that she doesn't see much. "I get so sick and tired of this dust," she will say, but one really wonders if she still means it. That window sill—what, indeed, is it for but the dust? What matters is not the view through the window, but the dust on the sill.

The Rites of Spring

The old man and the boy got on the train at Omaha. They walked
through the coach to the water cooler, where the old man let the
boy take the seat near the window while he stood in the aisle
picking his teeth with a match. He was a farmer, dressed in the
suit held in reserve for Sundays and travel, but the stripe in the
coat had disappeared from the knees of the pants. The bend at
the knee gave him the look of a man who was crouching, but
within the pants: for a man of his age he stood straight enough.
His name was Gudger, and he was the father of eight or ten kids,
he wasn't sure which. In the state of Texas, where he had a farm,
it didn't seem to matter.

The boy's name was Everett, but nobody ever called him that.
His mother had called him Candy, but she was now dead. As his
father was also dead there were people who referred to him as
the orphan, while others, like the old man, referred to him as
the little tyke. "What's going to be done about the little tyke?"
the old man had said. As nobody seemed to know, the old man
was taking him home to Texas where another little tyke wouldn't
matter so much.

Since the boy had never been to Texas, nor out of Omaha for
that matter, he kept his face pressed to the window, looking for
it. As time passed he realized it must be far away. Every hour or

so the old man told him that. "Don't git in such a hurry," the old man would say, and when the boy turned his head he might ask him, "How'd you like to butcher a hog?" The boy didn't know. But the old man was pleased at the thought of it. He would blink his pale, watery eyes and feel about in the air over his head for the wide-brimmed hat he had already taken off. It was there in his lap, with the ticket stubs sticking up in the band.

In the evening the old man took from his bag three hard-boiled eggs he had brought from Texas, cracked them on the chair arm, peeled them, and gave one to the boy. The other two he ate himself. Later he slept, snoring into the hat he had placed over his face, but with one heavy hand on the boy's knee as if to hold him there. It led the boy to reflect that losing a father had not been so much. Losing a mother, however, was another thing, and it also troubled the boy to know that he was now in Oklahoma but none the wiser for it. He kept himself awake, however, just to breathe the night air. It seemed to him colder, just as the darkness seemed more black. Under the lights on the station platform he looked for Cowboys, for Indians, and where the street lamps swung over empty corners he looked for tracks. Those that went off into the darkness single file.

It was still not light when they arrived in Texas and sat in a café, eating hotcakes, and looked at the red flares burning along the tracks. The old man spoke to the man behind the counter about the hog. He said he hoped he got back in time to help butcher it. Then he went off for his team to the livery stable and the boy stood at the window, facing Texas, and watching the daylight come slowly along the tracks. Nothing but space seemed to be out there beyond the flares. Right there in the street were the railroad yards with the pale flares still hissing, but beyond the yards, off there where a hog was about to be butchered, the sky went up like a wall and the world seemed to end. The boy didn't like it. Something about it troubled him.

When the old man came with the buggy and the team of lean mares with the fly-net harness, the boy wanted to ask just where they were going to. Would a team of old mares ever get them there? Here he was, at the end of his journey according to what it said on his ticket, but he felt in his stomach that his travels had just begun. From the rise where the buggy rocked over the tracks he could see that the road went off toward somewhere, but that it also trembled, and began to blur like a ribbon of smoke. "Buggy needs greasin'—" he heard the old man say, but the boy hardly noticed the creaking, as it seemed such a small sound in such a big world. In the soft road dust the wheels were quiet, and the lapping sound of the reins, on the rumps of the mares, was like water running under the wheels.

As the boy had never looked upon the sea, nor any body of water he couldn't see over, he had no word for the landscape that he faced. The land itself seemed to roll like the floors in amusement parks. Without seeming to climb they would be on a rise with the earth gliding away before them, and in the faraway hollow there were towns a day's ride away. The wheels turned, the earth seemed to flow beneath the buggy, like dirty water, but nothing else changed and they seemed to be standing still. Here and there white-faced cattle, known as Herefords, stood in rows along the barbed wire fence as if they had never seen a buggy, a horse, or a small boy before. They were always still there, as if painted on the fence, whenever he turned and looked. Then the road itself came to an end and they followed the wavering lines in the grass that the wheels had made the week before, on their way out. And when they came within sight of the farm—it seemed to recede, and they seemed to stalk it—the boy knew that he was nearing the rim of the world. What would he see when he peered over it? The hog. The hog seemed to be part of it. But the bleak house, with the boarded windows, was like a caboose left on a siding, and behind this house the world seemed to end. In the yard was a tree, but it would be wrong to say that the house and the tree stood on the sky, or that the body of the hog, small as it appeared, was dwarfed by it. The hog hung from the tree like some strange bellied fruit. Swarming about it in the yard were large boys with knives, sharpened pieces of metal, and small boys with long spears of broken glass. They all attacked the hog, hooting like Indians, and used whatever they had in hand to shave the stiff red bristles from the hog's hide. As the team of mares drew alongside, the boy in the buggy could see a small hole, like a third eye, in the center of the hog's dripping head. The mouth was curved in a smile as if the swarm of boys was tickling him.

"Guess we made it in time," the old man said, and using the crop of the buggy whip he tapped on one of the blood-smeared pails in the yard. A black cloud of flies rose into the air, then settled again. They made a sound as if the roaring wind had been siphoned into a bottle, leaving the yard empty and the flies trapped inside. They pelted the sides of the pail like a quick summer rain.

From his seat in the buggy—nobody called to him, or seemed to know that he was there—the boy watched the preparations for the butchering of the hog. A tall woman with a dough-colored face built a fire in the yard. There seemed to be no flesh on her lean body, and the dress she wore flapped in the wind as if hung from a hanger, or put out to dry on the line. Drawn low on her head was a stocking cap, and the stick with which she sometimes probed the fire was crooked like the handle of a witch's broom. Now and then a cloud of steam arose from the hog as a bucket of hot water was thrown on his body, or a puff of smoke, like a signal, arose from the fire. Now that the hog was shaved, the small boys carried wood, others put a new edge on the blades that had been dulled shaving him. An oil drum was carried from the house, and placed on the ground beside the fire, and over the fire was a large sheet of metal, making it a stove. The cutting of the hog began when the metal plate was hot. The old man worked from the ground up, first cutting off the feet at the knuckle, with the white knuckle showing like the milky eye of a blind horse. After the legs, he removed, carefully, the huge head. It was placed to one side, propped up in a pail, and although the hog's eyes were closed, it might be said that he attended his own barbecue. The smile was still on his face, as if he had long looked forward to it.

The light from the fire was like a coke burner on the greasy faces of the Gudger boys, but not the one who still sat in the buggy, out of the wind. The old man had spread the lap rug over him, and left him there. There was a lot going on, and a small city boy might get in the way. As he had eaten no pork his face was clean, but the smell of it was thick in his head and the shifting wind blew the savory smoke over him. At his back, when he turned to look, the state of Texas lay under the moon, and the thick matted grass was the leaden color of a dead sea. The house was an ark adrift upon it. Here and there, in the hollow of a wave or on a rise that appeared to be moving, lights would sparkle as if the sky was upside down. Behind him he could hear the crackling of the fire, and beyond the fire, strung up as if lynched, he could see the pale, strangely luminous body of the hog. But the great head, with the creased smiling eyes, seemed to be amused at the proceedings, and gazed at the scene in the manner of the boy. And it was this head, with its detached air, the upper lip curled back as if grinning, that led the boy to feel that he had something in common with it. He and the hog, so to speak, had both lost something. In each case they had given up more than what remained. The boy wondered how it was, in this situation, that the hog could look on the scene as he did, with what appeared to be a smile of amusement on his face. The joke seemed to be, if he could believe the hog, on everybody else. On the cursing old man with the sweating face, on his dough-colored wife, on his family of kids who stood around the fire with their faces oily with the hog himself. But when the boy closed his eyes to think about this he saw the grinning face of the hog before him, and the third small eye, in the middle of his forehead, seemed to wink. The fat that splattered in the fire that roared before him, crackled like burning twigs.

The cooking of the hog went on through the night. Small slices of the pork, no larger than a dollar, were dropped to fry on the metal sheet, and the fat ran off into the oil drum at the side. Into the fat the crisp slices of the pork were dropped. The drum filled up, layer by layer, in this way. When the fire died down the body of the hog would appear to recede into the shadows, then it would come forward, like a ghost, when the flames rose up. There was always less hog when the boy turned to look. But the smiling head of the hog seemed larger, the amusement increased on his shining face, and between the parted lips other sounds were sometimes heard. A throaty chuckle. Such as you might expect from a well-pleased hog.

In the cool of the night the dough-faced woman sometimes leaned over the fire for warmth, or stirred, with her pointed stick, the dying bed of coals. Something about it raised the small hairs on the boy's neck. It also brought, as it did to the hog, a smile to his face. The moonlit scene, the pale-faced butchers, the ghostly body of the hog, and the great milky emptiness of the night seemed bewitched. More was going on than met the eye, so to speak. But according to the hog, it was not serious. The boy and the hog both knew this, but nobody else.

Toward morning the fire died down, and the boy must have fallen asleep as the faint honking of geese woke him up. He saw their dark moving arrow on the morning sky. There was no longer noise around the fire, or the sound of hot fat spilling into the barrel, and when the boy raised his head he saw that he was alone with the hog. With the head, that is, and the two great hams that hung from the tree. Whether the head still smiled or not was hard to say. It was still there in the pail, gazing up at the now moonless sky, and the small black hole in the head was like an ornament. Somewhere to the east, blown thin on the wind, a rooster crowed. The lonely sound troubled the boy as it meant another day, no better than the last one, and maybe a day without the hog, was about to begin. Very likely the head of the hog, and the smile, would be cut up next. The ears would be made, as he had heard somewhere, into a purse. His feet would be put into barrels and sold in Omaha. His curly tail would make a tassel at the end of a whip. Everything would be used, nothing would remain, and thinking of that the boy sat up in the buggy as if a thought had occurred to him. On the pale morning sky he could see the rope that strung up the hams. This rope had been tied to a post in the yard, but it had been loosened from time to time in order to lower the shrinking body of the hog. The boy had seen how this was done. Even a city boy might learn the knack of it. He climbed from the buggy, using the spokes like rungs of a ladder, and as he loosened the rope he wrapped the coils around his waist. He had seen this done by the fat man in a tug of war. It was hard to say what the boy had in mind, if anything. He unraveled the rope until the great hams, taking up the slack with a snap, swept him from the ground like a dummy and swung him in a wide arc. The jolt had drawn the coils at his waist, and he hung like a sack, bent like a jack-knife, and the blurred movement of the earth sweeping past made him close his eyes. As he swung, the wind gave him a clockwise turn. As the boy didn't want to be sick with the hog still there smiling at him, he kept his mouth closed, and his eyes shut tight. His fingers swelled thick, and he could feel the pulse when he closed his hands. But he felt much better, nevertheless, and when another rooster crowed, there was a bright streak of daylight in the east. There was also a smile on the face of the hog, and as the rope stopped creaking a lamp in the house indicated another day had begun.

The Origin of a Species: 1942–1957

Part I

Time Past

Our story begins in California, on Sunset Boulevard, where a boy is seated on a bench with his Uncle Dudley, watching the cars with the good-looking women inside stream by. The man turns to the boy and says, "You had enough milk and honey?" "I guess I've had enough," the boy replies, and they get up and walk across the street.

That is the beginning of a venture in the Art of Improvisation, with Uncle Dudley as the master improvisateur. Improvisation, which seems to me one key to American character, rules nowhere with such authority as in California, and few American characters, to my knowledge, are so cut to its dimensions as my Uncle Dudley. He was—let us say he *is*—an early master of making-do. What is he up to in the land of milk and honey? Let us watch a man of his talents at work:

A boy selling papers held one out and my Uncle Dudley stopped to read. A fellow named Young has just won twenty-five thousand bucks. He's swum all the way from Wrigley's island to a place right on the coast. (For this he received $25,000.) There was a picture of him still covered with lard.

"You chew gum?" said Uncle Dudley.

"Sure," the boy said.

"Look what you've done," said Uncle Dudley, "look what you've done—ain't you ashamed?" We all looked at the fellow still covered with lard. Yesterday, it said, he hadn't a cent. Now he had twenty-five thousand bucks.

"Paper?" said the boy.

"No," Uncle Dudley said.

Life with Dudley is life played by ear. By ear, a motley group of characters is persuaded to put up the money to finance a car trip to the East. Skepticism and gullibility, American standbys, are delicately kept in balance by the Maestro. Against the hopes of one he plays the fears of another. And the Kid? He is learning the American game of life—the rules of walking on water.

It is the origin of this species—those lifelike characters that inhabit books—that I want to consider. Are they fiction, fact, or a blend of both? However character is conjured out of thin air, the reader wants the reassurance that he is *real*. Real as it is, life is seldom real enough. It seems to have no conception of its proper business until the writer, tampering with its nature, sets it straight. If he is one of the chosen, the origin of a new species is the result. Dudley is a character drawn from nature. But *whose* nature? At that time, an Uncle Verne, with proper mythic overtones, appeared out of the East and stopped in Omaha. He wore a blue serge suit, a soiled white shirt, a black hat with a wide brim, and shoes that he left unlaced so he could kick them off. He had been gassed in the First World War, rolled his eyes in an epileptic manner, chewed rather than smoked King Edward cigars, and carried in his vest pockets a large sampling of gold coins. He proved to be incurably shy, fond of me and pigeons, and generous. He liked to ride in the front seat of our car with his hat rolled back, a cigar clenched between his teeth, his hands clasped firmly between his knees, the harbor lights of Rangoon flickering in his bloodshot eyes. He seldom spoke, and he disappeared as strangely as he appeared, walking off in the rain one late fall day after putting in my hand what seemed a fortune in gold coins. He was, it seems to me now, my first heartbreak, and my first love.

He was also a seedbed of *characters*. But of my Uncle Dudley, that voluble improviser, we have in his archetype just one or two hints. He liked to get out and go. He liked to ride with his nose to the wind. The smell of gasoline was like wine in his blood. My own incurable passion for the almost–Open Road received its baptism in his company. We had, in the few weeks we were together, a fabulous time. All this while my father, blurred by the wind, slept fitfully in the wide back seat.

If Uncle Dudley passes muster as a species, his origins are very complex. We seem to begin with a blending of facts: my father, whose arms hung from his neck like chicken wings; my Uncle Verne with his nose to the wind; some pear-shaped sportsman I saw wearing knickers—and the voice, nothing more, of a jailed prophet in a South Carolina hoosegow.

What did I have in mind? I wanted more than these several cloths could supply. It is out of this need that my Uncle Dudley, that genial windbag, arises, a character who blends the happy fiction with the sorry facts. He was the man with whom I longed to take my imaginary trips. A mythic figure, part gold, part brass; an improvised master of improvisation; a man born to give the old shell game an all-American twist.

Such was my intention. Let's look at the results. Fiction and fact have been imaginatively blended, but the dish served up is a platter of clichés. We have that ne'er-do-well, the jocular bounder, who proves to have a heart of gold: he is just the sort of mythic uncle every boy should have. The factual ingredients are small compared with the fictional sources. The Kid is a latter-day Huck Finn afloat on the asphalt river of life, and the motley crew on the gasoline raft are all latter-day heirs to mythical kingdoms.

Uncle Dudley is a modified Duke of Bilgewater, with something of his rhetorical powers of persuasion, and the entire carload, without exception, are refugees from the world of Aunt Sally.

These are obvious facts all these years later, but they were well concealed from me at the time. I had read Tom Sawyer, along with Tom Swift, but Huck Finn and the Duke I did not get around to until some time after My Uncle Dudley. It hardly seems to matter. I was getting my Mark Twain out of the mouths of the characters his fiction had created. The hand that fashioned Huck Finn had also fashioned me. The Road to Xanadu is less mysterious than the river that runs, thanks to Mark Twain, through the fathomless caverns of the All-American Mind.

Sometimes a writer will give you, in his first book, the rough outlines of his matter, the elements, however rudimentary, with which he will grapple for the rest of his life. Rudiments is the word for Uncle Dudley. He is a simple character, but he sounds a characteristic note: audacity, however ill-advised, which lifts or ducks its head in most of the novels reappears, eleven books after Uncle Dudley, in a similarly mobile setting. Love Among the Cannibals would be read by him with relish now that he could pick it up at a drugstore counter.

Man and Boy is the title of one of my books. The question would seem to be: If these figures are archetypes, in what manner do they change their faces? How, and where, do they go on turning up? In The Man Who Was There, there is, prophetically enough, both a new boy and a new uncle: "A man with grass stains on his pants knocked at the door one April morning, called himself Uncle Kermit, and said he had come for Agee Ward. With his Uncle Kermit Agee Ward rode away." More important, there is a new car:

Agee Ward is seated at the steering wheel of a car with wire wheels and a brand new California top. . . . He has removed one hand from the steering wheel to point at Uncle Kermit and what he has just written on the side of the car. This is: CALIFORNIA HERE WE COME! On the running board are three large cans, labeled GAS—WATER—OIL . . . and a desert water bag hangs from a noose on the radiator cap and drips a dark stain on a new army-duck pup tent.

There is one more snapshot from this year. It is taken on Larrabee Street in Chicago, in front of a Y.M.C.A., and seems to mark the end—or the beginning—of something. Uncle Kermit is once more behind the steering wheel. . . . He wears the same black fedora, but the brim has so often been wiped from his face, or blown back, that it will not come down. . . . But the greatest change has taken place in the car. The California top lacks three panes of glass. . . . The windshield is shattered and held together with adhesive tape. . . . It has been somewhere, this car. . . . It will not let you forget where it has been. For it is not a car anymore; it is a character.

Like the old man and the Kid, it will go on turning up in my books.

Uncle Harry and Aunt Clara, the characters of the Home Place, are drawn as closely from life as my talents permitted. Eighty years of rural life had shaped this flesh so well there was little for the writer to do but observe it. In this book the author was both writing fiction and reporting on fiction become flesh. A vivid and moving example of nature, human nature, imitating art. A corset of character, as inflexible and predictable as the seasons, sustained them through almost a century of rural life. The ordeal of survival has placed them beyond either praise or blame, or questions of taste. I tried to speak with disinterest of such matters but I'm afraid the strain shows in the author's voice. On the Protestant nature of their lives he has this to say:

For thirty years I've know what the Home Place lacked . . . but I've never really known what they had. I know now. But I haven't the word for it. The word Beauty is not a Protestant thing. It doesn't describe what there is about an old man's shoes. The Protestant word for that is character. Character is supposed to cover what I feel about a cane-seated chair, and the *faded bib, with the ironed-in stitches, of an old man's overalls. Character is the word, but it doesn't cover the ground. It doesn't cover what there is moving about it, that is. I say these things are beautiful. . . . For this character is beautiful . . . there's something about these man-tired things, something added, that is, that's more than character. . . . Perhaps all I'm saying is that character can be a form of passion, and that some things, these things, have this kin d of character. That kind of passion has made them Holy things. That kind of holiness . . . is abstinence, frugality, and independence—the home-grown, made-on-a-farm trinity. . . . Independence, not abundance, is the heart of their America.*

I have repeated this small sermon not for its moral, which is questionable, but for what it tells us about the *character* who felt that way. Clyde, alias Agee, alias the Kid, is growing up, in his own fashion, and showing a tendency to brag about the things he once kept under the bed. He has found—or so he thinks—a consequential part of his *self*. *The Home Place* is a start. *The World in the Attic* is a summing up. This little book was intended to have photographs, like *The Home Place*, which will partially explain both its slightness and its quality. It is intended to have a memoir-like flavor. My reason for going back to the attic, though, is not to evoke nostalgia but rather to find the partial origin of several new species. They seem to ornament the text rather than to exist as part of the story. One is named Scanlon; one is a sort of handy man named Purdy; and the last is an old woman, Aunt Angie.

All are trial runs for characters who are central to *The Deep Sleep* and *The Field of Vision*.

In *The World in the Attic*, we get our first glimpse of Grandmother Porter:

A loud racket, like a shutter clattering, made me jump. I was wading through the garden, weedy now, but stopped and turned toward the racket, the large birdbox fastened to the window of the old man's room. A large, moth-eaten squirrel sat on top of it. He was biding his time, his mouth full, while a pointed stick, the sharp end of a cane, rattled up and down, back and forth, in the birdbox. Then the cane withdrew, and I heard the lid snap down.

Two novels later she appears in The Deep Sleep.

The arrival of the paper, like the rising of the sun, was one of the things that she observed, [the Grandmother] but she was under oath not to step out on the porch and reach for it. At that time in the morning it was known that she looked a sight. The heels and straps were worn off her shoes, and her apron, the loose strings dangling, hung like a curtain from her gobbler's neck. But there was no law to prevent her from fishing for the paper with her cane.

Later we see her at her ironing, in the basement:

In the cool of the basement, in the corner between the coalbin and the fruit cellar, the Grandmother stood with her back to the light, ironing. Her cane hung from the water pipe that passed over her head. Her apron—since she stepped on the strings—was folded over her arm, like a napkin, with the hard-candy pocket where she could get at it easily. On the broad end of the board sat another iron, on a rack for hot irons, although these irons were never hot enough to burn anything. Mrs. Porter had asked her to please stop spitting on them. But for eighty-five years, and maybe longer, the Grandmother had spit on the face of her irons, and what she had done that long she was still inclined to do. So she spit, whether the iron sizzled or not. Then she ironed, whether the iron was hot or not.

The origin of this species goes back to The Home Place, where we know her as a Cropper:

Grandmother Cropper had been showing my wife her Afghans. They were spread out on the floor, all around her, and my wife had a few squares, the size of pot holders, in her lap. . . . The old lady munched her teeth and said, "After the choir marched in he says, 'Now who is the oldest lady, the oldest mother here today?' Nobody said anything. Then he said, 'Mrs. Tillie A. Cropper is the oldest lady, the oldest mother, here today.'" Grandma fluttered her eyelids. "I thought the floor'd sink beneath my feet. 'I am now going to ask her,' he says, 'to please stand up.' I stood up. He walked across to the pulpit. There was a bouquet of fushia. He says, 'I present this to you today for being the oldest lady, the oldest mother, who is here today.' I made a bow, sat down. He called on the lady next to me, Mrs. Plomers, but she wouldn't get up." Grandma crooked her head, raised her left leg, then made a light pat on the floor.

I have mentioned Mr. Purdy, who comes into the full handyman flower in the character of Mr. Parsons in The Deep Sleep. He is a composite character in which can be seen the lineaments of an archetype. He is distantly related to all of those uncles, Verne, Kermit, and Dudley, since he exists, by stealth, on the rim of society. He lends an ear; he observes; he makes peace; he makes do. Improvising, in one form or another, is his life. I feel for him an affection that is rooted less in paternal pride than in the deep similarity of our roles in life. The writer, too, lives on society's periphery. He lends an ear; he observes; he makes both war and peace; he makes do. Improvising is the essence of his life.

But it is the character named Scanlon, who appears in three of the novels (The World in the Attic, The Field of Vision, Ceremony in Lone Tree), whose career proves to be of interest. He first appears in the Attic, in this context:

This fellow Tom Scanlon, for instance, was known to have slept in his clothes. He smoked a good deal, lying in bed, and left his cigars in a pile in the nightpot, which he kept on the chair at the side of his bed. When he got sleepy he would pull the quilt over his legs. Even in winter he seldom got between the sheets. An odd man, in many ways, he liked the small room at the back [of the hotel] where the only window opened on the west. Right straight down the tracks, the telephone poles, and the semaphores. . . . .

There was no excuse for this as there were comfortable chairs in the lobby, a brass rail for your feet, and a big window on the street. But in the winter, when it got dark early, Tom Scanlon was known to pull his bed, lazy as he was, over to the window so he could look out. Men walking down the tracks would see the glow of his cigar.

For all of its detail, this scene is "fiction." The character arises out of the need that author, and scene have for him. It is why he first appears as a character "offstage," to be heard about. I too am listening. I am trying him on for size.

Before both The Home Place and The World in the Attic, I was absorbed to the point of no return in the life and times of a man named Will Brady, a novel entitled The Works of Love. Several fragmentary versions of this novel run close to 200,000 words. The end product—if it can be called an end—left the attic of my mind strewn with fragmentary conceptions. One of them was Scanlon. The origin of this species was as much a part of the mystique of railroading as the telegraph ticker, the whistle of trains, and the stationmaster's green eyeshade.

Will Brady and Scanlon seem initially to arise from the same impulse, but then Brady, in his story, heads east, down the long road that leads to Chicago. Indian Bow and the view to the west are left to such a character as Scanlon. It is on this ever-receding horizon that his eyes are fixed. If Brady seems to point toward an intolerable future, Scanlon's gaze is fixed on the mythic past. It remains serene and uncorrupted because it keeps itself out of this world. Scanlon devotes his life to the preservation of the past, thawing fragments of it for his grandchildren, to whom this faraway music proves a disquieting legacy. Will Brady followed his gentle dream, and carried to its completion his innocent voyage; but Scanlon made a dark tower of his memories—which were only the memories of others—and made of himself, through his stubborn passion, a species of horseless Don Quixote. Of all this we see little in his early portrait, and must wait to hear his story in The Field of Vision, where the sanded navel of the bullring sets him off. Compare his daughter's memory of her father in The Field of Vision with Scanlon's picture in The World in the Attic: "By the time she had been old enough to wait on him, and run up the stairs with his food, her father had been known as the man in the room. In the bed, as a rule, fully clothed, propped up on a pillow so he could see out the window, or see in the mirror the body of the man stretched out on the bed."

Nor can we be sure the author has finished with him. The Works of Love opens in this manner:

In the dry places, men begin to dream. Where the rivers run sand, there is something in the man that begins to flow. West of the 98th Meridian—where it sometimes rains and it sometimes doesn't—towns, like weeds, spring up when it rains, dry up when it stops. But in a dry climate the husk of the plant remains. The stranger might find, as if preserved in amber, something of the green life that was once lived there, and the ghosts of men who have gone on to a better place. The withered towns are empty, but not uninhabited. Faces sometimes peer out from the broken windows, or whisper from the sagging balconies, as if this place—now that it is dead—had come to life. As if empty it is forever occupied.

These lines suggest not merely one man's preoccupation but something of the nature and function of the imagination. Where the rivers run sand we can look for the origin of a species. One like Tom Scanlon; one like Will Brady; and one like Author Morris.

Part II

Time Present

Time past, beginning with that blend of fiction and fact in My Uncle Dudley, is a mythic land of genial cliches, inhabited by a series of madcap uncles and ruled over by a "fiction" named Tom Scanlon. All of these worthies spend their time fleeing from

Aunt Sally and converting small fry to their nomadic vision of life. This is a durable dream. But what about time *present*? Where and how does one make the leap? In my own case, I think it has been less a leap than an approach through a series of partly concealed transformations: Agee Ward to Clyde Muncy, Muncy to Paul Webb in *The Deep Sleep* to Peter Foley of *The Huge Season* to Gordon Boyd of *The Field of Vision* to Earl Horter of *Love Among the Cannibals*. In Horter the circle rounds upon itself. How does the world look to him?

My story begins, like everything else, on the beach. Beaches are the same the world over, you peel down, then you peel off: they serve you up raw meat, dark meat, or flesh nicely basted in olive oil. A strip of sun and sand where the sex is alert, the mind is numb. . . . If it's world brother-hood you want, go to the beach. If you like parallels, the beach is where we came in, and where we'll go out. Having crawled from the sea, we're now crawling back into it.

How much does such a picture differ from the one that the Kid first sets eyes on?—the beach where the channel swimmer came up from the sea to receive $25,000 from the chewing-gum magnate. The past and present have more in common than we think. Uncle Dudley and the Kid, seated on a bench watching the cars stream by with the good-looking women in them, are not greatly removed from Mac and Horter—those unemployed cannibals sprawled on the beach among the cannybelles. And yet there is a difference. From his seat on the bench Uncle Dudley saw less of the present than of the past. For Mac and Horter, the past lies buried somewhere behind them or is drugged to a disquieting sleep within them. The day starts, as life starts, from scratch.

Love Among the Cannibals attempts to stand in the shifting and treacherous sands of the present, instead of fleeing into the past or the future. In that present, the Kid of *Uncle Dudley*, now transformed into Horter, tries to make out of what is phony something real. "The phony is: I mean it's here and now—you've got to take what's phony, if that's all you've got, and make it real." If Uncle Dudley seduced in the name of the past, the Greek, Horter's audacious girl friend, seduces in the name of the present. Although the present is castigated, the world in the attic is hardly mentioned: the drama enacted in earlier books has reversed itself. It is Time Present, in all of its contradictions, as summed up in the Greek, that carries the day.

In *The Man Who Was There* the buried past looks like this:

To find Lone Tree men came west and planted trees, planted men, planted corn—but the crops of men and corn returned to the east. . . . He could see that Lone Tree was a house divided, the old town facing the west, but the up- and-coming part of the town looking east. . . . Whatever remained on this edge of town did so at a risk, and a bad one, for only a huddle of old buildings had survived. They faced to the west—a row of old men who had walked to where the sidewalk ended and stood there thinking their thoughts, ignoring this firing squad of light.

In *The Home Place* like this:

Out here you wear out, men and women wear out, the sheds, the houses, the machines wear out, and every ten years you put a new seat in the cane-bottomed chair. Every day it wears out, the nap wears off the Axminster. The carpet wears out, but the life of the carpet, the Figure, wears in. . . . Under the carpet, that is, is the floor. After you have lived your own life, worn it out, you will die your own death and it won't matter. It will be all right. It will be ripe, like the old man.

In leaving the Home place we sense that Clyde Muncy has put much of the past behind him—but what about the world he left in the Attic, just a few miles down the road?

Was it possible that Gatsby's Daisy had lived in such a house? (The one in the hollow.) That anything like music had been heard in the yard, a hundred miles from water, or that girlish laughter, if there was such a thing, had blown anywhere? No man would believe it who had not just come, as I had, from the Hibbard basement, where sin and delight were preserved in amber, like the Lone Wolf. Where the sound of one word could bring back the music, the murmuring water music, the tinkling chimes on the porch, and the night as full of license as Cleopatra's barque.

Here is the seed of that strange passion that is central to the character of Boyd, and is something like the dream of a demon lover to the wife of McKee.

Out here there was lust enough, there was mind enough, but let there be no delight—no careening of the heart. Somewhere it had been resolved that the clapper be taken from the bell. That living, loving and dying should be done soberly.

In these words we anticipate the character of Boyd, in The Field of Vision, and the springs of his action: audacity. Audacity returns the clapper to the bell. Audacity, however ill-advised, culminates in the absurd impulses of Boyd and Horter—but time must pass before this impulse reaches such extremities. In Clyde Muncy we have no more than a sense that something vital is missing. If living, loving and dying soberly is not enough—then what is?

The Deep Sleep in the suburbs of Philadelphia seems far from The Home Place—but the word is seems.

It was all there in the mirror, but Webb could not describe the impression it made on him. He had been led through the house, room by room, so that this room had come as a symbolic climax, as if the house had gathered itself together in the lens of the mirror. Beginning at the back, beginning with the kitchen, each room seemed to open on a wider vista, a deeper, more ambitious prospect of American life. A sense of summer leisure, of sweetness and bounty, of innocence and promise without melancholy, seemed to pass through the house, blow in and out of the windows, as if he stood within a grove that Inness might have painted, and gazed out at life.

So the Schuylkill and the Platte, the suburbs and the sticks, are not so far apart as the map would have them. Not in *The Deep Sleep*. The world in the Attic has been shifted to the banks of the Schuylkil, where it is made real, as well as symbolic, and stairs are provided so the characters, when necessary, can retire there. In *The Deep Sleep* the American home has become the deep freeze of American life, where experience is stored until the new tenants, or the undertaker, hauls it away. In *Man and Boy* we are captive in the basement; in *The Deep Sleep* in the attic.

The Huge Season concerns three young men in the thrall of an even stranger captivity. This is how the narrator describes it:

I remember thinking, at the time, that we were like the iron filings in the field of the magnet that Lundgren liked to play with on his desk. But that was not it. Or rather it was more than that. All that does is give a name to the magnet—it doesn't explain the lines of force, or why it was that Lawrence, who was the magnet, became a captive himself.

Lawrence, the magnet, is dead, his mortal remains are at rest, but Peter Foley reassures us that his bones will go on chirping in a time that has stopped. In the large, sagging frame of Gordon Boyd we find the bones of Lawrence and some of his magnetism. That sober Everyman, Walter McKee, has never quite rid himself of the spell, and in a moment of compassion named his first-born son Gordon. Boyd's bohemian example is the ruin of Gordon—in the eyes of at least his mother, that girl on the summer porch whom Boyd, in a fit of audacity, once kissed. When Gordon, in turn, has a son, the child falls under the spell of old man Scanlon—the spell of the past—until he meets, in the bull ring, his

Uncle Gordon Boyd. It has been years since the bones of Boyd were chirping, but at the sight of the boy, in his coonskin hat, his youthful dreams are reactivated. He competes with Scanlon for the boy's admiration, and in an act of impulsive audacity, twirls the coonskin hat out into the ring, then lowers the boy over the fence to go out and get it. After he is salvaged, unhurt, from the bullring, McKee takes him by the hand to lead him out of danger.

"You know as well as I do, Boyd—" he began, but he could sense trouble coming. That wild streak in him. He took a fresh grip on the boy's hand and said, "This boy belongs to his Grandma."

"You're too late," Boyd replied. Did McKee see him shrug?

"Too late for what?" said McKee. Not that he wanted to know, God knows, but he just stood there. How did Mrs. McKee always put it? That Boyd had them bewitched.

"The kid's changed," said Boyd, as if the kid wasn't there. As if this change struck him as a sad one. "He's got a new pitch. He's just torn the pocket off Ty Cobb's pants."

"Don't you go putting ideas into this boy's head," said McKee, and gave the boy's hand a tug.

"You're too late," replied Boyd. "Whose boy you think he is?"

"You watch what you're saying, Boyd," said McKee, and dragged the boy up the aisle to get him out of earshot. "Right now," Boyd yelled, "he's the son of Davy Crockett, but any day now he may swap it for a pocket."

"When he does!" McKee hollered, shouting like an old fool, "I hope it doesn't do to him what it did to you." Then he wheeled and almost ran along the aisle dragging the boy.

In this scene the boy is wooed from the past to the terrors of the present—a triumph that saddens the winner more than it elates him. Boyd has no answer, but to win over the boy he risks, once more, walking on the water—defying the sober, sensible facts of life to set the heart careening, and the bell to ringing. The Field of Vision closes with McKee's awareness that the kid has changed. He is under the spell of the man who had been the ruin of them all.

. . . he could hear the boy yelling like his heart was broke. McKee could tell you, even though he couldn't hear it, just what it was that boy was yelling, and that it wasn't for a bull's horns, or anything like that. Not any longer. No, he was yelling for something else. He was yelling for something, McKee could tell you, that he couldn't buy even if he had the money, and gazing at McKee were the serene blue eyes of his wife. Ice-blue, Boyd called them. In matters like that he usually proved to be right.

Audacity, audacity triumphant—but to what purpose?

Gordon Boyd does not tell us. On this point The Field of Vision is vague. It seems a means of escape, primarily, from a life that has lost its savor, that seems to fear, above all else, the phantom of delight.

You will understand that I am speculating after the event. This is what I learn from my own books, not what I bring to them. Since the day Uncle Dudley first set eyes on California, through the spray thrown up by those mighty channel swimmers, it has never ceased to attract, repel and fascinate me. And with reason. It is the laboratory of the future. Both the sorcerer and the apprentice can learn from it.

So much for the scene. What about the characters? Here in the parallel is even more striking. The Kid is back—not merely in a new disguise—but as a latter-day Uncle Dudley, shepherding a latter-day crew of phonies across the dry places to the real McCoy. It is the Greek, however, not Horter, that calls the tune on this adventure, and the Greek is something more than audacity. If Scanlon is the personified *past*, the Greek is the personified *present*.

In these two figures we seem to have reached the world of pure contradiction. What bridge, real or imaginary, can possibly connect the beach at Acapulco with the old man Scanlon's hallucinated vision of Heaven as Hell?

At first viewing the *Cannibals* seems to consist of four characters—a sweet and sour pairing of cannibals and canny-belles. But what is it that we see right behind them?

This car the studio put at our disposal was in the quiet unassuming good taste of a hotrod parts manufacturer on his day off. Fireman's red, with green upholstery, it had a crushproof steering wheel, a crushproof dash, compartments in the doors for whiskey and soda, and a record player where the glove compartment usually is.

That is our first glimpse of this dream wagon before the front end drops into the ditch in Acapulco, and the process of stripping it down to the chassis begins. What happens to the car first happened to the cannibals on the beach. Day and night, the amiable destroyers keep their vigil in the ditch, boring from within like termites, reducing the car by degrees to the same condition as the occupants. It is this inanimate thing that symbolizes what the animate are undergoing. A shearing off of the clichés. A getting down to the essential facts.

. . . The men working beneath it were putting back the motor, the men working in it were putting back the dashboard, and the men not working were thinking of putting back the top. But they were sticking to the essentials. The little inessentials they were leaving off.

So the car is the link between the mythic past and the intolerable present, as it is also the link between Uncle Dudley and Earl Horter. It is the car that involves us in flight toward something—and flight away from it. Horter confronts the problem in this way:

When you hear people complain about custom regulations, passports, officials, and the rest of it, they are really telling you they don't want to leave the interior. They've come to a line, real and imaginary, they don't want to cross. When you bolt it helps to have one on the map, plainly visible. A threshold, like the door to that cabin in Malibu. When the Greek crossed that line she knew it, and kicked off her shoes. I like that. That's life as literature.

Who's talking? It might be Uncle Dudley, on his way to jail, it might be Webb, on his way to the Attic, it might be Foley reflecting on Lawrence, it might be Gordon Boyd reflecting on the springs of action in himself.

This does not imply a rejection of the Past so much as an escape from its crippling thralldom, such as Peter Foley believes he has experienced in his escape from the captivity of Lawrence. Devoid of nostalgia, Love Among the Cannibals takes place in a world where the past is non-existent: a moving back drop that appears to give motion to a car that is stationary.

After appearing in many disguises as the Hero, and his witness, and by the most circuitous fashion possible, Uncle Dudley and the Kid find themselves back at the starting point of their manifold adventures. Los Angeles, that City of Angels, that land of powdered milk and elusive honey which thirty years of time-present had transformed into a Disney Wonderland of the Phony. It was there that both adventures have their start in a transport of improvisation—the first in the picking up of men, the second in the picking up of women—and with full cargos both ships set sail for the Great Good Place. The beckoning green of Chicago's Lincoln Park, like the nostalgic green of Christmas jewelry, lures the traveler to the same pitfalls as the light-ringed bay of Acapulco, where what is phony, brought to its climax, can be sheared off.

Back in the twenties Uncle Dudley put it this way:

"You had enough milk and honey?" he said.
"I guess I've had enough," the Kid replied.

What is this if not characteristically American? Well enough is precisely the condition we will not leave alone. A tinkering, both appalling and sublime, is always going on. From her window at the sink the woman of the house, fenced in by all the comforts of technology, can see only the feet of the man who lies in the yard. He is *under* something, or he is into something, or he is building something, or he is tearing down something, and of only one thing can the woman of his life rest assured—milk and honey, homogenized and fortified, will not quiet him. *That* he now has—if he wants it—but what he seems to want is to make it new. Make it new in the hope that it will turn out to be what he wants.

But that is not likely. It is not, as we say, in the cards. The writer of fiction, dipping his hands into the swirl of our life, hears the disquieting roar of the disposal unit in his ears. Is the life that he loves, and tries to salvage, going down the drain? Little wonder, faced with this fact, that it is nostalgia that rules our hearts while a rhetoric of progress rules our lives. Little wonder that the writer, spinning his web over this drain like a spider, should indulge both himself and the reader in a singular conceit: that it is the web, not the drain, that transforms the raw material, the remains of spent lives, into a fiction of permanence. It is the last of those imaginative acts of audacity that give rise to the origin of a new species and the species, in turn, to a character. It will serve, for the time being, as one more answer to Crevecoeur's perennial question—but only until a new answer comes along. Only one thing seems certain. Stamped on its bottom will be the legend MADE IN U.S.A.

Excerpt from *Love Among the Cannibals*

My story begins, like everything else, on the beach. Beaches
are the same the world over, you peel down, then you peel off;
they serve you up raw meat, dark meat, or flesh nicely basted
in olive oil. A strip of sun and sand where the sex is alert, the
mind is numb. The beach in question, one of the best, is near
where Sunset Boulevard meets the sea. I don't mean to be ironic.
California is that way naturally. It's hard to do malice to California, but this particular strip might have been in Acapulco,
or down in Rio, or along the Riviera. If it's world brotherhood
you want, go to the beach. If you like parallels, the beach is
where we came in, and where we'll go out. Having crawled
from the sea, we're now crawling back into it. That solution of
salt in the blood is calling us home. And in a mammary age,
what better place to compensate for an unsuckled childhood?
Where else, these days, does the pretty matron shyly lower her
bra straps, hugging her charms? Not to nourish the future,
alas, but to preserve, in sun oil, the present. A season in the sun
before going under. Is that what we want? My friend Mac has a
colleague who wears on her tanned thigh the white shadow of
a man's hand—his own, as it happens. A climax, of course, to
her night-club act. A purely professional assist, in every respect.
They often pass the time at the beach together, and one man's

hand is as good as another's. She sings his songs, so he really belongs in the act.

When people ask me where I ran into Mac, I say the war. We have the stamp of things that came out of it. I've pieced together that Mac was born in Brooklyn, but I've never really heard him say so. He doesn't talk. I mean he doesn't articulate. If he's in a friendly, expressive mood he might sing his own songs, one of Cole Porter's, or variations on a number called *Dancing in the Dark*. That's Mac. If you add Noel Coward you've covered the field. If he has ever felt anything else I don't think he would recognize it. Which leaves me with a real problem. How to keep him up-to-date. I take an old cliché, soak him in it, then give it just that squeeze of the lemon that leads him to think he thought of it himself. In the flush of that sort of emotion he can speak.

"Man," he will bark, "it's great!"

In the song-and-dance business self-confidence helps.

Mac is thirty-eight, just three years my junior, but he looks a good deal younger. He has a round, bland, background-music sort of face. He tends to run a little heavy, his complexion is mottled with what I suppose was teenage smallpox, and he gives strangers the impression he's a little deaf. He isn't, but he seldom hears anything. When I'm in a rare sympathetic mood I tell the chicks that he's listening to his own music. But he's not. Nor is it what you would call a blank. The absence of any popular song to describe the vacant moods Mac passes his life in will leave most of his life a mystery. Two or three times a month he will roll over and say—he never thinks of anything unless he's lying down—"I ever tell you how I shot down that ME-109?"

In fifteen years you can shoot down a lot of 109's. But that event keeps coming back to him like the theme of one of his songs—a hit song, I suppose, he is still trying to find the music for. He looks to me for the words, but I don't have them. I never shot down an ME-109 myself.

I had lived with Irwin K. Macgregor for eight months in England without speaking to him. But that was not unusual. Nobody did. He was not the silent type, but the army had silenced him. Like a lot of silent men, he didn't have much to say, but in an inarticulate sort of way he can be fluent. This fluency consists of a theme and variation. The theme is, "Man, it's great!" The variation, "It's great, man!" If you know the army, you know what it would do to a vocabulary like that. "It's great, man!" will cover most of the verbal problems in the song business, but the army was no song, so Mac had nothing to say. Nothing at all, I mean, until he met me.

Mac was no great shakes as a pilot but we both fagged out the same cold winter, and we were sent upcountry to the same warm spa to recuperate. That's where we met. The place featured the usual lousy food, but some nice girls from Holland and a grand piano. I didn't know till he gave the stool a spin, and sat on it, that he played. I'd sit down at one end of the room, with a book, and watch this army-silenced guy dust off the stool with his knuckles, then squat on it and talk. A fluent keyboard lover. A real poet, of sorts, on the black keys. One day he played with a little more schmaltz than usual, and although we hadn't exchanged a word he looked up and said:

"Like that, eh?"

"It's not a bad tune," I said, since it sounded familiar.

"It's great, man!" he said. "I wrote it."

And he had. I could name you, but I won't, about a half-dozen tunes he had written before I met him. Not bad, not good. Lacking the master touch. The sort of *unheard* music you need to fill out a TV program. But his piano was good. It was the piano that gave him his start. He could have sat out the war in a Fort Dix jazz band but he got this idea that he wanted to fly. He thought the war had come along so he could pick up, without charge, the rudiments. He did, all right, and as he points out himself—that's where he met me. I couldn't do much for his talent, but I could give the lyrics a certain touch. If the lyrics were *good*—I mean if the clichés were coined before he was—he had the sort of talent that could almost live up to them. What I'm saying is, as he puts it, we make a great team.

There have been so many corny movies about jazz pianists I don't have to tell you about them. That's how he was. I mean he was like *all* of them. He believed. He even believed in his own stuff. After he met me there was some point in it—some point, that is, believing in *my* stuff—but up until then it was all a matter of faith. Until he met me all of his songs were songs without words. I took his music and pasted the right sort of labels on it. I used to do that sort of thing for nothing, what we referred to in my youth as amusement, and I found it more amusing than trying to read a book. Sitting there, day after day, I heard the same tunes over and over, and I found it entertaining to write a set of lyrics for some of them. One little tune I liked went something like this:

> Roses are nice, violets are too,
> But tulips are what I share with you.
> Stamen, pistol and pollen connect,
> The tulips of Kansas with old Utrecht.

I had reference to a particular piece of light meat from Utrecht. One day Mac played this tune and from my corner of the room I chipped in with the lyrics. It made quiet an effect.

"Man, it's great!" he barked, and with that modest statement the song team of Macgregor and Horter was born. It didn't help me with the maid from Holland, but it settled me with Macgregor. "You got talent, man!" he said. "You know what I mean?" As it happened, I did. We've been inseparable, as our billing says, ever since.

It's probably fair to say, as Mac often does, that I've made him whatever he is—is being a man with a fat check from ASCAP every month. In the trade we are sometimes referred to as the poor man's Rodgers & Hart, since the big-time money has a way of eluding us. It might be that my lyrics, like some cough drops, dissolve very pleasantly on the tongue but have a way of coming back, like the taste of onions, during the night. I don't really know. But something like the taste of onions is at the back of my mouth right now.

In the *Who's Who in the Missouri Valley*—in it at one time, that is—you will see my picture and find me listed as the Shelley of the corn belt. The next year I was drafted. That makes me sixteen years a poet *manqué*. I understand that the war made some poets the way a man is said to make a woman, but that wasn't my war, and it had another effect on me. The only poetry I now hear is when Mac brings a chick to the apartment and plays my recording of Eliot reading *The Waste Land*. He has the record nicked so it retracks when the voice says:

"Hurry up, please, it's time!"

Something about Eliot's Oxford accent seems to do the trick. It's never long before he gets up and turns the record off, and the lights on. Although I've stopped writing it myself, I'm responsible for spreading some pretty good lines. Trapped with a chick of the brainy type Mac will say:

> "Does the imagination dwell the most
> Upon a woman won or a woman lost?"

If she says lost, he dates her. If she doesn't, he claims he hasn't missed anything.

Before you feel sorry for either of us, let me tell you that we spend our time on the beach, where, if you had our time and money, you'd like to spend yours. We came here, instead of Bermuda, where the sun is also shining, because I had, and sold, this idea for a new musical. New? Well, something in the line of a Latin-American *Porgy and Bess*. Yankee money, Latin passion, good-neighbor policy, everything. I've been to Mexico, which takes care of that, and Mac has listened to a lot of Xavier Cugat. We don't want it so Latin it might alienate Uncle Sam. Three of the major studios fought for it, and we are now living in what they call a château, in one of the fire-trap canyons, with a view of all the water that is out of reach in case of fire. Mac has a piano, and I have all day at the beach. What I do, I can do anywhere, but Mac can only sound chords at night, or very early morning on the St. Regis roof. He sleeps under the beach umbrella most of the day, then we go out to eat where they have background music, with a girl in the foreground singing Macgregor & Horter's latest hit. A little after midnight we drive back up the canyon and go to work. Something Mac once read in a muscle magazine led him to feel that sex drains a man's creative energy. He means the same night. It doesn't seriously handicap a song writer. Sex is something he takes like vitamins, and it has nothing to do with immortal love, tenderness, loss of sleep, and songs like *Stardust*. As Mac says himself: "Sex is sex. You know what I mean?"

I do. It is part of my job. The problem is to find a nice respectable chick who needs a little push along, professionally, and who doesn't mind a little do-re-mi from a respectable guy. They're not too hard to find. A little French Bikini number, who needed a very long push, had been on Mac's hands for the past three weeks, but she had this idea that you don't need a voice in the song racket. You don't. But you need more than one close friend.

That side of my colleague's nature is cut and dried, offers little in the way of complications, and leaves him fairly famished for what he calls the *real thing*. The real thing is hard to define, but roughly it's what Charlie Chaplin found, beginning with Paulette Goddard. We might call it *The Million-Dollar Baby in the Five-&-Ten Weltanschauung*. I think he got it from the song, which he ran into a little early, but he was, and is, precocious about songs. As another man stumbles on *Jean Christophe*, Kahlil Gibran, or

Dale Carnegie, Mac stumbled on the Million-Dollar Baby in the five-and-ten. That did it. That's what he means by *heart*.

"It's GOT no heart, man!" he'll say, so I'll take whatever it is and slip in a few words about how he found her in the automat. A girl with a green stain on her finger from a piece of Christmas jewelry can name her price. Mac will double it.

Like a talent scout in Woolworth's basement, Mac likes to hang around the record department, waiting for some Million-Dollar Baby to buy one of his songs. When she does he will lean over and say, "Like that, eh?" As a rule she does, having bought it. He will then introduce himself as the author, and the next thing you know he asks the chick if she can sing. Did you ever hear of a girl in a dime store who couldn't sing? I suppose we have roughly half a million records proving that not one of them can, but the way some of them *can't* is interesting. Mac has turned up a dozen or so of them. Any one of these girls will tell you that Mac has a heart of gold, combined with the loftiest Father's Day sentiments. All of which is true. His Million-Dollar Babies are left untouched. They are all heart, having nothing in common with the chicks, of a respectable sort, who need a little practical push along. They can be found in dime stores, drugstores, hot-dog stands, orange-drink shops, and all those places Charlie Chaplin had the knack of turning them up. Nowadays they can also be flushed at the beach. Million-Dollar Babies with that spring-green Christmas jewelry look.

You never know the other side of an army man until you see him in mufti. But Mac has no mufti. He stepped out of one uniform into what I'll have to call another. If you have sometimes wondered who it is who really wears the two-tone ensembles that set the new car styling, Mac is your man. That's why I keep him down at the beach. He's quite a sight on the beach as well, in his Hawaiian shorts, made of coconut fiber, a cerise jacket with a bunny-fur texture, a sea-green beret, and something like an ascot looped at his throat. Those shops that have the latest thing for men always have something, hidden in one of the drawers, too early for anybody else but just right for Mac. On the beach I let him wear it. He still looks better with it on than off. He has one of those complexions that will never tan, so he passes the day under the beach umbrella. Having no complexion problems I lie in the sun and watch the chicks go in and out of the water. When the beach is crowded I listen for the up-and-coming clichés. That particular morning it wasn't crowded; we had a little morning fog, which is customary, but I rather like the beach in a cloud of fog. There you are; the sound of the sea is off behind the wall.

This little chick with her hair in a pony tail came up from behind us, sprinkled a little sand on me, then pitched her camp where the tide had smoothed the sand. She spread out her little towel, let down her straps, put on her gem-studded glasses with the built-in visor, daubed Noxzema on her nose, then lit up a Parliament and smoked. I thought the little leather case might have her lunch, her radio, and her sun-tan lotion, but this was no run-of-the-mill sort of chick. Not on your life. She opened it, cranked it, and put a record on the gramophone. Owing to the radio Mac was playing, we didn't hear her taste in music till he turned it off. A sultry-type songbird was crooning a number entitled "What Next?" That happened to be the last song we had written with a chance to catch on. The songbird was the not-so-little girl we call Pussy, the one with Mac's hand on her thigh, who specializes in what I call Music for Leching, without accompaniment. She sings under the name of Faith Amor. The one exception to my practice of using clichés, and not writing them, will be found in "What Next?" I had to write them. It explains the song's brand-new old look.

> What next?
> The life of love I knew
> No longer loves
> The things I do.
> What next?

When Mac heard those moving lines he sat up and barked, "Man, it's great! You know what I mean?"

This little chick really did.

"Ah think she is simply *wonnaful*," she said, modestly pulling up one suit strap. "If Miss Ah-moh does it, I just have to have it. Ah reahly do."

If you keep your ear to the ground for clichés, as I have to, you get these shockers. First you hear it, then you meet it in the flesh. Since Mac gives the impression of being a little deaf, she turned her blinkers on me.

"It's a nice song," I said. "What's the girl's name?"

Nothing rocks these chicks back so much as to hear they are mad about someone you never even heard of. She rocked back and said, "You nevah hurt of Miss Ah-moh?"

"You mean Pussy?" I said. "The chick on the strip?"

That cut her. You could see where she was cut.

"Pussy can do a nice piece, all right," I said, "if she's got the right material."

"Ah'm sho yoh can't mean Miss Ah-moh," she replied. "Ah nevah hurt Miss Ah-moh refurt to as Pussy."

"Her mummy calls her Pussy, her daddy calls her Pussy, her friends call her Pussy, and we call her Pussy."

"Yoh ackshilly know huh?"

"Mr. Macgregor here does," I said, giving Mac the nod. "He wrote the song foh huh." I have to watch myself with these Suthun belles, since I tend to imitate their lingo.

"Yoh ackshilly dit?" she said, looking at Mac. Mac ackshilly did, but I could sympathize with her. "Ah feel chus mortafite, Mistuh MacGraw—" she began, but if you're going to follow what it is she says I ought to stop telling you how she sounds. But if what she said really mattered, I'd translate it for you. It's all in how she sounds. What she went on to say was that if she had half the sense she was born with, a doubtful statement, she would have known it was the song, not just the ah-tist, that appealed to her. She managed to say that, then she looked at Mac as if talking to him would move him to speech.

"Pussy hams it up a little," I put in, "but it's not a bad piece."

She wiggled like a wet puppy on her towel, then she pinched herself and asked Mac if she was asleep or if she was awake. That was actually one that Mac might have answered, but he let it pass. Then she wanted to know if we thought she was crazy, a young unchaperoned little girl like herself, coming down to the beach with nothing but her record player and her Parliaments. I was about to answer that one when she sighed, then said:

"Mistuh MacGraw, ah get so sick an' tahd talkin' to mahself."

Mac generally looks so dead that any sign of life in him makes quite an impression. It made one on her. It made one on both of us. He suddenly sat up, leaning forward so far that the crucifix he wears around his neck swung free on its chain, showing the 18-carat stamp. He's not religious, but he believes in playing the odds. I could see the idea drip through his mind that there was a song here, a *great* one, and the words "so sick an' tired talkin' to myself" formed on his lips. Then it crossed his mind why he thought so. Someone had already done it. The wind of hope that had filled him seemed to leak out through his pores.

"Yoh know why ah come to the beach, Mistuh MacGraw? Ah come to thaw out. Ah was nevah so colt anywheah in mah life as ah am out heah."

She shivered. If I had half the brains I was born with, I would have heard the alarm right there. Mac's alarm, I mean. The buzzer that rings when one of his Million-Dollar Babies turns up.

"It's a nasty climate—" I said, edging away. "You freeze in the fog, then—"

"Honey—" she said, giving herself a little hug, "ah doan mean that climate. Ah mean the hu-man climate. Ah nevah crossed paths with so many colt shoulters in all mah life."

In a moment of excitement he can hardly bear, Mac will take off whatever hat he is wearing, run one hand through his hair, then put the hat back on, pulled down tight. He did that. Then he looked at me and said, "Crossed paths, man! Crossed paths an' cold shoulders!"

His eyes were one me, but they were actually leafing through our song-title file. If "Crossed Paths" wasn't there now, it soon would be.

"Miss—" I began, but she was telling Mac that the only friend she had was her little record player, and by that she meant it was the only friend she had of the masculine sex. Was she out of her mind to think her little gramophone was her boy friend? Well, she did. It just went to prove how lonely she was. She was one of these chicks who close or flutter their eyelids whenever their mouth is open, acting on the same principle as these dolls with the weights in their heads. I couldn't get a word in edgewise. Her pretty little cold shoulders were covered with duck bumps. I thought Mac would take his shirt off and wrap it around her, but he was too excited, too full of the *big* one, so all he did was jam the hat down around his ears, then say:

"Baby—you sing?"

"Mistuh MacGraw!" she said, shocked with recognition. "Why, Mistuh MacGraw."

"Miss—" I began.

"What in the wohld should evah make you think so, Mistuh MacGraw? Ah do sing. Ah suppose ah should say ah wanna sing."

"Miss Garland—" I said. That clicked. I mean that cut her to the quick.

"Harcum," she said. "Miss Billie Harcum. Ah'm a stootun of Marlene Mazda Joyce, although yoh-all probly know huh, an' refuh to huh as somethin' else."

"Muzzy Joyce has some nice contacts, Miss Harcum," I said. "We sometimes find a cage for her little songbirds. You dance?"

"Why, Mistuh—"

"Horter. Of Macgregor & Horter."

"Ah'm the awfullust fool, Mistuh Hortuh. Ah know yoh name as well as mah own."

"Let's focus on Mac here then," I said. "The name is Macgregor, not MacGraw, but he'll probably insist that you call him Mac."

"Oh, Mistuh Macgregaw!"

"My name is Earl," I went on, "but I don't insist on it."

"Uhl? Ah chus love Uhl as a name."

"We're not casting right now, Miss Harcum, but we have a small spot for some dark-complected dancers—Mexicali roses instead of Memphis roses, if you know what I mean."

She did. I waited to see if she could take it, and she took it.

"You'll need a little more color," I said, sizing her up. "The shade we're going to want is octoroon, or light mulatto—"

When I said mulatto she darkened to the shade I had in mind. Over the years I've noticed that a flush of indignation does more for a girl than Max Factor. There's more to flush in a woman, that is, than her face and eyes.

"You'll do if you can dance, honey," I said, and she suddenly saw right through me. I was a *card*. It had taken her all that time to catch on. I didn't really mean what I'd said about mulatto, it was just my way of pulling her pretty leg. She put it out where I could reach it, and said:

"Mistuh Hortah, ah'm essenchuly a singah. A singah of the contnental type."

Continental-type singers, *aus* Weehawken and Memphis, are almost as rare as girls who sing in dime stores.

"What we *need* is dancers, Miss Harcum," I began, but Mac sat up suddenly and barked:

"Baby, can you take it?"

"Take it?" echoed Miss Harcum. Fearing the worst, she turned to me.

"We have a little test number, Miss Harcum," I said. "If a girl can't take it—" I rolled my eyes, shrugged my shoulders.

"Can ah try—right heah, Mistuh Hortuh?"

"Sure, baby!" barked Mac. "If you'll turn that thing off—" and he wagged his hand at her whining record player. I don't sing our stuff often, but when I do Mac knows I like it quiet. Our little cannibelle number, as a matter of fact, is a litmus test. The chick can take it or leave it, and we can take or leave the chick. Miss Harcum wiggled over to switch off her machine, then she came over like a seal with a fish at its nose, and let me have the benefit of her pretty little duckies. I wet my lips, huskily crooned:

> "Baby cannibelle, once you try it,
> I'm the dark meat in your diet,
> You eat me while I eat you,
> Since it's the economical thing to do,
> Baby, baby can-ni-bellllle!"

Well, they don't do it so much any more, but she almost swooned. The Memphis type, *her* type, don't go in for playing it cool. She bit down on her lip, gasped for air, scooped little holes in the sand to hide her feet in, and gave no thought to the fact that both of her straps were down.

"Man," bellowed Mac, "she can take it! You know what I mean? She took it!"

"Oh, Mistuh Mac—"

"—gregor," I said. "The number's not particularly Latin-American, but it is *muy* Acapulco," giving the *muy* a roll that made it clear just what I meant.

"Aca-pulco?" she said. "Now did you evah—Ah'm invited to a pahty of some folks who just come from Acapulco. Theatuh people. You would know theah names. Ah'm invited but ah jus got too much self-respeck, I suppose."

"What kinda party is it, baby?" said Mac, since he loved non-respectable parties.

"It's not the kinda pahty a respectable gurl is seen at alone."

I got the picture pretty well, and said, "Too bad all our nights are sewed up, Miss Harcum, but since Mac, here—"

"Baby—" said Mac, "when is it?"

"This particulah pahty just so happens to be tonight, Mistuh MacGraw."

"Baby—" chanted Mac, but in his excitement he forgot what he meant to say. But I hadn't. When a chick has passed the Horter test, it's always the same.

"You happen to have a girl friend, Miss Harcum?" I said.

"Mistuh Hortuh—" she said, fluttered her eyes as if the idea of a girl friend left her nonplused. It gave me time to slip a pencil out of Mac's shirt pocket, tear off a piece of his score. When her eyes stopped fluttering it crossed her mind that she did have a girl friend, one she worked with, and being theatuh people they all more or less lived in the same house. I took the address, the telephone number, and to make sure we would find the place after dark we drove her home and dropped her off on our way to eat.

This car the studio put at our disposal was in the quiet, unassuming good taste of a hot-rod parts manufacturer on his day off. Fireman red, with green leather upholstery, it had a crush-proof steering wheel, a crush-proof dash, compartments in the doors for whisky and soda, and a record player where the glove compartment usually is. We didn't even have to buy our own records. They supplied us with them.

I'd say one of Mac's ideas of heaven is to have Eddie Duchin playing Cole Porter while we cruise along the coast highway toward Santa Barbara. You don't have to whistle at the girls in this car, just sit in it with the top down, the music going, while you drive along the strip. This little chick and her friends lived in Westwood, in one of those attractive slums for tomorrow, a cool arrangement of glass and tin sloped to catch the heat. This chick had sworn her girl friends would be dying to meet me, an actual living man who wrote song lyrics, but she came down the steps alone, and joined us in the front. I must say she looked sharp. You know how these little girls learn to walk so they make a sharp clack on the pavement, and almost whinny when they pull up alongside your fence.

She climbed in—she got in between us—then she said she just had to be frank with me, and that her girl friends didn't feel they should be running around with a man my age. "Well, what age am I?" I said, since I hadn't mentioned my age. "All ah said was you certainly weren't over forty," she replied. I could see she pulled that deal just to flatter Mac, in his baby-face thirties, and at the same time have the two of us to herself. All the time she put on this little act her hand was on my knee, not Mac's, indicating that a man my age offered certain advantages.

Anyhow, I went to this party without a chick. We drove back to Sunset, I remember, into that section they call Bel Air, then we drove into the hills where the movie stars live. You can't bring the Riviera over in crates, the way Citizen Kane would have liked to, but you can name the streets Cannes, Antibes, Monaco, with an Italian wing running from Amalfi to Sorrento. We took the French wing, that night, and followed it to the summit of the hill, where we curved along the vine-covered wall of a château. So that the effect wouldn't be lost, or if you came up at night and might have missed it, the drive in went across a drawbridge over a moat. Inside the open court, about the size of a gym, there were representative sports cars of all nations, with a patriotic sprinkling of Thunderbirds. On the East Coast that would mean money, but here on the West Coast a soda jerk, willing to choose between a chick and a Thunderbird, can have the Thunderbird. He lives in a closet, gulps his sandwich at the counter, and can't afford the salves for his athlete's foot, but when you see him on Sunset he's on a par with the movie stars. Unless they get off the highways, it leaves most movie stars with no place to turn.

Surrounded with all that quiet, imported good taste, our bright fire wagon had a certain class, and I left it where we could sneak off early, since I intended to.

One of these professional catering outfits had taken over the place. They had a fellow in the yard to lead you to the right door, a man at the door to size you up and frisk you, then one in the hall to guide you to the proper facilities. One of the minor dividends of forty-one years, fifteen of them passed among the gay counterfeiters, is that you can size up a piece of scenery pretty fast. The way these caterers knew their way around they probably lived in it. This mansion full of trophies—they had a viking sled with the reindeer harnessed in the main hallway—was probably rented out, furnished, for parties of this type. This one had been given an Acapulco flavor by stringing a fish net along the stairway, and scenting the place with the smell of Mexican cigarettes. They had a Mariachi outfit from Olvera Street, featuring an old man, his shoulders snowy with dandruff, who would let out that *yip* so characteristic of carefree, child-like, passionate Mexican life. The drinks were served in those blurred Mexican glasses, by waiters in creaky huaraches, and *aficionados* were encouraged to take their tequila straight. I'm nothing if not an *aficionado*, and I attracted more than the usual attention by scoffing at the plate of sliced limes, and crying for salt. I had spent most of one summer mastering tequila and salt. You sprinkle a little salt on the back of your hand, where you can lick it off, like a tourist, or by tapping the wrist, sharply, get the salt to hop into your mouth. I did, then raised my eyes to see—the way a man meets his fate in the movies—a woman, a young woman, who had just entered the room. The directness of her gaze caught me unprepared. I returned it, that is. The word chick—the word I *rely* on—did not come to mind. This tremendous girl—the scale of this girl made me step back a pace to see her—wore one of the flowers, one of the favors for the ladies, in her hair. That's all I could tell you. I turned away at that point to collect myself. It took me more than a moment. The jigger-size glass that held my tequila was slippery on the outside from what I had spilled. You know the feeling you have that in your grasp, *within* your grasp, you have the dream that has always escaped you—followed by the feeling that your eyes, and your heart, have cheated you again. When I turned she was gone. Gone. Had she really been there?

I walked back to the main hall where I could see up the curve of the stairs, where the women congregated; pretty good-looking women, in the main, thanks to the California sun. But this girl was not there. Looking up the flight of stairs it occurred to me that I wouldn't know this girl by how she looked—I didn't *know* how she looked—I would only recognize her by how I felt. How did I feel? The way I often feel in elevators.

Excerpt from *One Day*

To avoid people—the pattern of his life seldom departed from this constant—Cowie left the scene of the accident while it was still crowded. Time had changed many things, but it had not persuaded Cowie to turn from animals to people. Was there never an end of it? Murder most foul, the bell tolling another witches' sabbath? In the dark reaches of Cowie's mind a clanging sounded, like a crossing bell, and melancholy reflections were stored to hang head down, like bats. In the lights of the car as he approached his house he saw the raccoon posted at his nightly vigil, waiting for Cowie to sort out and serve his miserly garbage. Lacking garbage, Cowie had turned to such substitutes as TeeVee dinners. The raccoon preferred them served hot. If Cowie took pains with this offering, however, so did the guest. Cans and rubbish were left undisturbed once he felt he could rely on Cowie's judgment. Often by moonlight Cowie had watched him roll the garbage can down the drive like a beer barrel to where it would clatter with the sound of doom on the concrete wall. This impact would invariably pop off the lid. The problem had taxed Cowie's mind until he had stumbled on the brotherhood syndrome, and did to raccoons what raccoons would have done to themselves. On a compartmented plate he put out choice scraps, TeeVee dinners and thawed supermarket mince meat pies. A favorite.

The cats, who had expected him sooner, were not there at the door to greet him. The house was cold. Mrs. Warren had forgotten to turn on the heat. In the icebox, however, he found her can of Metrecal, pack of sliced Kraft cheese, and a loaf of dietary bread. A woman of Cowie's age—a point she liked to bring up—Mrs. Warren had raised four children, buried her husband, but valued her independence more than the comforts of living with her eldest son and his children in a tract. The first time she had pronounced the word tract Cowie had felt certain he misunderstood her. So Mrs. Ahearn would refer to the pesthouse where the doomed went to die.

His housekeeper for five years—after a year's trial run as his cleaning woman—Mrs. Warren didn't favor, as she said, much informality. He was still Mr. Gowie, as she preferred to pronounce it, and she was still Mrs. Warren. She used Cowie's bathroom to slip her plastic apron over her head. Otherwise, if he was in the house, she preferred not to use it at all, reserving part of her lunch period for a visit to Mrs. Opler, a friend up the road. To have something to say to Mrs. Warren on those occasions he found himself with her, Cowie had brushed up on her favorite subject, cholesterol. In spite of his familiarity with dietary problems he found this topic treacherously elusive. It seemed to lie in the mysterious distinctions between polyunsaturated oils, and saturated. Cowie grasped the meaning, but the application baffled him. Which one it was that was best for him he never seemed to know. That proved to be a help, since in that respect, if not in others, he was very much like her deceased husband: another man who failed to grasp what she knew to be best for him. Like Cowie he had smoked too much. Unlike Cowie he had killed himself swinging violently at a golf ball. Nor had he played the game. He had dropped dead in one of those places where you rent a bucket of the balls, and more than half the balls were still in the bucket when he dropped dead.

Mrs. Warren never tired of describing this event, leaving Cowie to draw his own conclusions. She had lived with him for twenty-four years, but the existence of this man seemed hard to establish. He was Mr. Warren. For eighteen of those twenty-four years he had served in the housewares department at Sears, which was why her kitchen had been the finest room in her house. As fine as it was, however, even her children knew she would not sit around in it all day and mope. In the Christmas season she helped out at Penney's, or worked in the notions counter at Woolworth's, where she saw all her friends more often than in all of those years she was tied down as a housewife. With Mr. Warren's unexpected passing she had begun a new life.

As he poured himself a glass of her skimmed milk, and spread poly-margarine on her dietary bread, Cowie wondered what the events of the day had meant to Mrs. Warren. Curious how often he referred them to her. Mrs. Warren's Tribunal. From her he would hear the judgment he feared to make himself. Death was not new to her. It seemed more accurate to say it did not exist. It would be that last extremity that did not lend itself to the cholesterol treatment, and with a certain embarrassed shrug of the brows would have to be faced.

When Mrs. Warren had come to Cowie it had been with many recommendations. Or rather connections. "I've connections all over," she had said. Connections all over she had, with the possible exception of her husband. She had them with the County, with the Purity Market, the girl who cashed her annuity checks at the bank, with Wade's Pharmacy, Sunset Magazine, the Blue Chip Stamp Store in Fairfax, and last but not least Dr. Cowie, who was now a connection she would list.

Visible ties, all of them. Mrs. Warren was independent but not a loner. She would be the first to sense that Lee Harvey Oswald would come to no good. Connections were precisely what he seemed to lack. The lines were down. Who in Dallas would cash his personal check? In Mrs. Warren's bland gaze Cowie saw mirrored his own trial by jury and its judgment: when it happened it would not be surprising, whatever it was. She knew his icebox, his dirty socks, his seldom slept-in bed. "I was his housekeeper for six long years," she would say, and the world would bate its breath for her comment. As it must to every man it would come to Cowie, polyunsaturated.

Did that sum it up? Connections were precisely what he did not have. Not with people. The lines were down with people, up with raccoons and cats. Was that not the clue to the new expanding age of pets? Those who did not go mad, or shoot somebody, or embrace a cause, or give away their babies, would discover the uses and abuses of a pet. Of FREE LOVE, as Evelina's cartons so profoundly said. Some would prove to be saturated, some unsaturated, but all would establish certain missing connections, supply heart's-ease in a daily vitamin dose. A connection. One could buy and oil them like a rawhide leash.

Quite by accident—giving the word its due—Cowie had been a pioneer in this movement, turning to animals as the ill would turn to oxygen. Lacking in passion, defective in aggression, subject to periods of internal bleeding, the problem of keeping up the connections was simply too much for Cowie. He could not live without them. But he could not see them torn down and then repair them. He had settled for connections not so easily broken, invisible lines of force. The raccoon waiting in the darkness, the cat in the doorway, dispensed with the mockery of understanding: the lines of give and take were always up.

Disturbing as it might seem, Cowie shared with Mrs. Warren certain fundamental articles of faith. A Bill of Wrongs—the small print at the bottom of the Bill of Rights. Chief among these wrongs was the right to give up. In each man's weary pursuit of happiness this right to give up loomed larger and larger. Cowie had given up people, Alec had given up her child, numberless lovers had given up love, and increasing numbers had given up their conscious lives. A non-conscious life they still lived, and the future looked bright for non-conscious dying. But to be fully conscious was to be fully exposed. Cause for alarm. As a matter of survival one gave it up. At one and the same moment this was an act of salvation and an act of destruction. Miltown. A cemetery with stop and go lights.

In representing nothing bigger than himself, Lee Oswald represented more than enough. He did in Texas. He did in all of America. A free man, he testified to the horrible burden of freedom: how connect with something? How relate to someone? It was no accident that he singled out the man who represented the maximum of human connections, and displaced this man, this symbol of connections, with himself. Lee Oswald had merely deprived another man of what, in his opinion, he had been deprived: his right to the pursuit and possession of happiness. As an American it was not necessary for him to speak for others: his life and happiness depended on his speaking for himself. His life, and as it so often happened, another man's death.

So this senseless crime not only made history: it made American sense. In each American ear the word from Dallas would acquire its own troubled burden of meaning, and its own intolerable burden of meaninglessness. What word was it? How well Cowie knew it. *Impotence.* The assurance that nothing said, nothing written or cabled, nothing accepted or rejected, nothing suffered or felt, nothing now up before Congress or still in the blueprints, nothing dug out of the past or prescribed for the future, would restore to a man his belief in his power to affect the course of human events. He might exert it, but believe in it he did not. Who should know better than Cowie, the inventor of the meaningful accident?

Hooded life a falcon, seen but unseeing, impotence persuaded Oswald not to strike out blindly but with cunning at the heart of the matter: a man who could act. The one man with the power to act as he could not. In its extremity such impotence made a man murderously potent. If he could not act he could *protest.* One side of this action bore the youthful face of Alec, the rebel face of Protest—on the other side, blindfolded, the face of impotence. Was this an American coin? A peculiarly American tragedy? In a vast arching lobby, in the stream of the world's traffic, a figure dressed like Uncle Sam extended toward Cowie an unlabelled can, with a slot at the top, soliciting anonymous contributions. Good will. Good will blindly feeding on itself.

So there was little that happened in Dallas that was stranger than what happened in Escondido, or what might happen anywhere under the sign of impotence. It seemed to Cowie there was one story only behind all the stories in the headlines—a vast sand pile wherein was lost one chameleon. *Finders Keepers, Losers Weepers,* as Irving had said. When this sotry was told it would prove to be a love and a horror story at once. On this day without end impotence and protest would lie down in darkness, like lovers, and issue from that union would turn up in Dallas, of them history was now being made. One thing for sure. Where such lovers lay down, such issue would turn up. In one voice they would cry for Havoc, in another for Help. Whoever told it this would prove to be a story as strange, or stranger, than that of Lee Oswald, common as the air that bathed the globe, inscrutable as death. An American story. No matter who told it, that's what it would be.

A Conversation with Wright Morris

JOSEPH J. WYDEVEN

The interview took place at Wright Morris's apartment at the Redwoods Retirement Community in Mill Valley, California, on October 21 and 22, 1995. Morris and I had settled into chairs, the tape recorder propped on a makeshift table between us. The view out the window showed a small patio and grass between the buildings; occasionally cats crossed the patio and the sound of crows was heard. On the wall next to us was a Weston Gallery poster picturing Morris's famous GANO grain elevator photograph. Some of the conversation took place on Saturday afternoon and evening, the remainder on Sunday morning. In the early evening, after we had eaten dinner in the cafeteria, we talked while darkness fell. The conversation was sometimes slow and halting and at other times spontaneous and quick. Occasionally Morris searched for words, lost his place, probed for appropriate references. He complained now and then of a faulty memory, but when he remembered well, he was articulate and often amusing, even when he was scolding. As Morris was now eighty-five and had reached — or surpassed — the age of some of the characters he created throughout his writing career, I wanted above all to explore his sense and experience of old age. The six-hour conversation veered and dodged — and it achieves coherence here by virtue of careful editing. Morris began with his favorite quotation from Samuel Beckett.

MORRIS: "From things about to disappear I turn away in time. To watch them of sight, no, I can't do it." That's my mantra for this decade. One of the first times I ran into it, I said "There goes

Morris!" It spoke so directly to me—basically I felt that it was just an imprint. And also, to me it's wonderful Beckett, because he's not losing himself in things that he understandably does. Those particular mannerisms of his—syntax, and all—seem to me to be absolutely right for that piece. "From things about to disappear I turn away in time." The whole music of the thing pleases me very much.

§

WYDEVEN: My sense is that the criticism and scholarship [of your work] is being done primarily on the Nebraska works. I think that that's probably reasonable. But I regret that nobody's done much on *The Deep Sleep* or *The Huge Season*—those two, in particular, strike me as important books. *Man and Boy* also. *The Deep Sleep*, especially, is a book that is horribly ignored.

MORRIS: I've got quite a few that I feel that way about.

WYDEVEN: Yes, but that one always struck me as sort of the classic American family novel. When the boys in Washington talk about American family values, they ought to go back and look at that book.

MORRIS: Well, it's interesting, how there is so much to be discovered about a writer who is so unread. Because, when you look at it, there are quite a few novels there that—however they've been acceptably received in a critical sense—have not been *read*. This is a simple fact that has been hard for me to accept, because these books are meant to be *read*! There's nothing in them that really conflicts with the reader. To my mind he needs only to have a desire to read good fiction. But, of course, I am counter here to what has been happening for about thirty years, the erosion of the number of readers left. Almost everybody who once read my stuff has been dead about fifteen years. That is an astonishing and disturbing fact to me. I'm supposed to be in a kind of *Sunset Magazine* closure of my life, you know, where people write rather pleasant reminiscences about their experiences. William Maxwell does some of this stuff very well. He's a very good writer. But, basically, that's one reason why I was anxious to get into this type of publication—because I simply will take any chance rather than feel that the work is just going to disappear from view.

WYDEVEN: It seems to me that right from the start you were interested in writing about old people.

MORRIS: Well, it's perfectly clear to me that my interest is in age itself. The elderly person, you have discovered, is an ongoing sort of empathy that I have—so when the occasion exists, I will slip it in. Very early, you see, I was reading Montherlant, who is a favorite of mine—a French novelist and poet, and a very radical figure. He had the women in France absolutely in a tizzy, because he wrote these novels which had to do with women. They are the most brilliant novels about women that exist; they're just absolutely incredible. I assigned these to some of my classes, and the girls were just so mad, you know, that they completely missed what it was he was doing as a writer. They just felt that he was bad-mouthing women, you see—but *brilliant!* He was a big figure in France, and there was a period when he was very much in league with figures that would have been thought of as being slightly fascistic, way back. And they were, because they were essentially blood-related, you see. And they thought they were dealing with a bunch of cheap grand slackers, mostly. Montherlant's pride is very great, and his talent is great. And the women in France *loved* this man, and *hated* him—because he was so *incredibly* sharp, and his talent for how to state these things—the attractions, and the unattractions, of aging.

WYDEVEN: Even as early as your second book, *The Man Who Was There*, you incorporated material that young men just don't deal with: people who are older.

MORRIS: You're right! It's more than inclination—the absolute necessity to shift the focus away from, let's say the contemporary, into something that had a little more space around it, where I really felt more comfortable—I've felt more comfortable with the older mind, than with trying to make—well, my own mind—interesting. It seemed to me that the young were shallow. And when I was empathizing with the elderly, I did my best work.

WYDEVEN: You seem to have come full circle. I'm thinking now about *Plains Song* and the short stories that you did in the eighties. At least four or five of those stories deal with people, like yourself, who are experiencing the aging process. Let's pursue these short stories for a little. I'm fond of some of those stories—but sometimes I'm baffled by them.

MORRIS: Now, this is a good point. I couldn't say it's a good point of the discussion, because we could get tangled up here in silence. Because I'm frequently troubled by your saying, "Now, what do you mean by this?" you know, and so forth, and I will say, "But, for Christ's sake!" And so, we don't get anywhere with that, because I simply feel that your approach to fiction really is on a level that is just a little below what you're reading.

WYDEVEN: Well, in order to *speak* about it, as a critic—

MORRIS: There is no—Aw, come on now, come on, come on, none of this "as a critic" and so on and so forth. That just muddies the water. Now, those stories actually constitute new beginnings at a time that I felt I'd had my say. And then I found out that I had these impressions . . . They were a little on the fragile side, but I felt that, in their fashion, they were all very revelatory—good Morris fiction; in short, I liked them. So I was glad to finally get them published. I began to place stories at the *New Yorker* with some regularity—and they published quite a few—mostly these small pieces, that make the most out of very relatively nonactive confrontations. But these were the pieces that precisely needed to be written. Actually, all of these pieces are an effort to bridge otherness. There's the one about the chickens. Do you remember the one about the chickens?

WYDEVEN: Are you talking about "Fellow Creatures"?

MORRIS: Yes.

WYDEVEN: I loved that story, the grackles in the trees.

MORRIS: What I could see, finally, in myself, was that I was writing the kind of pieces that were meant to establish new relations, in a more explicit sense. You see what I mean? One of those stories I think that is the most touching is that one about how the cows had come down and got on to the porch.

WYDEVEN: That's "Fellow Creatures." You told me that story when I was at your house a couple of years ago, that you actually *saw* those cows on your neighbor's back porch.

MORRIS: So I did!

WYDEVEN: That's a funny, funny scene. People who read that story remember that scene.

WYDEVEN: Well, you know, it's a wonderfully baroque scene, when the baroque is not particularly appropriate. But to see those old girls standing there—because there's nothing like a cow! There's nothing, nothing like a cow. And when you get these old girls standing there, together—just standing there—there is nothing like an absolutely *non-engaged* cow, standing in a field, looking at you. That is as far away as vision can get.

WYDEVEN: What you said about new connections, new relations—*that* story very clearly does that—and I think also "Glimpse into Another Country." Those two stories are so different in kind. I have no trouble understanding how all the details fit "Fellow Creatures," but not so with "Glimpse into Another Country"—which is probably my favorite story of the lot. And *probably* it's my favorite because it's the one that most *eludes* me.

MORRIS: Is that a fact? Well, now, I think the secret—if there is one, and of course there is one—I think the secret lies in your conviction—in terms of your own interests, and in terms of your own experience—that the writer who is any good should not *leave* you with these questions.

WYDEVEN: Oh, no! I don't think that's true! No, I don't think so—I don't have a problem with that.

MORRIS: Well, then, what is it you have the problem with?

WYDEVEN: I think I have a problem when I can't fit the parts together, when the parts seem to be lying there as if they're *supposed* to fit. I've read these stories over and over. I've read *that* story a *dozen* times!

MORRIS: That must make you mad as hell!

WYDEVEN: No, I like it each time I read it, and I always find something I missed before. When you and I were sitting in the cafeteria earlier, and I said, "What, you have a Halloween motif here?" I immediately thought of "A Glimpse into Another Country" because of that Halloween motif, and the witch-woman at the beginning of it, sweeping up the newspaper in the driveway with a broom! What a wonderful comment on contemporary civilization! So there are some wonderful things in that story, but I would like to be clearer about what that S-shaped woman *means*—as she departs on the bus. I was reminded of John Cheever's "The Angel on the Bridge" and thought of that S-shaped woman as "The Guardian of His Flight." I'm not sure if that makes sense or not.

MORRIS: Well, I think sometimes you're attempting to make connections that are *meant* to be elusive. Now, that may seem to be to you an inexcusable type of privilege on the part of the writer. But to me it is absolutely *essential* that the writer get himself into situations that are on the verge of being evasions. My preference is for the *unclarified*. When I feel that it is sounding a note that is essentially superfluous—if it isn't superfluous, I am puzzled as to why it's there.

Now we're coming back to a couple of things that were on my mind—words and photographs. I'm not as convinced as I was at one time that anyone really gives a damn about the relatively tentative, and sometimes even intrusively distracting, role of photographs—that I think I'm verging on distracting, rather than enhancing, with words. I'm not sure that the words are a clarification, because, in a sense, that is not my purpose! So that then I say, well, what the hell is your purpose, then? And my purpose, I would say, is to fashion exactly the story to which you take exception! I don't mean you! I mean, the reader takes exception to the way in which I do things. And this is one of the ways that I do things. There are a lot of times I'm clairvoyantly obvious because it seems that's the way things are. Then there are other times, when I feel that particular kind of tentativeness, that it's wrong for me to be defensive about, because it's the way that I find myself doing it. But many people express that a story should be *about* something—that the writer should be *clear*—and so on, and so forth. Now, none of these things, really, have ever meant anything to me, because I've never been that much interested in how the stories affect other people. But I've begun to be attentive to it when I could see that this is a predicament for me. And I do not want the predicament, because I *do* want the communication.

WYDEVEN: Take *Plains Song*. In *Plains Song* you seem to give us many pieces of evidence to put this all together—you bring the hairbrush scene back in, the biting of the hand—the woman bites her hand, and her husband tells the doctor that a horse bit her—and you bring those things together, and so one can take all those elements, ignore some that don't seem to fit, and still come up with a decent interpretation. I think a novel like *A Life* is pretty clear—first-time readers should be able to get that—lot of archetypal Jungian stuff, or whatever . . . and I think that "Fellow Creatures"—the grackles, the cows on the porch—offers little difficulty. But when you get to a story like "Glimpse into Another Country" there are so many elements that it's like trying to get the entire picture by getting three possible patterns to come together.

MORRIS: I understand you perfectly. What I do *not* understand . . .

WYDEVEN: is why I'm *bothered* by it.

MORRIS: It's the necessity you have to make the pattern. My answer would always be, "The way it is, is the way it is!" And I don't believe—I don't really—there is a further way to go, if you are a writer of my particular persuasion—there won't be many of them soon—because for me, the nonexplicit impression has a resonance about it that is more durable than that one which, presumably, would be a more sensible resolution of what seems to be open and available to the writer to play around with. What interested me about "Glimpse" was *exactly* the *over*complexity. The overcomplexity of it *delighted* me!

WYDEVEN: Right! Exactly! And as I say—having read those stories over and over—part of my delight is there's this puzzle that I just want to solve! How does this woman fit in here? And I'm saying that I want you, the writer, to answer that question in the text . . . but yet *not* answer it. .

MORRIS: Now you're getting closer to it.

WYDEVEN: But what I am suggesting is that *you* know why you put that character in there, and nobody else does! You can withhold that—that's fine—whatever you want—but do you understand what I'm saying? That's why people ask authors what things mean, because they're puzzled as hell, and they think, Well, I'm pretty close here, but I don't quite get the . . .

MORRIS: I think this is an unavoidable—and not to be really eliminated—difference between the writer and the reader. Otherwise you could say, "Well, the hell with the whole thing!" because the reason they "glimpse into another country" is to enter the imagination. And the manner in which—for the writer, as he brings these associations into a kind of focus—he knows that, it's better that I end this in here somewhere because it's going to get too disorganized—too apparently disorganized, and people are not going to like it. But, also, as I come down to the conclusion of "A Glimpse," the quality of the complexity excites me.

§

WYDEVEN: I seem to have the most fun with things I have difficulty with.

MORRIS: Oh, now you're very close to why it is as it is! You're very, very close. And what aggravates me is, why the hell don't you admit it?

WYDEVEN: I just *did!*

MORRIS: No, no—but first you want to *talk about* it! You want to know, Why did I do it this way, when all you had to do was go inside, and get a cup of water and come out and feed the horse, and forget about it. All right, in any case, that's all right, too—but, in fact, this is an excusable way of talking about fiction, as far as I'm concerned. So you go right ahead and probe me as much as you want to, because I think you're a *real reader*—but sometimes I think, for Christ's sakes, why does he *ask* that? That is just *intolerable!*

WYDEVEN: We were tracking your interest in aging characters.

MORRIS: I think my interest in older characters began to take on a life of its own. If I took a copy of *Solo* I could find the passage where I say, "Well, in Paris I found this book," and then I explain the surprise on the part of the young man that he was more interested in the *old* character . . . . There's a very popular French movie that deals with people who are growing old, you know, and I went to see it two or three times, and I bawled almost from the time it started, because I am so damned empathetic with some things about that life that my eyes begin to blur over just thinking about it. There isn't anything unusual about it. One of the things that aggravates me is the manner in which all of my emotions are on the surface now. I don't have to dig for them.

WYDEVEN: Is that something that occurs with aging?

MORRIS: I think so. I think so. I don't think there's anything unusual in this.

WYDEVEN: You don't have to guard your emotions—there's no *way* to guard them, is there? Do you find that troublesome, or . . .

MORRIS: Yes, sometimes—Oh, yes! I can be moved to tears. Oh, yes. And I have passages that I get into over my head, before I know I'm into it. And then, there I am, trapped. But I got most of this work done before these emotions took over. I ask myself, what is there biologically that produces this strange phenomenon? Because suddenly I'm very sensitive to sentimentality—because that's what it is—it's a type of excess of sentiment. And I say, where does it come from? Why do I feel this way? Because it does embarrass me. If I were teaching, I would be disturbed by it. Fortunately, I was not teaching when I was beginning to feel this particular type of insecurity. But it would surely have appeared if I had been teaching. They'd say, "Look at the old fool."

§

WYDEVEN: I think you were very much in control in the 1980s, in control of how you were publishing things; it seems that you were making your bid for posterity.

MORRIS: You think so?

WYDEVEN: In your autobiographies or memoirs, the collected short stories, the collected photographic essays, that wonderful book of photographs with the laser-scanned photographs [Photographs & Words].

MORRIS: That's a perspective I don't have on myself. But I can see exactly what you're saying. But, oddly enough, I perhaps felt I'd live another twenty-five years, you see. I had not drawn that kind of a bead on it, at any time.

WYDEVEN: Did you have a sense that when you were writing Plains Song you would be writing more novels after that?

MORRIS: No, I thought that Plains Song was the last echo. I stopped doing some things—this is where the coherence of your imagination, or your life, can be very gratifying. I suddenly stopped . . . and I have these opening words, about Plains Song, about getting this Clara, or this little impression of her and Harry, about that terrible incident, about their early lives . . . of which, of course, they're about as intimate as any of these people ever are. They see each other at breakfast but otherwise they don't have much to do with each other. There's no argument—there's none of that—but the role of the woman here is so subordinate and so accepted. This is one of the terrible things about America: we buried so many women in the plains, and what a place to be buried! Clara's situation was terrible because Harry was just terrible—absolutely terrible—until he was an old man, and had mellowed, mysteriously. When I came out to the home place as a boy, he did everything but cuff me. He didn't want any kid running around or sharing his—you know [Morris makes grunting sounds]—as he'd sit at the table. And though I was a kid, I just thought it was inexcusable. He had an awful mouth, it was always full of tobacco. I really hated his guts. I could hardly bear to see him. But then fifteen years passed and he's a different man! Absolutely a different man! Suddenly he's got his hats up there on one end of the stove. He's living in the nostalgic phase of his own life, and he'd put his hat on and he'd walk. I'd find him and he'd never say, "What are we doing now?" but, just "Well!" He'd stand around, he's just mobile, and that's about it. When I told him to walk through the barn, I hoped he wouldn't stumble over that damned bar of wood that goes across the door. I was just terribly afraid that he'd stumble, because I said, "Now, Harry, would you be kind enough to just walk in." It was wonderful how he knew what it was I wanted. But I thought, this is just a terrible door. I could fall right now, I would go around the garage to avoid it. And if *he'd* fallen, that could have . . .

WYDEVEN: How old was he at that time?

MORRIS: Eighty-two, eighty-three. Not old, but very old for him and Clara. They were old people at that time. Well, now, before we get away from our center here: what are we trying to clear up?

WYDEVEN: We were dealing with this idea of your coming full circle, the reality of this setting here—with the older people, especially. I always had the sense that you obviously have a fondness for women that you don't have for men.

MORRIS: Yes, this is right. There's no doubt about that. I'm very sympathetic with the female.

WYDEVEN: You're very good with them. I was noticing you, as you were talking with the various women as we were walking around here.

MORRIS: I get along with them fine! I'm just one of the family, really. They pick that up instantly! There's never a feeling about, "Where does this old fart really stand?" I have an instant rapport—never any problem!

WYDEVEN: Did you always have that?

MORRIS: I'm not sure. That's part of my own maturation, in some cunning way. Well, I've always been more sympathetic with women than men. But then I had very little access to them, you see. My father was—now, we're back where if I start talking about it, I would just be quoting from *The Works of Love*. I'd be very close to it.

WYDEVEN: It's very obvious that there is a difference in the way you sympathize with women and the guarded way you deal with your male characters. You were very hard on the men in *Plains Song*—so much that . . .

MORRIS: That you feel the edge there.-

WYDEVEN: That your focus is so much on women, and that you dismiss the men almost as animals.

MORRIS: Yes, I think that's right, Joe. I think that's right. I've begun to feel this son-of-a-bitching species is only half-civilized. In fact, I think, if we were going to discuss what is happening to this country, I would say the evolution of men has stopped.

WYDEVEN: Well, that's the point of your transfer of power to women, as you did in *One Day*, for example.

MORRIS: Yes, that's right . . . but, in any case . . . Now, this is a hard one: men have to grow old enough to really be almost useless, before they're . . .

WYDEVEN: Before they're of any use!

MORRIS: Before they realize that they're human.

WYDEVEN: Well, the ego gets in the way!

MORRIS: Well, yes. Oh, yes! Now, Harry had reached a stage, that was really a kind of an agreeable senility before he had loosened completely . . . and became this pale-eyed old man, who'd drop into this rattan chair, you know. Just as if, "Well, here I am—do something with me." And the girls: the younger members of the family would sit around behind—they just thought he was wonderful. He was just wonderful—an avuncular figure, you see—reaching for his hand, always wanting to be in touch with him. And he had simply become . . . it's unbelievable, what this man had become! He had just ripened, like something you had found in the earth. That's a reasonably accurate image. He was like one of those croquet balls, that I had kicked up . . .

WYDEVEN: Hidden in the grass.

MORRIS: Yes, exactly! And that's what he was. So that, when you get him up, he's a different man . . . it's a different ball. And, at this point, I began to be very fond of him. But he's so old; he's dead within a couple of years. And he would go in and lie on this cot. I liked all of this very much because as much as it distressed me, I liked the intricacy of the relationship, with materials, of his own life. All of this was just fine, for me. He had become a piece of farm machinery, actually—very much so. And that's why I felt almost obligated to explore this a little. That's why I'm saying, "Walk through this door with me, Harry." I wanted to, if possible, capture my sentiments about him. But, also, something about him . . . and that photograph [the final image in The Home Place] is marvelous to that extent. I think it's a real icon—it's right on the nose. I didn't have to do it over—didn't have to do anything! You can hear the tension in my voice, just thinking about him!

WYDEVEN: Yes, that's a very powerful photograph . . . and that whole series of photographs. But none of *Clara*.

MORRIS: Well, because she did not want to be taken under any circumstances, and so I just didn't do it. I spoke about her, in very realistic terms, from some of the first stops at the farm, before I had any idea of doing *The Home Place*. I'd come to the door, and she'd cover her bad eye, and say, "Well, which one are you?" . . . this kind of thing . . . always so neutral. Her neutrality was just so unimpeachable, you just felt—well, I liked her, I always respected her, but I felt, Is she alive? Is she really alive? Well, she was so brutalized by fifty years of living this life, and the children, and the manner in which she worked. I remember arriving, as a boy, and she's out in the yard, with this damned old tub-type clothes washer, which is run off a trolley that goes through one of the machines in the barn, under this tree! It is a photograph out of the 1840s!

WYDEVEN: From what you've been saying, you based Cora, of *Plains Song*, directly on Clara? Did I hear you using the two names interchangeably?

MORRIS: Oh, yes, there was no need for me to turn in any direction. I don't know, to what extent, there is even the need of a basing. It's just that—this was native, here—I'm just talking about family.

§

WYDEVEN: Did I tell you I finally got a first edition of *The Home Place*?

MORRIS: Well, that's an *achievement*, I'll tell you.

WYDEVEN: They were selling copies of *The Home Place* in Lincoln for $100.00, $125.00.

MORRIS: They were? I wouldn't have thought that, at one time, because that's the book about the text of which I have so many misgivings. But that's because I did not have the perspective on what it is I'm doing. So I am full of misgivings about how the manner in which my approach, which I feel to be responsive at the moment, later proves to be so basically defective in its limitation.

WYDEVEN: I'm not sure what you mean.

MORRIS: It just shows, to the point of barrenness, the manner in which the material is originating, and how it's being treated. It's a sentimentality. That, too, is . . . I'm off, in the dark, but I think you will see what I mean later. Most of the complaints I have about early stuff is the manner in which I *accept* the sentimentality—rather than having it there but not being used by it—you haven't been around me enough to see that I never use words that I don't *toy* with. —Because, frankly, I just find the speech is so barren, because of overuse—over-everything—that I literally *process* it while I'm thinking about it. That's not an exaggeration. People who are listening to me are constantly saying, "Would you repeat that, Mr. Morris?" They haven't the vaguest idea . . . But it is the process of my *thinking and feeling* about the material, so that, admittedly, it should come out in a more V. S. Pritchett manner, but it doesn't. It works its way up through layers of association, and I'm not really disturbed by it at all. That is, I'd be perfectly willing to let the repetition go by. And in the early works this is just about the way I did it. I wouldn't think about it, I would just repeat it. And I'd said, "Well, there's perhaps a good reason for my repeating it here." And partially, I thought, If I'm wrong about that, well then, I'll knock it out later—something like that. But at least it is a different way of thinking of how to deal with material that is over-processed.

WYDEVEN: Do you think you over-processed *The Works of Love*, one of my favorites?

MORRIS: Sometimes, yes, I think there's a good deal—now, I shouldn't say this so often. We make these adjustments to the language while we're listening to it. But when it's written down, you feel it is, instead of systemic, it's statementic, you know, something like this. They become statements. And they become . . . for that reason, they're . . . When I come across them, they just make me wince, because they have an emphasis that I *never* had in mind. But I realize that my speech is full of these exaggerations—or, let us say, unnecessarily loose uses of phrase—because that's the manner in which words will form themselves in my mouth, or in my mind, and while I'm talking. I do not want it to be so refined. I'd *like* it to be, but I don't want it to show the effects of my concern. It *is* a mannerism of mine—the particular way that I have become *one* writer, not another. That's about it. When I'm teaching, it's off the top of my head.

WYDEVEN: The last time we talked, three or four years ago, you thought *The Works of Love* was too sentimental.

MORRIS: I'm glad you thought of that. It *is* sentimental, as I am. Here's the way it happens. *The Works of Love* goes back about ten years, and when I first read it again, it's a shock! I'm very unsympathetic. Then I come back to it ten, fifteen years later, and I *like* it. There's nothing unusual about it. I was just responding as a reader, rather than as a writer. I'm writing about this young man, who has a kind of past—I'd really have to go back and look at the book, to see what the first twenty-five pages were like, because suddenly I'm into this vein of repeating, and being responsive to, my own experience, which I found to be quite . . . I thought it was rather good, at the time, because I thought, I don't believe this shows as badly as I think it might, that I'm trying to rewrite my own fiction. I've a tendency to that. Then I look at it again and I *like* it! I was remembering things that I hadn't thought of before. Like when he goes to a library: he's still a kid, and he goes in, and this woman is speaking to him. And he's speaking to her. But it's all a *new* scene. It doesn't derive from experience. I don't have a picture of the woman, I don't have her face, or anything. But I find myself writing in a manner as if the scene—as if the fictive scene is the way the experience fell out. And it didn't. This is . . . actually, this is fiction being processed. But when I found that I liked it, because it made Brady and Lincoln Park possible, walking around in the evening, and the manner in which I'm suddenly sympathetic with these people, and what this man seems to be seeing—not the boy, anymore—the man, and there's a family here—the woman—she's a big woman—tired, she's leaning forward, and the language—the manner in which I'd fallen into this—seemed to preserve me from the intrusion that I didn't want. I didn't want the thoughts, I wanted it to be *as is*, which seemed to be true for this scene and what follows, so it should not be connected.

WYDEVEN: Yes, you were doing what Wayne Booth calls "free indirect style": you're inside of the mind of this character, but it's not exactly a first-person approach.

MORRIS: Well, actually, it's . . . this must be a very contemporary form of sympathy on the part of the fiction writer, who is in his own element—in there with his own language—so that to fall back into, for instance, this attitude—would not have been bearable in *The Home Place*. But then, there is a moment when it is, and I want the reader to share a sentimental experience, to tolerate it. There's a moment when I'm very sensitive to the excesses of *The Home Place*, of the *over-simplified* responses of the language. I'm thinking now of how this experience finds itself easing into *The Works of Love*, at different levels. And each time it will be a little different for me, as well as for the reader.

§

WYDEVEN: When we first started, you talked about "the problem of sentimentality." You seemed to think that sentimentality is a serious American problem.

MORRIS: I do think it is. This I have to get back to . . . this is why this is a problem for me. Because I can look around and say, basically, what is wrong is our gross over-sentimentality. Nothing is real; everything is built into "I'll love you, forever" or "Let's run off to Tahiti." It's sentimentality! The old boys weren't drawn to these extremes; the extremes are there, and they have been settled badly. If I was writing essays now I would write one on sentimentality.

WYDEVEN: I think we're too suspicious of sentiment.

MORRIS: We're too cold about sentiment, that's all! But bring it up and we don't have a problem!

WYDEVEN: Is that your case against Norman Rockwell [in *The Territory Ahead*]? The sentiments that Norman Rockwell is dealing with are decent enough. It's that he stretches and carries.

MORRIS: Then, of course, you get into everything that happens, if it's American. Then it's the product, then it gets into hype. It cannot be controlled. It slides into hype automatically!

WYDEVEN: Sentimentality leads to Ricky Lake, on television, or Oprah Winfrey, Phil Donahue, . . .

MORRIS: Yes, this is right. Suddenly there is an edge that has simply been filed off of the sensibility so that the distinction between sentiment and sentimentality is not made. Well, now, there was a time, you see, that it just simply couldn't be reduced to such absurdities right away. You would just say, "Well, all right, all right." But it was sentiment, and it would be just accepted. You'd know that this was the far reach of a sentiment that you had to go behind the curtain to blow your nose! Now this is where I think things are profoundly out of hand. I don't see any solution except among a handful of very scrupulous, careful artisan-minded people who will continue to write books that are about something and without excesses. There's a Rockwell poster down here on the door of the woman who sort of runs the place, and she's sophisticated, but like most of the women here almost all of them have to give up the distinction between sentiment and sentimentality—just to be peaceful, you know, just to be at rest with it.

WYDEVEN: To keep the distinction really requires the sharpest mind.

MORRIS: It does. And then it's fatiguing and unnecessary, because when the distinction becomes a problem you say, "Put it all in the file, I'll get back to it later."

WYDEVEN: I was reading something you wrote in *Time Pieces*, that you thought whatever is going on in our culture—the image of the thing, whatever the *thing* is—was replacing the thing itself. This is a large part of postmodern communication theory: that so much of what we live with is *images*, rather than reality.

MORRIS: Well, this is at the root of my essential despair, about what I can't bear to face. That is, that this tremendous human experiment is going to fail. We just can't help but fail, because we are weak. We are terribly weak—I could be wrong about this—it's just, what is it, just my impression? But it has led me to feel that a good deal of the tolerance I've had for myself, or let us say, for books, that I feel have a future—this kind of thing—the agreeable, civilized sentiments—which I now see, are sentimental as ever, if not more so. These things are written on water, like everything else.

§

WYDEVEN: I was thinking of your book *The Huge Season*, which is set in the early 1950s.

MORRIS: Now, that's a good example, because I think there's a good deal of coherence about *The Huge Season* as a book. It's an unusual book. All books have this particular limitation: they have their moments, and then they don't have their moments. But *The Huge Season*—there could be a time when *The Huge Season* can be seen for what it is—which is a very clear—an unusually clear grasp of a very murky situation—and very important to Americans who, all of the time, believed they had it clear. And this is what gives the book a certain texture, a sense of being more than a piece of fiction. But when Foley got used to me, at that time, because he could afford to be almost as serious as I thought the situation was—not quite—because then it would be bathos, you know, right off the bat. But, I don't think it ever quite fell into it. This is not consequential, because you're living this role, you know. All they lack are the banners that are being manufactured by insurance companies to be held by people who are riding horses, as they come toward the cameras. This is how artificial it's become; this is the kind of thing I'm talking about, without mentioning it. This is despair, my sense of despair, because people who do this all think they're pretty good, pretty sharp, pretty capable. And, if anything else, they're honest. But they aren't within a mile and a half of knowing what the hell it is to be honest! It's so far out of hand that we don't know what's wrong with us. We have no notion what's wrong with us. The fakery is just terrible.

WYDEVEN: The fakery?

MORRIS: Yes. The fakery that we think of as culture. Well, all of this is occurring simultaneously. That's why this culture—for this culture, this century is very important, because it has been jammed with remarkably, wonderfully, self-revelatory moments of confrontation—just incredible. There are a dozen of them you could spend a life just sitting down with them. Take R. P. Blackmur. There were men at the time who could face this. We had a lot of them, an assembly of intelligent men. They could have held their opinions and not have felt they had to be awarded praise, because they had them. I suffered from this, too, because I too felt this way about the culture. I felt, all right, we're just human, you know, so what? But I didn't think we were rotten.

WYDEVEN: *A Bill of Rites, A Bill of Wrongs, A Bill of Goods*—you were pretty negative there.

MORRIS: Yes, that's pretty goddamn negative, too negative for what we think is American sentiment.

WYDEVEN: What if I were to say that right *now* you seem to me to be too severe on the culture? Isn't it normal for people—especially as they grow older—to feel that their own culture is in a worse state than anything ever before?

MORRIS: Right! But what if they are right? There are certain patterns I can't escape, I mean, there are certain ways in which people grow old, and certain ways in which society grows old . . . cultures. And then there are moments when we know what we're talking about. So are we talking about what we don't know anything about, or are we talking about something we do know too much about? And I know what *I'm* talking about. We're shot through with dry rot right now, when very capable minds—a few very capable minds—are reasonably in grasp of what is going on. They haven't lost touch, but they are not *in* touch. I put it like that because we *look* as if we are in touch because we have been a quite remarkable culture, for about a century.

§

WYDEVEN: That piece on you in the *San Francisco Chronicle* in 1991 suggested that your mother was still much on your mind. Do you speculate about what you might have been if she had lived?

MORRIS: Luckily, I don't—because I couldn't carry it anywhere. It just ends, right there. It ends as she stoops to put a kiss on the child, who's praying . . .

WYDEVEN: You have a lot of surrogate mothers in your books. I particularly notice this in *Will's Boy*, a book I—admire.

MORRIS: You like *Will's Boy*.

WYDEVEN: A lot! I always see it as kind of the adverse of *The Works of Love*, where the focus is on Will Brady having a surrogate father.

And then *Will's Boy* has the focus on Will. There are some passages in there that are just astonishing. The egg candler scenes, where you're talking about your father in that semi-darkness, with the light flashing out from inside the candler, almost like a photographic darkroom. You describe your father as "more than a father"—almost a mythic figure. That's what interests me.

MORRIS: It is interesting, probably, because that is the way I'm feeling as I write that scene. I ordinarily would be—later, without any time at all—I'd become very critical. But at that age I was still able to see him with sufficient detachment.

WYDEVEN: Almost with awe, in that scene.

MORRIS: Well, that would, perhaps, be the skill of the writer, rather than what his intentions might have been. The candling room, and what goes on in the candling room, could be made into a separate chapter, if I had written just a little longer, at the right time . . .

WYDEVEN: I wish you had—really liked that chapter. I'm intrigued by your idea of light, your emphasis on "Lampglow and Shadows." I think of it as your "Camera Obscura." I did a piece dealing with that image of light. My first critical piece, I think, where I let my feelings go, so that it was more than just a scholarly paper.

MORRIS: I can see that the candling room/the darkroom are just so wonderfully juxtaposed. If I got into this, it would be a little bit excessive, but it would be of interest . . . because that situation sets itself up, and is more than it should be, just in its very non-specificity. The boy is looking on, and he sees more than is there, as he should. Then out there—out just to the side—what a wreck this building was! My father simply couldn't give up these deep dreams about chance. He was a very handsome man, and he was destined to be the head of the Union Pacific Railroad. But, right at that time, he gets this dream about chickens, and loses every dime he's got. In a couple of months he'd lost about seven or eight thousand pullets. He had the demeanor and the manner, the aura of a railroad man. And something of his personality was flowering at that time in the manner he was sporting around with some attractive theatrical women. Near the end of my stay with the Mulligans, my father would take me with him on weekends when he went to the theater. And up on the stage would be two of these women he was courting. And they were very sophisticated women—they were sharp. I don't have a vision of them at all. I didn't think, are they good looking or aren't they? I was not really even appreciative of what he saw in them. But my father would sit in his high collar—which came so far out that his head was always elevated, as if he was a Roman—but, eager that I should share, just a little, his new status. He'd bought me a suit—these are some of the last indulgences he made as a father, just before the egg empire—I don't know quite what happened. He probably got into a bad deal—he probably didn't pay for eggs that he shipped. He was fairly unscrupulous in a very innocuous way. He was almost without any ordinary sense of morality.

WYDEVEN: I was reading Loren Eiseley's memoir, *All the Strange Hours. He* had an egg room scene—not an egg candler. Apparently he worked inside a room, in the semi-darkness, where his job was to watch the eggs?

MORRIS: That's what he did. I remember listening to Eiseley talk about this, and trying to figure out what was really taking place. But there was this place where they had chickens—that's the only clear image I have. It was at night, and so it's dark . . .

WYDEVEN: Right, and there's that light, like a Rembrandt light. I don't know where it's coming from.

MORRIS: Yes, that's right. Well, it captured my fancy, too, and, of course, Schmerzie [Morris's fond name for Eiseley] would immediately see its possibilities, as an extension of something more than just appearance.

WYDEVEN: I thought maybe he'd borrowed that scene from you.

MORRIS: I think he may have simply been alerted to the fact that there are chickens back there! It was out of his ordinary ken, so that some of the enterprises that I would make more out of, he wouldn't, because he just didn't see them in the light of their possibilities. Oh God, the bleakness of that country! Do you know, have you read carefully, the last story in *The Collected Stories?*

WYDEVEN: "The Origin of Sadness"? Yes, I've read it—and written on it.

MORRIS: Well, that owes a great deal to Eiseley. But it owes mostly . . . and it's interesting, because, if I hadn't stayed for three weeks in Kansas, I wouldn't have fallen into reflections of that sort. And the reflections took hold of me, in a very secure and assured way—which Eiseley must have contributed a good deal to, just by being Eiseley—because I knew and liked him. So that when the occasion occurred, that took the shape of this story, which I liked very much.

WYDEVEN: I thought that story was your act of homage to him—that you were encasing him in ice.

MORRIS: Well, it's a little hard to say to what extent. At a certain moment you don't really know where you're taking a story over, or where it just is having a little flourish on its own.

WYDEVEN: I had the sense that in writing it you were doing your bit to keep him alive—to keep that memory alive.

MORRIS: Right! To keep the memory alive is what it's all about.

The Safe Place

This story, originally published in the Kenyon Review *in 1954, reappears—in an abbreviated form and with a different ending—near the close of* Ceremony in Lone Tree, *as part of Boyd's novel.*

In his fifty-third year a chemical blast burned the beard from the Colonel's face, and gave to his eyes their characteristic powdery blue. Sometime later his bushy eyebrows came in white. Silvery streaks of the same color appeared in his hair. To his habitually bored expression these touches gave a certain distinction, a man-of-the-world air, which his barber turned to the advantage of his face. The thinning hair was parted, the lock of silver was deftly curled. The Colonel had an absent-minded way of stroking it back. As he was self-conscious, rather than vain, there was something attractive about this gesture, and a great pity that women didn't seem to interest him. He had married one to reassure himself on that point.

When not away at war the Colonel lived with his wife in an apartment on the Heights, in Brooklyn. She lived at the front with her canary, Jenny Lind, and he lived at the back with his two cats. His wife did not care for cats, particularly, but she had learned to accept the situation, just as the cats had learned, when the Colonel was absent, to shift for themselves. The cleaning women, as a rule, were tipped liberally to be attentive to them. The Colonel supplied the cats with an artificial tree, which they could climb, claw, or puzzle over, and a weekly supply of fresh catnip mice. The mice were given to the cats every Thursday, and on Friday the cleaning woman, with a broom and the vacuum, would try to get the shredded catnip out of the rug. They would then settle back and wait patiently for Thursday again.

The blast improved the Colonel's looks, but it had not been so good for his eyes. They watered a good deal, the pupils were apt to dilate in a strange manner, and he became extremely sensitive to light. In the sun he didn't see any too well. To protect his eyes from the light he wore a large pair of military glasses, with dark lenses and something like blinders at the sides. He was wearing these glasses when he stepped from the curbing, in uptown Manhattan, and was hit by a pie truck headed south. He was put in the back, with the pies, and carted to a hospital.

He hovered between life and death for several weeks. Nor was there any explanation as to why he pulled through. He had nothing to live for, and his health was not good. In the metal locker at the foot of the bed was the uniform in which he had been delivered, broken up, as the doctor remarked, like a sack of crushed ice. The uniform, however, had come through rather well. There were a few stains, but no bad tears or rips. It had been carefully cleaned, and now hung in the locker waiting for him.

The Colonel, however, showed very little interest in getting up. He seemed to like it, as his wife remarked, well enough in bed. When he coughed, a blue vein would crawl from his hair and divide his forehead, and the salty tears brimming in his weak eyes would stream down his face. He had aged, he was not really alive, but he refused to die. After several weeks he was therefore removed from the ward of hopeless cases and put among those who were said to have a fifty-fifty chance. Visitors came to this room, and there were radios. From his bed there was a fine view of the city, including the East River, the Brooklyn Bridge, part of lower Manhattan, and the harbor from which the Colonel had never sailed. With his military glasses he could see the apartment where his wife and cats lived. On the roofs of the tenements that sprawled below there daily appeared, like a plague of Martian insects, the television aerials that brought to the poor the empty lives of the rich. The Colonel ordered a set, but was told that his failing eyes were too weak.

On the table at his side were a glass of water, boxes of vitamin capsules and pills, an expensive silver lighter, and a blurred photograph of his cats. A bedpan and a carton of cigarettes were on the shelf beneath. The Colonel had a taste for expensive cigarettes, in tins of fifty, or small cedar boxes, but his pleasure seemed to be in the lighter, which required no flint. The small gas cartridge would light, it was said, many thousand cigarettes. As it made no sound, the Colonel played with it at night. During the day he lit many cigarettes and let them smoke in the room, like incense, but during the night he experimented with the small wiry hairs on his chest. Several twisted together, and ignited, would give off a crackling sound. It pleased him to singe the blonde hairs on his fingers, hold them to his nose. When not playing with the lighter the Colonel slept, or sat for hours with an air of brooding, or used his army glasses to examine the teeming life in the streets. What he saw, however, was no surprise to him. To an old Army man it was just another bloody battlefield.

Having time on his hands, the Colonel was able to see through the glasses what he had known, so to speak, all his life. Life, to put it simply, was a battleground. Every living thing, great or small, spilled its blood on it. Every day he read the uproar made in the press about the horrors of war, the fear of the draft, and what it would do to the lives of the fresh eighteen-year-olds. Every moment he could see a life more horrible in the streets, dangers more unjust, risks more uncalculated, and barracks that were more intolerable. Children fell from windows, were struck by cars, were waylaid and corrupted by evil old men, or through some private evil crawled off to corrupt themselves. Loose boards rose up and struck idle women, knives cut their fingers, fire burned their clothes, or in some useless quarrel they suffered heart attacks. The ambulance appeared after every holiday. The sirens moaned through the streets, like specters, every night. Doors closed on small fingers, windows fell, small dogs bit bigger dogs, or friends and neighbors, and in the full light of day a man would tumble, headfirst, down the steps into the street. If this man was a neighbor they might pick him up, but if a stranger they would pass him by, walking in an arc around him the way children swing wide of a haunted house. Or they would stand in a circle, blocking the walk, until the man who was paid to touch a dead man felt the wrist for the pulse, or held the pocket mirror to the face. As if the dead man, poor devil, wanted a final look at himself.

All of this struck the Colonel, an old soldier, as a new kind of battleground. "That's life for you," the doctor would say, when the Colonel would trouble to point out that the only safe place for a man, or a soldier, was in bed. Trapped there, so to speak, and unable to get up and put on his pants. For it was with his pants that a man put on the world. He became a part of it, he accepted the risks and the foolishness. The Colonel could see this very clearly in the casualties brought to the ward, the men who had fallen on this nameless battlefield. They lay staring at the same world that seemed to terrify the Colonel, but not one of these men was at all disturbed by it. Everything they saw seemed to appeal to them. Every woman reminded them of their wives, and every child of their own children, and the happy times, the wonderful life they seemed to think they had lived. When another victim appeared in the ward they would cry out to ask him, "How are things going?" although it was clear things were still going murderously. That it was worth a man's life to put on his pants and appear in the streets. But not one of these men, broken and battered as they were by the world they had left, had any other thought but a craving to get back to it. To be broken, battered, and bruised all over again. The Colonel found it hard to believe his eyes—both inside and outside the window—as the world of men seemed to be incomprehensible. It affected, as he knew it would, his feeble will to live. He did not die, but neither did he live, as if the world both inside and outside the window was a kind of purgatory, a foretaste of hell but with no possibility of heaven. Once a week his wife, a small attractive woman who referred to him as Mr. Army, brought him cookies made with blackstrap molasses, pure brewer's yeast, and wheat-germ flour. The recipe was her own, but they were made by the cleaning woman. As Mrs. Porter was several years older than the Colonel, and looked from eight to ten years younger, there was no need to argue the importance of blackstrap and brewer's yeast. The Colonel would ask how the cats were doing, read the mail she had brought him, and when she had left he would distribute the cookies in the ward. A young man named Hyman Kopfman was fond of them.

Hyman Kopfman was a small, rabbit-faced little man who belonged in the hopeless ward, but it had been overcrowded and he couldn't afford a room of his own. When he appeared in the ward he had one leg and two arms, but before the first month had ended they had balanced him up, as he put it himself. He stored the cookies away in the sleeve of the arm that he wore pinned up. Something in Hyman Kopfman's blood couldn't live with the rest of Hyman Kopfman, and he referred to this thing as America. Raising the stump of his leg he would say, "Now you're seeing America first!" Then he would laugh. He seemed to get a great kick out of it. Largely because of Hyman Kopfman, there were men in the ward, some of them pretty battered, who looked on the world outside as a happy place. Only the Colonel seemed to see the connection. He didn't know what Hyman Kopfman had in his blood, or where it would show up next, but he knew that he had picked it up, like they all did, there in the streets. What Hyman Kopfman knew was that the world was killing him.

Hyman Kopfman was in pain a good deal of the time and sat leaning forward, his small head in his hand, like a man who was contemplating a crystal globe. During the night he often rocked back and forth, creaking the springs. While the Colonel sat playing with his lighter, Hyman Kopfman would talk, as if to himself, but he seemed to be aware that the Colonel was listening. Hyman Kopfman's way of passing the time was not to look at the world through a pair of field glasses, but to turn his gaze, so to speak, upon himself. Then to describe in considerable detail what he saw. As the Colonel was a reserved, reticent man who considered his life and experience private, Hyman Kopfman was something of a novelty. He spoke of himself as if he were somebody else. There were even times when the Colonel thought he was. At the start Hyman Kopfman gave the impression that he would describe everything that had happened; which he did, perhaps, but all that had happened had not added up to much. He was apt to repeat certain things time and time again. There were nights when the Colonel had the impression that he went over the same material the way a wine press went over the pulp of grapes. But there was always something that refused to squeeze out. That, anyhow, was the Colonel's impression, since it was otherwise hard to explain why he went over the same material time and again, here and there adding a touch, or taking one away.

Hyman Kopfman had been born in Vienna—that was what he said. That should have been of some interest in itself, and as the Colonel had never been to Vienna, he always listened in the hope that he might learn something. But Hyman Kopfman merely talked about himself. He might as well have been born in the Bronx, or anywhere else. He had been a frail boy with girlish wrists and pale blue hands, as he said himself, but with something hard to explain that made him likable. His father had it, but only his mother knew what it was. Hopelessness. It was this, he said, that made him lovable.

The Colonel got awfully tired of this part of the story since Hyman Kopfman was hopeless enough. Too hopeless, in fact. There was nothing about him that was lovable. It was one of the curious conceits he had. His skin was a pale doughy color, and his general health was so poor that when he smiled his waxy gums began to bleed. Thin streaks of red, like veins in marble, showed on his chalky teeth. His eyes were very large, nearly goatlike, with curiously transparent lids, as if the skin had been stretched very thin to cover them. There were times when the eyes, with their large wet whites and peculiarly dilated pupils, gazed upon the Colonel with a somewhat luminous quality. It was disturbing, and had to do, very likely, with his poor health. It was because of his eyes, the Colonel decided, that Hyman Kopfman had picked up the notion that there was something appealing about his hopelessness. Some woman, perhaps his mother, had told him that.

At a very early age Hyman Kopfman had been brought to America. With him came his three brothers, his mother, Frau Tabori-Kopfman, and the roomful of furniture and clothes that his father had left to them. They went to live in Chicago, where his Uncle Tabori, his mother's brother, had rented an apartment. This apartment was four flights up from the street with a room at the back for Uncle Tabori, a room at the front, called a parlor, and a room in which they lived. In the parlor there were large bay windows but the curtains were kept closed as the light and the circulating air would fade the furniture. It would belong to Paul, if and when he married someone. In the room were chests full of clothes that his mother had stopped wearing, and his father, a gentleman, had never worn out. They were still as good as new. So it was up to the children to wear them out. It so happened that Mandel Kopfman, the father, had been comparatively small in stature, and his fine clothes would fit Hyman Kopfman, but nobody else. So it was that Hyman Kopfman was accustomed to wear, as he walked between the bedroom and the bathroom, pants of very good cloth, and on his small feet the best grade of spats. French braces held up his pants, and there was also a silver-headed cane, with a sword in the shaft, that he sometimes carried as he swaggered down the hall. He didn't trouble, of course, to go down the four flights to the street. Different clothes were being worn down there, small tough boys cursed and shouted, and once down, Hyman Kopfman would have to walk back up. He simply couldn't. He never had the strength.

His older brother, Otto, went down all the time as he worked down there, in a grocery, and returned to tell them what it was all about. He also went to movies, and told them about it. His brother Paul had been too young to go down to the street and work there, so he made the beds and helped his mother around the house. He cooked, he learned to sew, and since he couldn't wear the clothes of Mandel Kopfman, he wore some of the skirts and blouses of his mother, as they fit him all right. It didn't matter, as he never left the rooms. No one but Uncle Tabori ever sat down and talked with them. He worked in the railroad yards that could be seen, on certain clear days, from the roof of the building, where Frau Kopfman went to dry her hair and hang out their clothes. From this roof Hyman Kopfman could see a great park, such as they had known in Vienna, and in the winter he could hear the ore boats honking on the lake. In spring he could hear the ice cracking up.

Was that Hyman Kopfman's story? If it was, it didn't add up to much. Nor did it seem to gain in the lengthy retelling, night after night. The facts were always the same: Hyman Kopfman had been born, without much reason, in Vienna, and in Chicago he had taken to wearing his father's fancy clothes. Not that it mattered, since he never went down to the street. He spent day and night in the apartment, where he walked from room to room. Concealed in the shaft of the cane was a word, and when he stepped into the dim gaslit hallway, Hyman Kopfman would draw out the sword and fence with the dancing shadow of himself.

Ha! the Colonel would say, being an old swordsman, but Hyman Kopfman had shot his bolt. He could do no more than wag his feeble wrist in the air. His gums would bleed, his goatlike eyes would glow in a disturbing manner, but it was clear that even fencing with his shadow had been too much for him. Nothing had really happened. The Colonel doubted that anything ever would.

And then one day—one day just in passing—Hyman Kopfman raised his small head from his hand and said that the one thing he missed, really missed, that is, was the daily walk in the blind garden.

In the what? the Colonel said, as he thought he had missed the word.

In the blind garden, Hyman Kopfman replied. Had he somehow overlooked that? Hadn't he told the Colonel about the blind garden?

The Colonel, a cigarette in his mouth, wagged his head.

At the back of the building there had been a small walled garden, Hyman Kopfman went on, a garden with gravel paths, shady trees, and places to sit. Men and women who were blind came there to walk. There were also flowers to smell, but they couldn't see them of course.

Well, well—the Colonel had replied, as he thought he now had the key to the story. One of the Kopfmans was blind, and Hyman Kopfman was ashamed to mention it. What difference did it make what Hyman Kopfman wore if his brother Paul, for instance, couldn't see him, and if Paul was blind he would hardly care how he looked himself. What difference did it make if he wore his mother's skirts around the house?

Your brother Paul was blind then—? the Colonel said.

Blind? said Hyman Kopfman, and blinked his own big eyes. Who said Paul was blind?

You were just saying—the Colonel replied.

From the window—interrupted Hyman Kopfman—what he saw below was like a tiny private park. There were trees along the paths, benches in the shade where the blind could sit. The only thing you might notice was how quiet and peaceful it was. Nobody laughed. The loud voices of children were never heard. It was the absence of children that struck Hyman Kopfman, as he was then very young himself, and liked to think of a park like that as a place for children to play. But the one below the window was not for bouncing balls or rolling hoops. No one came to this park to fly a kite, or to skip rope at the edge of the gravel, or to play a game of hide-and-seek around the trees. In fact there was no need, in a park like that, to hide from anyone. You could be there, right out in the open, and remain unseen. It was Paul Kopfman who pointed out that they might as well go down and sit there, as nobody would know whether they were blind or not. Nobody would notice that Hyman Kopfman was wearing celluloid cuffs and pearl-gray spats, or that Paul Kopfman was wearing a skirt and a peasant blouse. Nobody would care, down there, if their clothes were out of date, or that when Hyman Kopfman talked his wax-colored gums were inclined to bleed. It was the talking that made him excited, and the excitement that made his gums bleed, but down there in the garden he was not excited, and nobody cared. There were always flowers, because nobody picked them. There were birds and butterflies, because nobody killed them. There were no small boys with rocks and sticks, nor big boys with guns. There was only peace, and his brother Paul sat on the wooden benches talking with the women, as he didn't seem to care how old, and strange, and ugly they were. In some respects, he might as well have been blind himself.

How long did this go on—? the Colonel said, as he knew it couldn't go on forever. Nothing out of this world, nothing pleasant like that, ever did.

Well, one day his brother Otto—Hyman Kopfman said—his brother Otto put his head out the window and . . .

Never mind—! said the Colonel, and leaned forward as if to shut him up. He wagged his hand at the wrist, and the blue vein on his forehead crawled from his hair.

A man like you, Hyman Kopfman said, an old soldier, a Colonel, a man with gold medals—

Never mind! the Colonel had said, and took from the table his silver lighter, holding it like a weapon, his arm half-cocked, as if ready to throw.

Was Hyman Kopfman impressed? Well, he just sat there: he didn't go on. He smiled, but he didn't repeat what Otto had said. No, he just smiled with his bleeding gums, then raised the pale blue stump of his leg, sighted down the shinbone, pulled the trigger, and said *Bang!* He was like that. He didn't seem to know how hopeless he was.

For example, this Kopfman had only one foot but he sent out both of his shoes to be poished: he had only one arm, but he paid to have both sleeves carefully pressed. In the metal locker at the foot of his bed hung the pinstripe suit with the two pair of pants, one pair with left leg neatly folded and pinned to the hip. Some people might ask if a man like that needed two pair of pants. It was strange behavior for a person who was dying day by day. Not that he wanted very much, really—no, hardly more than most people had—all he really seemed to want was the useless sort of life that the Colonel had lived. To have slept with a woman, to have fought in a war, to have won or lost a large or small fortune, and to have memories, before he died, to look back to. Somehow, Hyman Kopfman had picked up the facts, so to speak, without having the fun. He always used the word "fun" as he seemed to think that was what the Colonel had had.

Night after night the Colonel listened to this while he played with his lighter, or smoked too much, but he said very little as he felt that Hyman Kopfman was very young. Not in years, perhaps, but in terms of the experience he should have had. His idea of fun was not very complicated. His idea of life being what it was, the Colonel found it hard to understand why he hadn't reached out and put his hands on it. But he hadn't. Perhaps this thing had always been in his blood. Or perhaps life in America had not panned out as he had thought. At the first mention of Chicago, Hyman Kopfman would wave his stubby arm toward the window, roll his eyes, and make a dry rattle in his throat. That was what he felt, what he seemed to think, about America. But there was nothing that he wanted so much as to be out there living in it.

The case of Hyman Kopfman was indeed strange, but not so strange, in some respects, as the case of the old man in the bed on his right. The Colonel had been failing; now for no apparent reason he began to improve. Now that Hyman Kopfman was there beside him—a hopeless case if there ever was one—the Colonel's pulse grew stronger, he began to eat his food. He sat propped up in bed in the manner of a man who would soon be out. Here you had the Colonel, who had nothing to live for, but nevertheless was getting better, while Hyman Kopfman, who hungered for life, was getting worse. It didn't make sense, but that was how it was. Not wanting to live, apparently, was still not wanting to die. So the Colonel, day by day, seemed to get better in spite of himself.

The very week that Hyman Kopfman took a turn for the worse, the Colonel took that turn for the better that led the doctor to suggest that he ought to get up and walk around. Adjust himself, like a newborn babe, to his wobbly legs. So he was pushed out of the bed, and the terrycloth robe that hung for months, unused, in the locker was draped around his sloping shoulders and a pair of slippers were put on his feet. In this manner he walked the floor from bed to bed. That is to say he toddled, from rail to rail, and the effort made the sweat stand on his forehead and the blue vein crawl like a slug from his thinning hair. But every-body in the ward stared at him enviously. He could feel in their gaze the hope that he would trip, or have a relapse. But at least they were courteous on the surface, they remarked how much stronger he was looking, and made flattering comments on how well he carried himself. They spoke of how fine he would soon look in his uniform. All this from perfect strangers; but Hyman Kopfman, the one who had spoken to him intimately, snickered openly and never tired of making slurring remarks. He referred to the Colonel's soft arms as chicken wings. He called attention to the unusual length of the Colonel's neck. Naturally, the accident that had nearly killed the Colonel had not widened his shoulders any, and there was some truth in the statement that he was neck from the waist up. Nor had the Colonel's wide bottom, like that of a pear, which seemed to hold his figure upright, escaped Hyman Kopfman's critical eye. Nor his feet, which were certainly flat for an army man. A less disillusioned man than the Colonel would have made an official complaint, or brought up the subject of Hyman Kopfman's two-pants suit. But he said nothing. He preferred to take it in his stride. One might even say that he seemed to wax stronger on it. It was this observation, among others, that upset Hyman Kopfman the most, and led him to say things of which he was later ashamed. It was simply too much, for a dying man, to see one getting well who had nothing to live for, and this spectacle always put him into a rage. It also considerably hastened his end. It became a contest, of sorts, as to whether the Colonel would get back on his feet before Hyman Kopfman lost another limb, or managed to die. In this curious battle, however, Hyman Kopfman's willpower showed to a great advantage, and he deteriorated faster than the Colonel managed to improve. He managed to die, quite decently in fact, during the night. A Saturday night, as it happened, and the Colonel was able to call his wife and ask her to bring a suitable floral offering when she came.

Glimpse into Another Country

Hazlitt's wife carried a broom to ward off the neighbor's dogs as she walked with her husband down the drive to the waiting taxi. Too old now to attack, the dogs barked hoarsely from behind a screen of bushes. "I'll outlive them if it kills me," she remarked, and she stooped for the morning paper, flattened by the garbage pickup. "No ethnic food," she told Hazlitt. "You hear me? You remember what happened in Phoenix." From his shoulders, as he stooped to kiss her, she removed the gray hairs.

Hazlitt was reluctant to fly, anywhere, but he wanted something in the way of assurance—of life assurance—that he hoped to get from a specialist in New York. "If that's what you want," his own doctor, in San Francisco, had advised him, "and you can afford it, go get it." Could he afford it? He had that assurance from his wife. "You're worth it," she said.

She had made considerable fuss to reserve Hazlitt a seat at one of the plane's windows, which turned out to be near the center of the right wing. A stewardess helped him out of his coat, and held it while he felt through the pockets for his glasses. A woman with quick searching eyes came along the aisle to stop at his row, then turned to hiss at her companion. The habit of hissing at people had always dismayed Hazlitt.

The woman's hair looked as if she had just blow-dried it. The man with her, by appearance a cultivated person, wore a smart suède cap and carried their coats. His rather abstracted manner led Hazlitt to feel he might be a teacher, off to an academic meeting. As he reached her side, the woman slipped between the seats to the one beside Hazlitt, without glancing at him. She registered his presence, however, as she would a draft from the window, by shifting in the seat toward her companion. She wore knit gloves. With one hand she clutched a paperback book.

Hazlitt had not flown enough to know if her indifference to him was part of the etiquette of plane travel, where so many strangers were jammed in together: why start up something with a person who might well prove to be tiresome? He himself was guarded even with his colleagues at the university. The woman at his side had an appealing intactness, and her profile seemed intelligent. A perfume, or it might be a powder, was faintly scented with lilac.

Advised to buckle his seat belt, he observed that the palms of his hands were clammy. At the takeoff he faced the window with closed eyes. Perhaps the tilted wing spared him the vertigo that might have been part of the liftoff, and as the plane set its course he caught glimpses of the far blue horizon. The woman beside him browsed in a copy of the New York Times, picked up in the airport. Her interest seemed to be in the ads. At one point, he was screened off behind the paper but able to check the market quotations on his side. Finished with the paper, she stuffed it between the seats on her left, away from Hazlitt. He thought that rude, since he made it a point to share newspapers with his traveling companions. As she relaxed for a moment, closing her eyes, he was able to appraise her profile further—a little sharp to his taste, but attractive. From the pink lobes of her ears he received faintly erotic signals.

Suddenly, perhaps feeling his gaze, she turned to look directly past him, as if someone had tapped on the window. Now she would speak, he thought, but she didn't. She turned away, with a birdlike quickness, and leafed through the pages of her paperback book. Idle riffling—the sort of thing Hazlitt found irritating. At the back of the book, she paused to read a few words about the author, then turned to read the book's concluding page. That done, she read the next-to-last page, then the one before it. As she read, she nibbled at the corner of her lip.

Hazlitt was flabbergasted. He had discovered that the book she chose to read backward was *The White Hotel*. He could not fully believe what he had seen, yet there was no question he had seen it. She did manage to read most of the final chapter before turning the book back to its opening page, which she placed face down in her lap. What did she want now? Something to drink. Her husband raised his hand to signal one of the stewards.

Surely a more worldly traveler than Hazlitt would not have been so appalled by what he had witnessed. How justify this scanning of a book in reverse? Could it not be argued that a sensible person, of a sensitive nature, might want to know what was in store before making a full commitment? Perhaps, but the practice was new to Hazlitt, a sworn and outspoken enemy of speed-reading.

At the announcement that they were passing over Lake Tahoe, the woman leaned toward the window as if she might see it. Her seeming unawareness of Hazlitt had a calming effect on him. He made way for her. He was at pains not to be there. Leaning forward, she had crushed several pages of her book, but this too was a matter of indifference to her. She put the book aside to accept, from her companion, a news magazine. She leafed through the pages, then stopped to consider an article on crime, with illustrations.

"Oh, my God!" she exclaimed, crumpling the page, and turned to fix Hazlitt with an intense, green-eyed stare. Did she think him a criminal? It seemed to him that her eyes moved closer together. "There's no place to go!" she cried. "Just imagine!" She had ignored Hazlitt; now he felt cornered by her. "Where would *you* go?" she barked.

His lips were dry. He wet them, and said, "My wife and I were recently in Oaxaca—"

"*Mexico?* Are you crazy?" She saw that he might be. "There is *nowhere* . . . " Her voice trailed off. Her husband had placed his hand on her lap to calm her.

"I was at a party in the forties—" Hazlitt began.

"In the forties!" she cried. "Who lives in the forties?"

Fortunately, he divined her meaning. "The *nineteen*-forties—the party was in the East Seventies. Musicians, writers, composers, and so on. Do you remember Luise Rainer?" Clearly she did not. "At the time," he continued, "she was an actress—"

"You write?" she asked him.

Hazlitt did write scholarly articles; he asked himself if she considered that writing. "I was with a friend," he said, "a painter. We all agreed there was nowhere to escape to. The war was everywhere, or soon would be. Then one of them said, 'You know what? There *is* no *where*. All the wheres have vanished.'"

Perhaps the woman felt there was more to the story. Her lips parted, but she said nothing.

"We have friends in Buenos Aires," he went on, "but I would never go so far as to recommend it."

"It's like no *air*. That's what it's like. It's like there's less air."

"As a matter of fact—" began Hazlitt, but she had turned from him to her crumpled magazine. Carefully, as if she meant to iron it, she smoothed it out on her lap. "That book you were reading," he continued. "I've met the author. A very respectable chap." (Everything he was saying was the purest hogwash.) "I know that he would consider it a personal favor if you read his book as it was printed, from the front to the back."

What had come over him? In her green, unblinking stare he caught the glimpse of a chill that might excite a lover. She turned from him to lean on her companion, who peered over her frizzly hair at Hazlitt. The man wore tinted bifocals. His expression was mild. "My wife said you had a question?"

Returning his gaze, Hazlitt knew he had been a fool. "It's just that I happen to know the author, and took the liberty of speaking for him."

"He's crazy," said the wife. "Don't rile him."

Calmly the man removed his glasses and polished the lenses with a fold of his tie. Unmistakably, Hazlitt recognized one of his own kind. A physicist, perhaps, with those hairy fingers. Or a member of a think tank. "Theoretically," the man said, breathing on a lens, "there is something in what you say, but, as a practical matter, having bought the book my wife is free to read it as she pleases, or to ignore it. Wouldn't you agree?"

Particularly galling to Hazlitt was the way the fellow had turned the tables on him. It was usually he who was the cool one, the voice of reason in the tempest, the low-keyed soother of the savage breast. Worse yet, this fellow was about half his age.

"Of course! Of course! Stupid of me. My apologies to Mrs. —"

"Thayer. I'm Dr. Thayer."

Across the lap of Mrs. Thayer, who shrank back to avoid him, Hazlitt and Dr. Thayer clasped hands, exchanged the glances of complicit males. If there was a shred of solace in it for Hazlitt, it lay in Mrs. Thayer's full knowledge of this complicity.

"Take the filthy book!" she said, thrusting it at him. "And read it any way you like!"

Hazlitt let it fall to the floor between them. He fastened his gaze on the glare at the window. Sometime later, the stewardess, serving his lunch, had to explain to him how to pull out the tray from the seat in front of him, and pry the lid from his salad dressing.

Hazlitt would say for this woman—when he discussed it with his wife—that she maintained to the last his nonexistence. He remained in his seat until the plane emptied, then wandered about the airport. He caught a glimpse of Dr. Thayer, on one of the escalators, helping his wife into her coat. The sharpness of her elbows troubled Hazlitt. Thin and intent as a cat, she reminded him of someone. Was it his wife? She groped in her purse for a piece of tissue, pressed it to her nose.

In the taxi to Manhattan, Hazlitt was moved to chat a bit with the driver, but the Plexiglas barrier between them seemed intimidating. Through the tinted windshield, as they approached the city, the October evening skyline was like the opening shot of a movie. Hazlitt had often told his wife that if the sun never rose he might like city living. In the car lights the streets glittered like enamel. It pleased him to note, as they drew near the Plaza Hotel, the horse-drawn hacks lined up along the curb. One of the drivers was a young woman with pigtails, frail as a waif. She held a leather feed bag to the muzzle of her horse, whose pelt shone like patent leather where the harness had worn off the hair.

The hotel porter, elderly himself, took a proprietary interest in Hazlitt. He led him into the bathroom to explain that the knobs on the faucets might confuse him if he got up at night for a drink of water: they turned contrary to the usual directions. A sign of the times, Hazlitt thought.

He thanked the porter, then stood at the window listening to the sounds of the street. A warm, moist breeze stirred the curtains. The tooting horns put him in mind of the radio plays of the forties. Turning to phone his wife, he saw his reflection in the mirror on the closet door. Something about the light, or the mirror, altered the impression he had of himself. A pity his wife couldn't see it. He would call her later; it was early still in California, and such talk could make her uneasy. What she feared the most when he traveled without her was that he might do something foolish, if not fatal, and end up hospitalized where she could not get at him. As he washed his hands—taking care with the faucets—he remembered her final caution: not to walk the streets at night, but if he did, not to be caught without money.

She had given him a hundred dollars in twenties on the under-standing he was not to spend it, so that when the muggers looked for money they would find it.

Hazlitt meant to stroll a bit—he needed the exercise—but when he left the hotel the young woman with the pigtails and her black spotted horse were still there. Frequent tosses of the horse's head had spread oats on the street and sidewalk. Jovially, Hazlitt inquired, "This rig for hire?"

"That depends where you're going." She spoke to him from her perch in a tone of authority.

"Bloomingdale's," he said, "before it closes."

"That's where I'm headed," she replied, ignoring his playful tone, and watched him climb into the cab. Hazlitt must have forgotten the leisurely pace of a weary horse. He leaned forward in the seat as if that might urge it along. As they approached Bloomingdale's, he saw that peddlers had spread their wares out on the sidewalks.

The girl stopped the horse so that the hack blocked the crosswalk, and a stream of pedestrians swirled around it. As Hazlitt arose to step down from the cab, it teetered slightly, and he peered about him for a helping hand. One of the peddlers—a tall, swarthy fellow wearing a pointed hat made of a folded news-paper—had taken a roll of bills from his pocket to make change for a customer. This person, lights reflected in her glasses, peered up at Hazlitt with a look of disbelief. Did he seem so strange? A moment passed before he recognized Mrs. Thayer. She wore tinted horn-rimmed glasses, and a babushka-like scarf about her hair, tied beneath her chin. To take her change, while holding her purse, she gripped one of her knit gloves between her teeth, where it dangled like a third hand. The sight of Hazlitt had, in any case, left her speechless. He could think of nothing better to do than slip one hand into his coat front and strike the comical pose of a public figure welcomed by an admiring throng. The tilt of the carriage may have led him to misjudge the step down to the street. He toppled forward, both arms spread wide, and collapsed into the arms of the peddler, knocking off his paper hat. Over the man's broad shoulder he caught a glimpse of Mrs. Thayer, her hand clamped to her mouth now in either astonishment or laughter. She was gone by the time Hazlitt's feet were firmly planted on the street.

The peddler, after recovering his hat, was remarkably good-humored about it. "She knows you, eh?" he said, giving Hazlitt a leer as he smoothed the rumpled front of his coat. Hazlitt pondered the query as he selected, from the peddler's display, a French-type purse for his wife, a woman reluctant to buy such things for herself.

"Don't you worry!" the peddler added. "She'll be back. I still got her three dollars!" From his wad of bills he peeled off several and passed them to Hazlitt, giving him the smile of a collaborator. "You O.K.?" he said, and steadied the older man's arm as he stepped from the curb.

In Bloomingdale's foyer, where the doors revolved and Hazlitt felt well concealed by the darkness, he paused to spy on the peddler. There was something familiar about him—a big, rough fellow who turned out to be so gentle. In his sophomore year at college, Hazlitt had been intrigued by a swarthy, bearded giant, wearing a faded orange turban and a suit coat over what appeared to be his pajamas, who used to cross the campus directly below the dormitory window on his way to a shack in the desert wash. He walked with a limp, and carried a sack of groceries over his shoulder. As he passed beneath Hazlitt's gaze he would crook his head around, revealing his dark, hostile expression, and then beam directly at him the wide-eyed, toothy smile of a child beholding a beloved object. These extremes of temperament were like theatrical masks of contrary humors slipped on and off his face. Hazlitt learned that the man was a Sikh, one of a sect of fiercely independent warriors in India. What had brought him to California? Everything about him was out of scale and seemed disconcerting—even his smile. There were rumors that he kept his wife captive, that he trapped and ate coyotes. But what did all of that have to do with Hazlitt spying on a peddler from Bloomingdale's foyer so many years later?

Nevertheless, the incident had aroused him, agreeably. This state, he thought, might be what his younger colleagues called "having a buzz on"—an expression that had previously mystified him. He wandered about the store's crowded aisles. In the cosmetic section, the customers and the clerks chattered like birds in an aviary. They leaned to peer into mirrors as if uncertain who they were. Hazlitt paused at a counter displaying bracelets set with semiprecious stones. A young woman with dark bangs to the edge of her eyes spoke to him. She opened the case to lift out several of the items. In her opinion, they cost practically nothing—a special purchase at seventy-nine dollars. He would have guessed a price a third of that, but he showed no surprise. One by itself was very nice, she advised him, but two or more enhanced their beauty. To illustrate, she placed two about her broad wrist, above a hand with blunt fingers and cracked nails.

"Very well," Hazlitt said, feeling nothing at all, and waited as she wrote up the order. Was it cash or card? Card, he replied, and searched it out in his wallet.

"Oh, I'm so sorry," she said, "but we don't take Visa."

Hazlitt's astonishment was plain. He wondered if it might be a cunning revenge of the East on California. Would they accept his check? Of course. As he filled one out, his wife's face materialized suddenly, then receded. He wrote so few checks that she had cautioned him to make certain he did it correctly.

His driver's license was also needed, the clerk told him. Ah, he was from San Francisco? She had spent a summer with a friend in Carmel, where she nearly froze. Hazlitt explained that the summers might run cooler than the winters, which was why some people found it so attractive. She did not follow his reasoning, her attention being on other matters. "I've got to get this O.K.'d," she said. "Would you just like to look around?"

Hazlitt looked around. Having already spent so much money, he could do without further temptations. To get out of the crowded aisles he wandered into an adjoining department. Against a pillar he saw a canvas chair, apparently meant for the lover of horses: it was made with stirrups, bridles, bits and strips of harness leather. He sagged into it. Nearby, a TV screen glowed like the sun at a porthole. He made out the image of a dense throng of people moving about in a large, dimly lit building. The flowing garments of the women, the density of the crowd suggested it was somewhere in India. As his eyes adjusted, Hazlitt saw that the floor seemed to be strewn with bodies, to which the passing crowd was indifferent. Some were alone. Others were gathered in crumpled heaps. The milling of the figures among these fallen creatures gave the scene an unreal, dreamlike aspect. Were they dead? No, they were sleeping. The film gave Hazlitt a glimpse into a strange country where the quick and the dormant were accustomed to mingle. Perhaps, he thought, it was not the walkers but the sleepers who would range the farthest in their travels.

He was distracted by a stream of jabbering, excited people, most of them young, who hurried down the store aisles toward the front exit. Then, rather suddenly, the place was quiet. He delayed a moment, expecting further excitement, then came out of the shadows and returned to the jewelry counter. The clerk was not there. Other departments also appeared to be abandoned. Through the glass doors of a side entrance he saw hurrying figures and flashing lights. A young man in shirtsleeves, with a perplexed expression, ran toward Hazlitt, waving a flashlight. He took him by the arm and steered him down the aisle. "Out! Out!" he cried. "We're emptying the building!"

"The clerk still has my driver's license," said Hazlitt, but in his agitation the man ignored him. He urged him along through the empty store to where several policemen stood at the exit.

"The clerk has my driver's license!" Hazlitt repeated.

"Don't drive," the man replied. "Take a cab."

Police vans and patrol cars blocked off the street. He stood for some time under one of the awnings waiting for something dramatic to happen. The revolving beacons on the cars lit up the faces of the crowd like torches. Several men in helmets and olive-drab uniforms entered the building carrying equipment. Hazlitt heard someone call them a bomb squad. The awareness that he had no driver's license, no positive identification, touched him with an obscure elation. He strolled along with a noisy group of young people who had just exited from a movie, and they seemed to take his presence for granted. When someone asked him the time, he said, "Nearly nine," and was reminded that he had not yet called his wife. "You won't believe this," he would say, knowing she would.

To get his call so early in her evening startled her. "Where are you?" she cried. It was his custom to report the events of the day—or the nonevents, if so they proved to be—and this time he really had a story to tell. But, hearing the note of concern in her voice, he changed his mind. Any mention of the bomb scare would disturb her rather than amuse her.

He explained—feeling the need to be explicit—that he was in his hotel room, seated on the bed, facing the partially opened window. A cool breeze stirred the curtain. He asked her if she could hear the car horns in the street below. If she had been with him, he said, they would have gone to a play—she loved the theater. As she spoke to him—how well he saw her—she would be seated at the kitchen table, behind the lazy Susan, with its clutter of vitamin bottles, and several of the squat candle glasses set out in anticipation of the first seasonal storms and blackouts. Hazlitt knew so exactly just how it all was that he could hear the sound of the wall clock—stuffed with a towel to mute the tick-ing—and he could read the pressure (falling) on the barometer at her shoulder. He continued to talk, in a way that soothed her, about his short ride in the horse-drawn hack (a thing they had done together), and about the swarthy peddler selling his wares on the Bloomingdale's corner—for some reason, he avoided mention of Mrs. Thayer—until she spoke up to remind him that he was phoning from New York, at his own expense, and not from his office at the college. Before he replied she had hung up.

He was aware, with the lights switched off, how the sounds at the window seemed magnified. In the play of reflections on the ceiling he glimpsed, as through a canopy of leaves, the far-away prospect he had seen on the Bloomingdale's TV—bustling figures swarming soundlessly among the bodies strewn about a station lobby. Somehow the spectacle was full of mystery for him. None of this was a dream—no, he was awake; he heard the blast of the horns below his window—but the dreamlike aura held him in its spell until those sleeping figures arose to continue their journey.

In the doctor's waiting room the next morning, Hazlitt faced a wall of brightly colored children's paintings, goblinlike creatures with popped eyes, short stumpy arms, stiltlike legs. It was his wife who once remarked that this was probably how most children saw the world—like specimens under the lens of a microscope. In the suspended time that Hazlitt sat there, he held and returned the gaze of a purple-faced goblin, preferring it to the pale, ghostly image of the old man reflected in its covering glass.

The specialist's assurance, spoken at Hazlitt's back between thumps on his ribcage, drew more from its offhand manner than from what the man said: he showed little real concern. Every hour, Hazlitt gathered, the doctor saw patients more deserving of attention. His assistant, a well-coifed matronly woman with sinewy legs and the profile of a turkey, shared with Hazlitt her opinion that "a reprieve is the best one can expect, at our age."

He was down in the street, flowing north with the current, before he sensed that he was free of a nameless burden, and seemed lighter on his feet. He crossed to Park Avenue for a leisurely stroll through the Waldorf lobby, for the pleasure of its carpet and the creak of expensive Texas luggage. Approaching Bloomingdale's again, he paused to reconsider the previous evening's scene: Hazlitt himself teetering in the hack, the dark-skinned peddler in his paper hat, and Mrs. Thayer reaching for her change, with one of her knit gloves still dangling from her teeth.

Back at Bloomingdale's jewelry counter, he found that the girl with the bangs had the morning off. In her place, an older and more professional clerk requested some further identification before she could give him his license back with the bracelets. She reminded him that one couldn't be too careful. Last night's bomb scare—a telephone call from the Bronx—proved to be without foundation, but the entire building had had to be vacated. What was this country coming to, she asked him.

Before Hazlitt could reply, his attention was distracted by a display in the case he was leaning on—a short strand of pearls on a headless bust. Was it some trick of the lighting that made them seem to glow? "These are real?" he asked the saleswoman. They were real. Would he like to see something less expensive? Her implication piqued him, because it was accurate. She took the strand from the case and let him hold it. He knew nothing about pearls, but he was dazzled. He saw them on his wife—he saw her wide-eyed astonishment, her look of disbelief. "If it's not too inconvenient," he said, "I'd like to return the bracelets and take the pearls."

He had not troubled to ask the price, and the clerk gave him a glance of puzzled admiration. "We'll just start all over," she said, "but I'm afraid I'll have to ask you once more for your driver's license."

Right at that point, Hazlitt might have reconsidered, but he did not. From his wallet he removed a second blank check, and waited for the woman to present him with the bill. The sum astounded but did not shock him. Writing the numbers, spelling the sum out gave him a tingling sense of exhilaration. Again he saw his wife, seated across the table from him, gaze at him open-mouthed, as she would at a stranger.

"This will take a few minutes," the clerk said, and went off into the crowded aisles.

Hazlitt's elation increased. He drummed his nails on the case as he peered about him. One might have thought that he had propositioned the clerk, that she had accepted and gone off to pretty up a bit and get her wrap. His exhilaration persisted as he moseyed about. In the bakery department, he flirted with the clerk, who served him a croissant he could eat on the spot.

Back at the jewelry counter, he found everything in order. Was there anything else? His wife kept her jewels in pouches, he said—would they have a small pouch? The woman found one, of a suèdelike material, into which the pearls nestled.

He was out of the building, under an awning that dramatized his own reflection in the shop window, before he again remembered the incident with the peddler on Fifty-ninth Street. He wanted to ask him if Mrs. Thayer had come back for her change, but the fellow was not there.

In the early years of their marriage, while he was doing his graduate work in the city, Hazlitt had loved to walk up Fifth Avenue with his wife for lunch at the Met. The museum itself confused and tired her; she did not like mummies, or tombs, or religious paintings. But Hazlitt liked to watch the people as they strolled about looking at objects, the stance they assumed when contemplating an artwork. Secret translations were encouraged there, he felt, and a burden of culture was enlarged or diminished. An hour or so of this spectacle always left him so fatigued he was eager for the comforts of the dim Fountain Court lunchroom, the buzz of voices, and the splash of water.

Heading for the museum now, Hazlitt was already at Seventy-eighth Street before he was aware of the almost stalled bumper-to-bumper traffic. Passengers riding downtown in the buses and cabs made no faster progress than those who were walking. Some waved and exchanged remarks with the pedestrians. Hazlitt sauntered along, hardly caring that it had started to drizzle. Puddles had formed on the steps of the Met, and the sleeves and shoulders of his coat were wet. He checked the coat, then strolled about in a crowd like that in Grand Central Terminal. Just off the lobby, to the right, a new book department was jammed with shoppers. Hazlitt was attracted by the displays and the brilliant lights. On one of the tables, someone had opened, and left, a large volume—Fauve paintings, as bright as Christmas candy. Across the table another browser, sniffling slightly, her face partially veiled by the hood of a transparent slicker, had paused to dip into a collection of van Gogh's letters. She read the last in the book, which she seemed to like; she tried the next-to-last, then the next. Her slicker clearly revealed the unfortunate S-curve of her posture, and the purse that she clutched to her forward-thrusting abdomen. She pressed a wad of tissue to her nose as she sneezed.

Hazlitt wore a tweedy wool hat that concealed, his wife insisted, his best features. Mrs. Thayer passed so close behind him that he felt and heard the brush of her slicker. Was it possible that she found his reappearance as unsurprising as he found hers? Then he saw her at a distance, looking at cards, and her cheeks appeared flushed. It troubled him that she might have a fever. The short-sleeved dress she wore under her transparent raincoat exposed her thin arms. Later, in one of the admission lines, he watched her remove one of the knit gloves by gripping the tips of the fingers with her teeth, then tugging on them like a puppy. Hadn't her husband explained to her about germs?

Although it was still early, and Hazlitt was not fatigued, he made his way toward the Fountain Court lunchroom. He was standing at the entrance for a moment or two before he noticed the renovation. The dusky pool and its sculptured figures were gone. The basin was now a mere sunken pit, of a creamy color without shadows, and it was already bustling with diners crowding its tables. Instead of the refreshing coolness and splash of the water, there was the harsh clatter of plates and cutlery. Hazlitt just stood there, until he was asked to move. There was a bar to his right—he could have used a drink—but the flood of creamy light depressed him. He backed away, and out of long habit found the stairway that led down to the basement.

The dark and cool lavatory in this wing of the building used to be one of Hazlitt's regular stops. The high windows were near a playground, and he could often hear the shrill cries of the children outside. He thought he heard them again now as he opened the door, but the babble stopped as he entered the washroom. Six or seven small boys of assorted colors and sizes, their arms and faces smeared with gobs of white lather, stood facing the mirror at the row of washbowls. Their wide-eyed, soapy faces seemed to stare at Hazlitt from an adjoining room. The stillness, like that of a silent movie, was broken only by the sound of lapping water. A thin film of water covered the tiles at Hazlitt's feet.

As if he found this circumstance more or less normal, he crossed the room to the nearest booth and pushed open the door. A youth, older than the others, was crouched on the rear of the fixture with his feet on the bowl's edge. With the thumb of his right hand he depressed the handle. The water spilled evenly from the rim of the clogged bowl to splash on the floor.

In the dark of the booth, Hazlitt saw little but the cupped whites of the boy's eyes. The youth raised his free hand slowly to his face as if to wipe away a lingering expression. Something in this gesture, like that of a mime, revealed to Hazlitt that the boy was stoned. In the deep void of his expanded pupils was all the *where* that the world was missing. The eyes did not blink. Hazlitt turned from him to face the mirror, and the boys, who had formed a circle around him. One had opened his shirt to expose his torso, creamy with lather. With the light behind them, all Hazlitt saw was the patches of white, like slush on pavement. Still, it pleased him to have their close attention.

The smallest boy thrust a hand toward him, its wet palm up. "Trick or treat," he said gravely. Two of those beside him hooted like crows.

"Well, let's see," Hazlitt said, and drew some coins from his pocket. He exposed them to the light, the silver coins glinting, just as the boy gave his hand a slap from the bottom. The coins flew up, scattering, then fell soundlessly into the film of water.

"Hey, man, that's no treat!" the boy scoffed, and he rolled his eyes upward.

From the pocket of his jacket Hazlitt withdrew the suède pouch; he loosened the noose and let the string of pearls fall into the boy's coral palm. How beautiful they were, as if just fished from the deep! The boy's hand closed on them like a trap; he made a movement toward the door as one of the others grabbed him. Down they both went, slippery as eels, with their companions kicking and pulling at them. They thrashed about silently at Hazlitt's feet like one writhing, many-limbed monster. He was able to leave unmolested and track down the hall in his squishy shoes.

In the gift shop off the lobby he bought a pin, of Etruscan design, that he felt his wife would consider a sensible value. Carrying his coat—the drizzle had let up, and the humid air seemed warm—he walked south under the trees edging the park to the Seventy-second Street exit. Held up by the traffic light, he stood breathing the fumes of a bus and listening to the throb of its motor. At a window level with his head, one of the riders tapped sharply on the glass. Hazlitt was hardly an arm's length away, but he saw the woman's face only dimly through the rain-streaked window. What appeared to be tears might have been drops of water. The close-set green eyes, as close together as ever, were remarkably mild, and gave him all the assurance he needed. As he stared, she put a wadded tissue to her nose, then raised her gloved hand, the palm toward him, to slowly wag the chewed fingertips. Its air brakes hissing, the bus carried her away.

Letter to a Young Critic

David Madden's friendship with Wright Morris began in 1957 with a letter full of questions. Morris's answers were later published in this interview.

Wayne, Pennsylvania
December 7, 1957

Dear David Madden:

On the assumption, gratefully assumed, that you have made your way both in and out of Darkest Morris, I greet you at the edge of the clearing with a bottle of cherry phosphate and some fatherly advice. I take it you have a copy of your map in hand, so let's begin at the beginning:

[What is your estimation of Wayne C. Booth's essay ("Two Worlds in the Fiction of Wright Morris," *Sewanee Review* [Summer 1957]: 375-99) on your novels?]

Booth's report strikes me as sound, in the essentials, and it had much of interest to say to the author. The theme of audacity, as I would describe it, in one or several disguises, and many variations, emerges from all of the books. We begin with it in *Uncle Dudley*, and we last confront it in *The Cannibals*, where both Horter and the Greek improvise on the "act of bolting." *The*

Cannibals seems to have thrown you off stride, as it did many of my readers, who were happily nested in the groves of Nostalgia. It is the purpose of that book to shake the sentimental leaves from all those mythic limbs. You will not find this achievement of much interest until you have processed your own past, and come to terms with your inheritance of raw material. Having written ten books on this subject, I can appreciate your engagement. But there can, and in my opinion, should, be an end. In "The Territory Ahead," [incorporated into a book with the same title published by Harcourt Brace in 1958] an essay in *The Living Novel*, just published by MacMillan, you will find a summarizing statement on American writing and writers, on technique and raw material, that will answer many of the questions you have about Morris—and raise others. Insofar as my books and opinions interest you, I cannot urge it on you too strongly. It should serve as a statement, to which these notes may be appended.

[Are your novels in the "realistic" genre?]

Realistic etc.—all of my books testify to the function of *verisimilitude:* the life-like look that conveys the sense of life. No theories here: this is how the mind works, or how it doesn't. What I want is a sense of life so real it evokes a little more than life.

[You use some of the same character names, and indeed some of the same characters, throughout the novels; different characters have some of the same very particular memories, sometimes almost verbatim. How intentional is this common memory store?]

In putting my puzzle together—a fairly literal description—I began with no conception that a pattern might emerge, or that this emergence was a latent, groping form of conception. (See "Territory.") The pieces of the jig-saw that keep turning up (figures like Tom Scanlon; the unemployed heroes, Charles Lawrence, Boyd, etc.; men who feed birds, open cans with forks; bowls that contain the past, like an urn; paper weights where it is forever snowing, and clearing, and snowing)—these are the keys to the house of fiction. A writer shapes them to open doors with them. The room and the view will be different, but the key is the same. In *The Field of Vision* you see me arranging familiar pieces in a new pattern. A beginning. Much still to be done. It could not be done at all, however, while I was trapped in my own material. In those self-dug graves lie the bearded giants—face down.

On this subject we might prattle happily forever. It is both denser and more complex (the life of these fragments) than is evident in the published books. *The Works of Love*, a key book in this matter, in an early, wonderfully incoherent draft, contained the gist of all these potsherds in a flow reminiscent of Bridie Murphy. By the way—and a very *large* by—the University of California at Berkeley has a quantity of Morris manuscripts in their library, just waiting for the likes of Madden. . . . In the many drafts of the key books you will find some questions answered, others raised. But there, my boy, is the site of Morris-Troy. Bring up your wooden horse!

[One of your finest qualities is the subtlety of your underwriting, by which some large feelings and ideas are generated; but sometimes one gets lost. For instance, Dudley's audacious behavior is often enigmatic.]

Dudley is caught in the Morris field of vision, that magnet that buzzed in Lawrence, Boyd, [Agee] Ward, and [Earl] Horter, obliging him to be something of a damn fool in order to be himself. Blake plagiarized me here, as he does elsewhere, when he said that a fool who persists in his folly will become wise. I that know what you want to know is WHY—the simple, bare-faced motives, and indeed they are bare. The old fool merely wants to show himself a man. Underwriting—which seems to be a species of underwater swimming—has its many disadvantages, and that is one. Is the pool empty? That is how it often looks. I still have, in my possession, a *very* early manuscript that appears to be in Hindu. It is also *very* long. There were giants in the earth in those good old days.

[Why do so many characters—the Boy and Lipido in *Man and Boy*, for instance—resemble birds? Is this motif related to the image of the wetting of the bread with spittle before feeding it to the birds?]

I seem to find birds a sympathetic and lucid form of symbolism. The old man and the spittle is an instance. Fact and imagination, dream and reality, the caged and the uncaged—flight with feathers on it.

[And eggs. The novels are well-stocked with eggs. The theme of Sherwood Anderson's "The Triumph of the Egg" seems dominant in *The Works of Love*, which you dedicated to Anderson.]

And EGGS. Let us, my dear Boswell, clear this matter up. That damn Anderson EGG has long haunted me. Long before either Morris or Anderson hoped the egg would triumph or break, my father had the dream—à la Brady—of a chicken farm in Nebraska. About 1916. *The Works of Love* is true to the atmosphere. The egg—from which all birds come (see above) entered my life the HARD WAY, and that is very much the way it is working out. HARD. I will NOT say we have seen the last of them. It may seem hard to credit, with my affection for Anderson, but I had never read "Triumph of the Egg" until a review of *The Works of Love* called it to my attention! So there we have it. The small, small world, the large, LARGE egg. I suppose it was the dedication to Anderson that encouraged the tie-in. Well, HE would love it. What egg could triumph better than that?

[What other writers have influenced you?]

On the subject of writers and influences—very tricky at the best—a clarifying point. I read madly in college (where I discovered books) but nothing at all contemporary. (To correct this oversight a dear overseeing lady gave me a copy of The Fountain by Charles Morgan!) I began to write without a model or style, without any useful notion of form and conception, which will help to explain a very long five years of apprenticeship. I wrote novels of childhood, several of them, then I began to write the dense, prose-poem sort of things . . . that eventually appeared in such a book as The Inhabitants, facing the photographs. It is writing that led me to photography—and you will see why if you study the prose pieces. I was trying to lay my hands on the object itself. The photograph seemed the logical way to achieve such ends. It was one way, of course, but a writer's way is another, and these artifacts, thousands of them, go on turning up in my books. That Uncle Dudley, my first published novel, resembles no other book so much as itself, is due to the background I have described. Your nostalgia, I'm afraid, kept you from sensing the close affinity, both in style and substance, that Love Among the Cannibals has for Uncle Dudley. We have come full circle—I came, that is, full circle without being aware of it—and The Cannibals marks a fresh engagement with the present, rather than the past, which has now been re-experienced. I am not, in any sense, through with it—The Field of Vision is the first act of organization—but I am finished with immersion. In the waters of my fathers I have been dipped. This may be the great American baptism, since all our writers of consequence have to go through it. In my opinion (vide "The Territory") damn few survive. Immersion is immolation.

I admire writers as diverse as Hemingway and Camus, Mann and Joyce, Kafka and Lawrence, but I observe, increasingly, that this admiration is remote from imitation, and may have little to do, as in the case of Lawrence, with the major novels, or the public figure. One book, or a few pages, may suffice to include a man in the personal pantheon. The writer who writes more than he reads, as I do, will develop the faculty of appraising, in a short exposure, what it is that he seeks, and what it is that nourishes him. Whether the twig bends to water or not, the writer bends to the currents that feed him. All others are merely distractions. He truly *learns* only what he can use.

In this matter, as in many others, I refer you again to "The Territory Ahead," where I have stated, as clearly as I know how, relevant opinions on writing and writers.

[One of your major and unique abilities is to achieve dramatic intensity and interest without the crutch that action often becomes in American literature. Why do you eschew action and focus retrospectively upon a few memorable events?]

The notion of what is dramatic, novelistically speaking, is apt to be either fashionable or clichéd: the meaningful object, or the meaningful event, is precisely what the writer must imagine, and in this *act of the imagination* are such elements of drama as he finds necessary. It is the *imaginative act*, not the action of events, that reveals the artist of stature—the action of events can be learned by formula, and often is. My problem as a writer is to dramatize my conception of the experience, and it may often exclude, as it often does, the entire apparatus of dramatic action. The impassive life of Brady is instructive in this point. His life, for me, is full of meaningful action on the level of awareness. This is also true of *The Cannibals*—with its pattern of surface action—as it is of *The Works of Love*, where the action is submerged. (See chapter 3 of *The Territory Ahead*.) What a writer *does*, not what he should do, not even how well or badly he does it, is the only imaginative fact of any consequence. This is now all but forgotten. It is assumed books are written to provoke discussion. Actually, they are conceived to make discussion irrelevant.

[Even while you were a photographer, did you feel yourself becoming a writer?]

This is answered in my remarks on an earlier question. I began as a writer. In my effort to possess the *ding an sich* I tried the resources of photography. They are considerable but limited. Reality is not a *thing* but a *conception*, and the camera cannot conceive. I tried to overcome this limitation by a marriage of sensations in the mind of the beholder: *The Home Place* and *The Inhabitants*.

[A dirty question, but one raised emphatically by your works: how do you regard women in our society?]

Women? A very dirty question, indeed. But *Woman*, that is another matter. My opinions on this subject have been formulated, with my problem in mind, by Henry James. (Vide: *The American Scene*.) Betrayed by Man (deprived of him, that is), woman is taking her abiding revenge on him—unconscious in such figures as Mrs. Ormsby [in *Man and Boy*] and Mrs. Porter [in *The Deep Sleep*], where she inherits, by default, the world man should be running. Since only Man will deeply gratify her, the Vote and the Station Wagon leave something to be desired. One either sees this, or one doesn't. As of now both man and woman are tragically duped: the Victor has no way of digesting the spoils.

[What explains Webb's very moving act of kindness in *The Deep Sleep* when he lays the watch where Mrs. Porter can find it?]

Webb's act reflects his respect for the forces that both salvage human life and destroy it: the pitiless compulsion that testifies, in its appalling way, to the spirit's devious ways of survival.

[Your novels declare that you are haunted by Nebraska, the region of your childhood. Not since Thomas Wolfe has such lucid and meaningful nostalgia pervaded a body of work.]

Not since Thomas Wolfe? My dear Boswell, Mr. Wolfe tried to do the impossible—and failed, naturally. Mr. Morris is much more ambitious. It is the possible he wants, and sometimes he gets it. . . .

[How have your novels been received outside the United States?]

Too early to say. German editions just now appearing. *The Deep Sleep* seems to be the most exportable. It did very well in England, and has been translated into German and Italian. The English critical scene has a familiar incoherence. *The Field of Vision* was the object of considerable irrelevant abuse. . . .

[In what direction are you now heading in your work? *Love Among the Cannibals* doesn't seem to begin a direction that you would be likely to follow very long.]

I have been dropping hints all along the way. The biggest hint you preferred to ignore, since it didn't suit your pattern. *The Cannibals*. A deliberate putting aside of the familiar nostalgic pattern. An effort to confront, in Lawrence's terms, the poetry of the present, where the strands are all flying, and the waters are shaking the moon. When a writer does that rare thing—stops doing what he knows how to do, and endeavors to do something more—it is instructive that those who hold an interest in his work should be the first to cry havoc. When we are less engaged with the nature of our pasts, and have unreeled our minds to come to terms with the present, we will, I suspect, find *The Cannibals* a much different book. If I should prove to be a writer of some interest, it will prove to be one of my most interesting books.

Technique and Raw Material

"God alive, Sir Knight of the Mournful Countenance," said Sancho, "I cannot bear in patience some of the things that your Grace says! Listening to you, I come to think that all you have told me about deeds of chivalry and winning kingdoms and bestowing islands and other favors and dignities is but wind and lies, all buggery or humbuggery or whatever you choose to call it. For when anyone hears your Grace saying that a barber's basin is Mambrino's helmet, and after four days you still insist that it is, what is he to think except that such a one is out of his mind?"

We have that barber's basin, more crushed and dented than ever, among us today. It symbolizes the state of the imagination in the raw material world of facts. Like Sancho, the modern temper distrusts the processes of the imagination, but it has great faith in the alchemy of the laboratory. High octane and low imagination are the order of the day.

The romantic agony of the poet has been displaced by the agony of the test tube—the compulsive commitments of the poet have given way to the compulsive behavior of atomic fission. The hallmark of the true agony is that extinction is preferable to self-examination. The end of life, public and private, is preferable to the end of the pursuit of such knowledge.

Technique and raw material are essential to both the study and the laboratory. By raw material I mean that comparatively crude ore that has not been processed by the imagination—what we refer to as *life*, or as experience, in contrast to art. By technique I mean the way that the artist smelts this material down for human consumption.

A new world, in these terms, will contain more raw material than an old one. America, that is, is rawer than Europe. This rawness is comparative, however, since the brave new world that the explorer discovers contains, on the whole, only what he comes prepared to find. But a permissible illusion of rawness exists on each frontier. And in a nation of expanding frontiers, the illusion of rawness expands along with them. Technique, in this pioneer picture, is therefore little more than a clearing operation—the raw material is the thing, and the technique is a method of collecting it. There usually appears to be an inexhaustible supply of it. But if you happen to run out of it where you are, why then you move on to where it is waiting. It *exists*, that is. It is not something the artist conjures up.

If the world is a collection of crude barbers' basins which the artist must transmute into gold, both Cervantes and Norman Rockwell, "the most popular, the most loved, of all contemporary artists," give us a lesson in how the trick is done.

"Do you know what I think, Sancho?" said Don Quixote. "I think that this famous piece of that enchanted helmet must by some strange accident have fallen into the hands of someone who did not know, and was incapable of estimating, its worth, and who, seeing that it was of the purest gold and not realizing what he was doing, must have melted down the other half for what he could get for it, while from the remaining portion he fashioned what appears, as you have said, to be a barber's basin."

It is Cervantes who takes us behind the scenes and shows us how the imagination works: we are not merely told that the world is a stage, but how it operates. Technique and raw material are dramatized at the moment that the shaping imagination is aware of itself. We see the way in which the world—in Whitehead's sense—is processed into reality. The transitory, illusive facts are shaped into a fiction of permanence. At the moment that the mind takes the step we think of as characteristically modern, we are taken offstage, into the very wings of the mind itself. We are allowed to see the world, as the raw material, and Don Quixote, the transforming technician. The author, whom we do not see, is the discipline that turns the Mournful Knight's mad antics to the service of the heart's desire, the intelligence. Both technique and raw material—the processed fiction and the raw fact—confront each other in Don Quixote and Sancho, a legend of the labyrinthine way of the imagination itself.

II

The history of fiction, its pursuit of that chimera we describe as reality, is a series of imaginative triumphs made possible through technique. In *Mimesis*, Erich Auerbach has charted this course from Homer to Joyce. In aesthetic terms, *facts* are those sensations that have been convincingly processed by the imagination. They are the materials, the artifacts, so to speak, that we actually possess.

At the summit of technique we have such a craftsman as Joyce. There is so little craft in fiction on this scale that so much craft seems forbidding. Is the end result—we are inclined to ask ourselves—still alive? Is life, real or imaginary, meant to be processed as much as that? In Joyce the dominance of technique over raw material reflects one crisis of the modern imagination. Raw material has literally dissolved into technique.

In *Finnegans Wake* the world of Dublin happens to be the raw material that Joyce puts through his process—but the process, not Dublin, is the thing. It is the process that will give the raw material its enduring form. A parallel transformation is still taking place in what we call modern art. In Manet's portrait of Clemenceau the subject has vanished into the method—the method has become painting itself. Both Dublin and Clemenceau are processed into means, rather than ends, since the artist's problem is not to reconstruct the old, but to construct the new. It is characteristic of the mind of Joyce that the city of Dublin, shaped by his ironic craft, should not merely disappear but prove hard to find.

The brave new world has had its share of able craftsmen, but with the exception of Hawthorne and James, both closely linked to the old, they usually lacked what we would call the master touch. Raw material, usually the rawer the better, seemed to be their forte. On certain rare and unpredictable occasions craft might break through this devotion to raw material, but the resulting masterpiece had about it the air of an accident; not so much a crafty man-made thing, as a gift from above. The author usually took pains not to repeat it, or to learn from his experience. *Walden*, *Leaves of Grass*, *Moby Dick*, and the *Adventures of Huckleberry Finn* have in common this sense of isolation. Something of a mystery to both the author and the public, they resemble some aspect of a natural force—a pond, a river, a demonic whale—rather than something cleverly contrived by man. They seem to have more in common with Niagara Falls, Mammoth Cave, or Old Faithful than with a particular author, or anything so artificial as art. They are wonders, but *natural* wonders, like the Great Stone Face.

This notion of the natural, the unschooled genius who leaps, like a trout, from some mountain stream, seems to be central to our national egotism. It reappears every day in the child—or the backward, untutored adult—who draws, writes, strums a saw or plays a piano without *ever* having taken a lesson. That lessons might corrupt his talent, and ruin his promise, goes without saying. We believe in doing only what comes naturally.

But those natural moments in which we take so much pride—*Walden*, *Leaves of Grass*, *Moby Dick*, and *Huckleberry Finn*—are, without exception, moments of grace under pressure, triumphs of craft. The men who produced them are artists, innovators, of the first magnitude. Each of these statements is a contemporary statement, and each is unique. They represent new levels where, in the words of D. H. Lawrence, the work of art can ". . . inform and lead into new places the flow of our sympathetic consciousness, and it can lead our sympathy away in recoil from things that are dead."

If we now ask ourselves under what pressure these moments of grace are achieved, I believe it is the pressure of the raw material itself. Each of these men felt the need to domesticate a continent. In his essay on Hawthorne, Melville observed: "It is not so much paucity as superabundance of material that seems to incapacitate modern authors."

He had reason to know. It was not lack of material that silenced Herman Melville. The metaphysical woods that he found mirrored in the sea, and which drew him to it, of all aspects of the brave new world were the least inhabited.

III

With the passing of the last natural frontier—that series of horizons dissolving westward—the raw-material myth, based, as it is, on the myth of inexhaustible resources, no longer supplies the artisan with lumps of raw life. All of it has been handled. He now inhabits a world of raw-material clichés. His homemade provincial wares no longer startle and amaze the world. As a writer he must meet, and beat, the old world masters at their own game. In his "Monologue to the Maestro," Hemingway states the problem in his characteristic manner:

There is no use writing anything that has been written better before unless you can beat it. What a writer in our time has to do is write what hasn't been written before or beat dead men at what they have done. The

only way he can tell how he is going is to compete with dead men . . .
the only people for a serious writer to compete with are the dead that he
knows are good. . . .

With this credo the Portrait of the Artist as a Young American is
permanently revised. The provincial is out. The dyed-in-the-wool
professional is in. Not only do we have to meet the champ, we
have to beat him. That calls, among other things, for knowing
who he is. Such a statement could only come from a writer who
knows you have to beat the masters with style and technique, and
it is on these terms that he has won his place in the pantheon.

If raw material is so bad, if it is the pitfall and handicap to
the artist that I am suggesting, why is it that American writers,
through, rather than in spite of, this handicap, are one of the
germinal forces wherever books are read. Here, I think, we have
an instructive paradox. It involves us in the problem of good and
bad taste. Not the good or bad taste of the artist, but the good or
bad taste we find in his raw material. Good taste—*good* in the
sense that it is fashionable and decorative—usually indicates an
absence of the stuff of life that the artist finds most congenial.
Both the Parthenon and the urban apartment decorated with
Mondrian and Van Gogh resist more than a passing reference,
usually ironic in tone. The over-processed material, what we
sense as overrefinement, is an almost fatal handicap to the artist:
we feel this handicap in James—not his mind, but in his material—and it is at a final extremity in Proust. Only a formidable
genius, only a formidable technique, can find in such material
fresh and vital elements.

Bad taste, on the other hand, is invariably an ornament of
vitality, and it is the badness that cries out with meaning, and
calls for processing. Raw material and bad taste—the feeling we
have that bad taste indicates *raw* material—is part of our persuasion that bad grammar, in both life and literature, reflects *real*
life. But bad taste of this sort is hard to find. Bad "good taste" is
the world in which we live now.

In reference to Joyce, Harry Levin has said: "The best writing of our contemporaries is not an act of creation, but an act of evocation peculiarly saturated with reminiscences." This observation pertains to Joyce and Proust as it does to Fitzgerald and his dream of Gatsby, or to Hemingway's Nick on "The Big Two-Hearted River." In our time, that is, nostalgia is not peculiarly American.

But the uses to which the past is put allow us to distinguish between the minor and the major craftsman. The minor artist is usually content to indulge in it. But the labyrinthine reminiscence of Proust is conceptual, *consciously* conceptual, in contrast to the highly unconscious reminiscence in *Huckleberry Finn*. Not *knowing* what he was doing, Mark Twain was under no compulsion to do it again.

Twain's preference for *real* life—*Life on the Mississippi*—is the preference Thoreau felt for facts, the facts of Nature, and Whitman's preference for the man-made artifact. Something *real*. Something the hand, as well as the mind, could grasp. Carried to its conclusion this preference begins and ends right where we find it—in autobiography. On this plane raw material and art appear to be identical. *I was there, I saw, and I suffered*, said Whitman, sounding the note, and the preference is still dear to the readers of the *Saturday Evening Post*. Wanting no nonsense, only facts, we make a curious discovery. Facts are like faces. There are millions of them. They are disturbingly alike. It is the imagination that looks behind the face, as well as looks out of it.

Letting the evidence speak for itself, the facts, that is, of the raw-material myth, the indications are that it destroys more than it creates. It has become a dream of abuse rather than use. We are no longer a raw-material reservoir, the marvel and despair of less fortunate cultures, since our only inexhaustible resource at the moment is the cliché. An endless flow of clichés, tirelessly processed for mass-media consumption, now give a sheen of vitality to what is either stillborn or secondhand. The hallmark of these clichés is a processed sentimentality. The extremes of our life, what its contours should be, blur at their point of origin, then disappear into the arms of the Smiling Christ at Forest Lawn. The secretary with the diaphragm in her purse, prepared to meet any emergency, will prove to be a reader of Norman Vincent Peale or Kahlil Gibran. Ten minutes of her luncheon will be turned over to *The Mature Mind*. The raw-material world of facts, of *real* personal life, comes full circle in the unreal phantom of who spends real time seeking for his or her self in the how-to-do-it books—How to Live, How to Love, and, sooner or later, How to Read Books.

What was once raw about American life has now been dealt with so many times that the material we begin with is itself a fiction, one created by Twain, Eliot, or Fitzgerald. *From Here to Eternity* reminds us that young men are still fighting Hemingway's war. After all, it is the one they know best: it was made real and coherent by his imagination.

Many writers of the twenties, that huge season, would appear to be exceptions to the ravages of raw material, and they are. But it is the nature of this exception to prove the rule. In inspiration, the twenties were singularly un-American. An exile named Pound established the standards, and the left bank of Paris dictated the fashions. This lucid moment of grace was Continental in origin. With the exiles' return, however, it came to an end. The craftsmen who shaped and were shaped by this experience—Eliot, Fitzgerald, Crane, Hemingway, and so on—maintained their own devotion to the new standards, but they had little effect on the resurgent raw-material school. Whitman's barbaric yawp, which Pound had hoped to educate, reappeared in the gargantuan bellow of Wolfe and a decade of wrath largely concerned with the seamy side of life.

Once again that gratifying hallucination—the great BIG American novel—appeared in cartons too large for the publisher's desk. Once again the author needed help—could one man, singlehanded, tame such a torrent of life? If the writer caged the monster, shouldn't the editor teach him to speak? The point was frequently debated; the editor-collaborator became a part of the creative project, the mastering of the material as exhausting as mastering life itself. In a letter to Fitzgerald, who had suggested that there might be room for a little more selection, Thomas Wolfe replied: "I may be wrong but all I can get out of it is that you think I'd be a better writer if I were an altogether different writer from the writer I am."

Time and the river—was Fitzgerald suggesting they reverse themselves? That a writer swim against the very current of American life? He was, but the suggestion has never been popular. Tom Wolfe didn't take it, and the writer who does take it may find himself, however homegrown, an exile. He swims against the current; and the farther he swims, the more he swims alone. The best American fiction is still *escape* fiction—down the river on a raft, into the hills on a horse, or out of this world on a ship—the territory ahead lies behind us, safe as the gold at Fort Knox.

IV

Raw material, an excess of both material and comparatively raw experience, has been the dominant factor in my own role as a novelist. The thesis I put forward grows out of my experience, and applies to it. Too much crude ore. The hopper of my green and untrained imagination was both nourished and handicapped by it.

Before coming of age—the formative years when the reservoir of raw material was filling—I had led, or rather been led by, half a dozen separate lives. Each life had its own scene, its own milieu; it frequently appeared to have its own beginning and ending, the only connecting tissue being the narrow thread of my *self*. I had been *there*, but that, indeed, explained nothing. In an effort to come to terms with the experience, I processed it in fragments, collecting pieces of the puzzle. In time, a certain over-all pattern *appeared* to be there. But this appearance was essentially a process—an imaginative act of apprehension—rather than a research into the artifacts of my life.

The realization that I had to create coherence, conjure up my synthesis, rather than find it, came to me, as it does to most Americans, disturbingly late. Having sawed out the pieces of my jigsaw puzzle, I was faced with a problem of fitting them together. There is a powerful inclination to leave this chore to someone else. In the work of Malcolm Cowley on William Faulkner, we may have the rudiments of a new procedure. Let the critic do what the author fails to do for himself. As flattering as this concept might be—to both the author and the critic—it must be clear that the concept is not tenable. The final act of coherence is an imaginative act—not a sympathetic disposal of parts—and the man who created the parts must create the whole into which they fit. It is amusing to think what the mind of Henry James would make of this salvage operation, a surgical redistribution of the parts of a patient who is still alive. Mr. Cowley's service to the reader is important—what I want to put in question is his service to the writer. This is implicit, if unstated, in any piece of reconstruction that attempts to implement what the writer failed to do himself.

This act of piety toward the groping artist—a desire to help him with his raw-material burden—is one with our sentiment that he labors to express the inexpressible. Like a fond parent, we supply the words to his stuttering lips. We share with him, as he shares with us, an instinct that our common burden of experience, given a friendly nudging, will speak for itself. At such a moment the mind generates those evocations peculiar to the American scene: life, raw life of such grace that nature seems to be something brought back alive. Out on his raft Huck Finn muses:

Two or three days and nights went by: I reckon I might say they swum by, they slid along so quiet and smooth and lovely. Here is the way we put in the time.

In what follows we are putting in our own time. We are there. Memory is processed by emotion in such a way that life itself seems to be preserved in amber. But we know better; we know that it is more than life, and it is this knowledge that makes it so moving—life has been imagined, immortal life, out of thin air. Not merely that boy out on the river, but the nature of the world's imagination, there on the raft with him, will never again be the same. But at the end of his adventures, at the point where the fiction—like the reader—merges into fact, Huck Finn sums it all up in these pregnant words:

But I reckon I got to light out for the Territory ahead of the rest, because Aunt Sally she's going to adopt me and civilize me, and I can't stand it. I been there before.

So has the reader. Aunt Sally has his number, but his heart belongs to the territory ahead.

The Ram in the Thicket

This story, originally published in Harper's Bazaar *in 1948, is an early beginning to the 1951 novel* Man and Boy.

In this dream Mr. Ormsby stood in the yard—at the edge of the yard where the weeds began—and stared at a figure that appeared to be on a rise. This figure had the head of a bird with a crown of bright, exotic plumage, only partially concealed by a paint-daubed helmet. Mr. Ormsby felt the urgent need to identify this strange bird. Feathery wisps of plumage shot through the crown of the helmet like a pillow leaking sharp spears of yellow straw. The face beneath it was indescribably solemn, with eyes so pale they were like openings in the sky. Slung over the left arm, casually, was a gun, but the right arm, the palm upward, extended toward a cloud of hovering birds. They came and went, like bees after honey, and there were so many and all so friendly, that Mr. Ormsby extended his own hand toward them. No birds came, but in his upturned palm he felt the dull throb of the alarm clock, which he held tenderly, a living thing, until it ran down.

In the morning light the photograph at the foot of his bed seemed startling. The boy stood alone on a rise, and he held, very casually, a gun. The face beneath the helmet had no features, but Mr. Ormsby would have known him just by the stance, by the way he held the gun, like some women hold their arms when their hands are idle, parts of their body that for the moment are not much use. Without the gun it was as if some part of the boy had been amputated; the way he stood, even the way he walked was not quite right.

Mr. Ormsby had given the boy a gun because he had never had a gun himself, not because he wanted him to shoot anything. The boy didn't want to kill anything either, and during the first year he found it hard to: the rattle of the BBs in the barrel of the gun frightened the birds before he could shoot them. And that was what had made him a *hunter*. He had to stalk everything in order to hit it, and after all that trouble you naturally try to hit what you're shooting at. He didn't seem to realize that after he hit it it might be dead. It seemed natural for a boy like that to join the Navy, and let God strike Mr. Ormsby dead to hear him say so, nothing ever seemed more natural to him than the news that the boy had been killed. Mother had steeled herself for the worst, the moment the boy enlisted, but Mr. Ormsby had not been prepared to feel what he felt. Mother need never know it unless he slipped up and talked in his sleep.

He turned slowly on the bed, careful to keep the springs quiet, and as he lowered his feet he scooped his socks from the floor. As a precaution Mother had slept the first few months of their marriage in her corset—as a precaution and as an aid to self-control. In the fall they had ordered twin beds. Carrying his shoes—today, of all days, would be a trial for Mother—he tiptoed to the closet and picked up his shirt and pants. There was simply no reason, as he had explained to her twenty years ago, why she should get up when he could just as well get a bite for himself. He had made that suggestion when the boy was just a baby and she needed her strength. Even as it was she didn't come out of it any too well. The truth was, Mother was so thorough about everything she did that her breakfasts usually took an hour or more. When he did it himself he was out of the kitchen in ten, twelve minutes and without leaving a pile of dishes around. By himself he could quick-rinse them in a little hot water, but with Mother there was the dishpan and all of the suds. Mother had the idea that a meal simply wasn't a meal without setting the table and using half the dishes in the place. It was easier to do it himself, and except for Sunday, when they had brunch, he was out of the house an hour before she got up. He had a bite of lunch at the store and at four o'clock he did the day's shopping since he was right downtown anyway. There was a time he called her up and inquired as to what she thought she wanted, but since he did all the buying he knew that better himself. As secretary for the League of Women Voters she had enough on her mind in times like these without cluttering it up with food. Now that he left the store an hour early he usually got home in the midst of her nap or while she was taking her bath. As he had nothing else to do he prepared the vegetables and dressed the meat, as Mother had never shown much of a flair for meat. There had been a year—when the boy was small and before he had taken up that gun—when she had made several marvelous lemon meringue pies. But feeling as she did about the gun—and she told them both how she felt about it—she didn't see why she should slave in the kitchen for people like that. She always spoke to them as *they*—or as *you* plural—from the time he had given the boy the gun. Whether this was because they were both men, both culprits, or both something else, they were never entirely separate things again. When she called *they* would both answer, and though the boy had been gone two years he still felt him *there*, right beside him when Mother said *you*.

For some reason Mr. Ormsby could not understand—although the rest of the house was neat as a pin—the room they *lived* in was always a mess. Mother refused to let the cleaning woman set her foot in it. Whenever she left the house she locked the door. Long, long ago he had said something, and she had said something, and she had said she wanted one room in the house where she could relax and just let her hair down. That had sounded so wonderfully human, so unusual for Mother, that he had been completely taken with it. As a matter of fact he still didn't know what to say. It was the only room in the house—except for the screened-in porch in the summer—where he could take off his shoes and open his shirt on his underwear. If the room was *clean*, it would be clean like all the others, and that would leave him nothing but the basement and the porch. The way the boy took to the out-of-doors—he stopped looking for his cuff links, began to look for pins—was partially because he couldn't find a place in the house to sit down. They had just redecorated the house—the boy at that time was just a little shaver—and Mother had spread newspapers over everything. There hadn't been a chair in the place—except the straight-backed ones at the table—that hadn't been, that *wasn't*, covered with a piece of newspaper. Anyone who had ever scrunched around on a paper knew what that was like. It was at that time that he had got the idea of having his pipe in the basement, reading in the bedroom, and the boy had taken to the out-of-doors. Because he had always wanted a gun himself, and because the boy was alone, with no kids around to play with, he had brought him home a thousand-shot BB gun by the name of Daisy—funny that he should remember the name—and five thousand BBs in a drawstring bag.

That gun had been a mistake—he began to shave himself in tepid, lukewarm water rather than let it run hot, which would bang the pipes and wake Mother up. When the telegram came that the boy had been killed Mother hadn't said a word, but she made it clear whose fault it was. There was never any doubt, *any* doubt, as to just whose fault it was.

He stopped thinking while he shaved, attentive to the mole at the edge of his mustache, and leaned to the mirror to avoid dropping suds on the rug. There had been a time when he had wondered about an Oriental throw rug in the bathroom, but over twenty years he had become accustomed to it. As a matter of fact he sort of missed it whenever they had guests with children and Mother remembered to take it up. Without the rug he always felt just a little uneasy in the bathroom; it led him to whistle or turn on the water and let it run. If it hadn't been for that he might not have noticed as soon as he did that Mother did the same thing whenever anybody was in the house. She turned on the water and let it run until she was through with the toilet, then she would flush it before she turned the water off. If you happen to have old-fashioned plumbing, and have lived with a person for twenty years, you can't help noticing little things like that. He had got to be a little like that himself: since the boy had gone he used the one in the basement or waited until he got down to the store. As a matter of fact, it was more convenient, didn't wake Mother up, and he could have his pipe while he was sitting there.

With his pants on, but carrying his shirt—for he might get it soiled preparing breakfast—he left the bathroom and tiptoed down the stairs.

Although the boy had gone, was gone, that is, Mother still liked to preserve her slipcovers and the kitchen linoleum. It was a good piece, well worth preserving, but unless there were guests in the house and the papers were taken up, Mr. Ormsby forgot it was there. Right now he couldn't tell you what color the linoleum was. Stooping to see what the color might be—it proved to be blue, Mother's favorite color—he felt the stirring in his bowels. Usually this occurred while he was rinsing the dishes after his second cup of coffee or after the first long draw on his pipe. He was not supposed to smoke in the morning, but it was more important to be regular that way than irregular with his pipe. Mother had been the first to realize this—not in so many words—but she would rather he did anything than not be able to do *that*.

He measured out a pint and a half of water, put it over a medium fire, and added just a pinch of salt. Then he walked to the top of the basement stairs, turned on the light, and at the bottom turned it off. He dipped his head to pass beneath a sagging line of wash, the sleeves dripping, and with his hands out, for the corner was dark, he entered the cell.

The basement toilet had been put in to accommodate the help, who had to use something, and Mother would not have them on her Oriental rug. Until the day he dropped some money out of his pants and had to strike a match to look for it, he had never noticed what kind of a stool it was. Mother had picked it up secondhand—she had never told him where—because she couldn't see buying something new for a place always in the dark. It was very old, with a chain pull, and operated on a principle that invariably produced quite a splash. But, in spite of that, he preferred it to the one at the store and very much more than the one upstairs. This was rather hard to explain since the seat was pretty cold in the winter and the water sometimes nearly froze. But it was private like no other place in the house. Considering that the house was as good as empty, that was a strange thing to say, but it was the only way to say how he felt. If he went off for a walk like the boy, Mother would miss him, somebody would see him, and he wouldn't feel right about it anyhow. All he wanted was a dark, quiet place and the feeling that for five minutes, just five minutes, nobody would be looking for him. Who would ever believe five minutes like that were so hard to come by? The closest he had ever been to the boy—after he had given him the gun—was the morning he had found him here on the stool. It was then that the boy had said, *et tu, Brutus*, and they had both laughed so hard they had to hold their sides. The boy had put his head in a basket of wash so Mother wouldn't hear. Like everything the boy said there were two or three ways to take it, and in the dark Mr. Ormsby could not see his face. When he stopped laughing the boy said, *Well, Pop, I suppose one flush ought to do, but*

Mr. Ormsby had not been able to say anything. To be called Pop made him so weak that he had to sit right down on the stool, just like he was, and support his head in his hands. Just as he had never had a name for the boy, the boy had never had a name for him—none, that is, that Mother would permit him to use. Of all the names Mother couldn't stand, Pop was the worst, and he agreed with her; it was vulgar, common, and used by strangers to intimidate old men. He agreed with her, completely—until he heard the word in the boy's mouth. It was only natural that the boy would use it if he ever had the chance—but he never dreamed that any word, especially *that* word, could mean what it did. It made him weak, he had to sit down and pretend he was going about his business, and what a blessing it was that the place was dark. Nothing more was said, ever, but it remained their most important conversation—so important they were afraid to try and improve on it. Days later he remembered what the boy had actually said, and how shocking it was but without any *sense* of shock. A blow so sharp that he had no sense of pain, only a knowing, as he had under gas, that he had been worked on. For two, maybe three minutes, there in the dark, they have been what Mother had called them, they were *they*—and they were there in the basement because they were so much alike. When the telegram came, and when he knew what he would find, he had brought it there, had struck a match, and read what it said. The match filled the cell with light and he saw—he couldn't help seeing—piles of tinned goods in the space beneath the stairs. Several dozen cans of tuna fish and salmon, and since *he* was the one that had the points, bought the groceries, there was only one place Mother could have got such things. It had been a greater shock than the telegram—that was the honest-to-God's truth and anyone who knew Mother as well as he did would have felt the same. It was unthinkable, but there it was—and there were more on top of the water closet, where he peered while precariously balanced on the stool. Cans of pineapple, crabmeat, and tins of Argentine beef. He had been stunned, the match had burned down and actually scorched his fingers, and he nearly killed himself when he forgot and stepped off the seat. Only later in the morning—after he had sent flowers to ease the blow for Mother—did he realize how such a thing must have occurred. Mother knew so many influential people, and they gave her so much that they had very likely given her all this stuff as well. Rather than turn it down and needlessly alienate people, influential people, Mother had done the next best thing. While the war was on she refused to serve it, or profiteer in any way—and at the same time not alienate people foolishly. It had been an odd thing, certainly, that he should discover all of that by the same match that he read the telegram. Naturally, he never breathed a word of it to Mother, as something like that, even though she was not superstitious, would really upset her. It was one of those things that he and the boy would keep to themselves.

It would be like Mother to think of putting it in here, the very last place that the cleaning woman would look for it. The new cleaning woman would neither go upstairs nor down, and did whatever she did somewhere else. Mr. Ormsby lit a match to see if everything was all right—hastily blew it out when he saw that the can pile had increased. He stood up, then hurried up the stairs without buttoning his pants as he could hear the water boiling. He added half a cup, then measured three heaping tablespoons of coffee into the bottom of the double boiler, buttoned his pants. Looking at his watch he saw that it was seven thirty-five. As it would be a hard day—sponsoring a boat was a man-size job—he would give Mother another ten minutes or so. He took two bowls from the cupboard, set them on blue pottery saucers, and with the grapefruit knife in his hand walked to the icebox.

As he put his head in the icebox door—in order to see he had to—Mr. Ormsby stopped breathing and closed his eyes. What had been dying for some time was now dead. He leaned back, inhaled, leaned in again. The floor of the icebox was covered with a fine assortment of jars full of leftovers Mother simply could not throw away. Some of the jars were covered with little oilskin hoods, some with saucers, and some with wax paper snapped on with a rubber band. It was impossible to tell, from the outside, which one it was. Seating himself on the floor he removed them one at a time, starting at the front and working toward the back. As he had done this many times before, he got well into the problem, near the middle, before troubling to sniff anything. A jar that might have been carrots—it was hard to tell without probing—was now a furry marvel of green mold. It smelled only mildly, however, and Mr. Ormsby remembered that this was penicillin, the life giver. A spoonful of cabbage—it had been three months since they had had cabbage—had a powerful stench but was still not the one he had in mind. There were two more jars of mold; the one screwed tight he left alone as it had a frosted look and the top of the lid bulged. The culprit, however, was not that at all, but in an open saucer on the next shelf—part of an egg—Mr. Ormsby had beaten the white himself. He placed the saucer on the sink and returned all but two of the jars to the icebox: the cabbage and the explosive-looking one. If it smelled he took it out, otherwise Mother had to see for herself as she refused to take their word for these things. When he was just a little shaver the boy had walked into the living room full of Mother's guests and showed them something in a jar. Mother had been horrified—but she naturally thought it a frog or something and not a bottle out of her own icebox. When one of the ladies asked the boy where in the world he had found it, he naturally said, *In the icebox*. Mother had never forgiven him. After that she forbade him to look in the box without permission, and the boy had not so much as peeked in it since. He would eat only what he found on the table, or ready to eat in the kitchen—or what he found at the end of those walks he took everywhere.

With the jar of cabbage and furry mold Mr. Ormsby made a trip to the garage, picked up the garden spade, walked around behind. At one time he had emptied the jars and merely buried the contents, but recently, since the war that is, he had buried it all. Part of it was a question of time—he had more work to do at the store—but the bigger part of it was to put an end to the jars. Not that it worked out that way—all Mother had to do was open a new one—but it gave him a real satisfaction to bury them. Now that the boy and his dogs were gone there was simply no one around the house to eat up all the food Mother saved.

There were worms in the fork of earth he had turned and he stood looking at them—they both had loved worms—when he remembered the water boiling on the stove. He dropped everything and ran, ran right into Emil Ludlow, the milkman, before he noticed him. Still on the run he went up the steps and through the screen door into the kitchen—he was clear to the stove before he remembered the door would slam. He started back, but too late, and in the silence that followed the BANG he stood with his eyes tightly closed, his fists clenched. Usually he remained in this condition until a sign from Mother—a thump on the floor or her voice at the top of the stairs. None came, however, only the sound of the milk bottles that Emil Ludlow was leaving on the porch. Mr. Ormsby gave him time to get away, waited until he heard the horse walking, then he went out and brought the milk in. At the icebox he remembered the water—and he left the door open and hurried to the stove. It was down to half a cup but not, thank heavens, dry. He added a full pint, then put the milk in the icebox; took out the butter, four eggs, and a Flori-gold grapefruit. Before he cut the grapefruit he looked at his watch and seeing that it was ten minutes to eight, an hour before train time, he opened the stairway door.

"Ohhh, Mother!" he called, and then he returned to the grapefruit.

"*Ad astra per aspera*," she said, and rose from the bed. In the darkness she felt about for her corset, then let herself go completely for the thirty-five seconds it required to get it on. This done, she pulled the cord to the light that hung in the attic, and as it snapped on, in a firm voice she said, "*Fiat lux*." Light having been made, Mother opened her eyes.

As the bulb hung in the attic, the closet remained in an afterglow, a twilight zone. It was not light, strictly speaking, but it was all Mother wanted to see. Seated on the attic stairs she trimmed her toenails with a pearl-handled knife that Mr. Ormsby had been missing for several years. The blade was not so good any longer and using it too freely had resulted in ingrown nails on both of her big toes. But Mother preferred it to scissors, which were proven, along with bathtubs, to be one of the most dangerous things in the home. *Even more than the battlefield, the most dangerous place in the world. Dry feet and hands before turning on the lights, dry between toes.*

Without stooping she slipped into her sabots and left the closet, the light burning, and with her eyes dimmed, but not closed, went down the hall. Locking the bathroom door she stepped to the basin and turned on the cold water, then she removed several feet of paper from the toilet-paper roll. This took time, as in order to keep the roller from squeaking it had to be removed from its socket in the wall, then returned. One piece she put in the pocket of her kimono, the other she folded into a wad and used as a blotter to dab up spots on the floor. Turning up the water she sat down on the stool—then got up to get a pencil and pad from the table near the window. On the first sheet she wrote—

Ars longa, vita brevis
Wildflower club, sun. 4 p.m.

She tore this off and filed it, tip showing, right at the front of her corset. On the next page—

ROGER—
Ivory Snow
Sani-Flush on thurs.

As she placed this on top of the toilet-paper roll she heard him call "First for breakfast." She waited until he closed the stairway door, then she stood up and turned on the shower. As it rained into the tub and splashed behind her in the basin, she lowered the lid, flushed the toilet. Until the water closet had filled, stopped gurgling, she stood at the window watching a squirrel cross the yard from tree to tree. Then she turned the shower off and noisily dragged the shower curtain, on its metal rings, back to the wall. She dampened her shower cap in the basin and hung it on the towel rack to dry, dropping the towel that was there down the laundry chute. This done, she returned to the basin and held her hands under the running water, now cold, until she was awake. With her index finger she massaged her gums—*there is no pyorrhea among the Indians*—and then, with the tips of her fingers, she dampened her eyes.

She drew the blind, and in the half-light the room seemed to be full of lukewarm water, greenish in color. With a piece of Kleenex, she dried her eyes, then turned it to gently blow her nose, first the left side, then with a little more blow on the right. There was nothing to speak of, nothing, so she folded the tissue, slipped it into her pocket. Raising the blind, she faced the morning with her eyes softly closed, letting the light come in as prescribed—gradually. Eyes wide, she then stared for a full minute at the yard full of grackles, covered with grackles, before she actually saw them. Running to the door, her head in the hall, her arm in the bathroom wildly pointing, she tried to whisper, loud-whisper to him, but her voice cracked.

"Roger," she called, a little hoarsely. "The window—run!"

She heard him turn from the stove and skid on the newspapers, bump into the sink, curse, then get on again.

"Blackbirds?' he whispered.

"Grackles!" she said, for the thousandth time she said *Grackles*.

"They're pretty!" he said.

"Family—" she said, ignoring him, "family *Icteridae* American."

"Well—" he said.

"Roger!" she said. "Something's burning."

She heard him leave the window and on his way back to the stove, on the same turn, skid on the papers again. She left him there and went down the hall to the bedroom, closed the door, and passed between the mirrors once more to the closet. From five dresses—*any woman with more than five dresses, at this time, should have the vote taken away from her*—she selected the navy blue sheer with pink lace yoke and kerchief, short bolero. At the back of the closet—but in order to see she had to return to the bathroom, look for the flashlight in the drawer full of rags and old tins of shoe polish—were three shelves, each supporting ten to twelve pairs of shoes, and a large selection of slippers were piled on the floor. On the second shelf were the navy blue pumps—*we all have one weakness, but between men and shoes you can give me shoes*—navy blue pumps with a Cuban heel and a small bow. She hung the dress from the neck of the floor lamp, placed the shoes on the bed. From beneath the bed she pulled a hat box—the hat was new. Navy straw with shasta daisies, pink geraniums, and a navy blue veil with pink and white fuzzy dots. She held it out where it could be seen in the mirror, front and side, without seeing herself—*it's not every day that one sponsors a boat*. Not every day, and she turned to the calendar on her night table, a bird calendar featuring the natural-color male goldfinch for the month of June. Under the date of June 23 she printed the words, FAMILY ICTERIDAE—YARDFUL, and beneath it—

Met Captain Sudcliffe and gave him U.S.S. Ormsby

When he heard Mother's feet on the stairs, Mr. Ormsby cracked her soft-boiled eggs and spooned them carefully into her heated cup. He had spilled his own on the floor when he had run to look at the black—or whatever color they were—birds. As they were very, very soft he had merely wiped them up. As he buttered the toast—the four burned slices were on the back porch airing—Mother entered the kitchen and said, "Roger—*more* toast?"

"I was watching blackbirds," he said.

"Grack-les," she said. "Any bird is a *black*bird if the males are largely or entirely black."

Talk about male and female birds really bothered Mr. Ormsby. Although she was a girl of the old school Mother never hesitated, *anywhere*, to speak right out about male and female birds. A cow was a cow, a bull was a bull, but to Mr. Ormsby a bird was a bird.

"Among the birdfolk," said Mother, "the menfolk, so to speak, wear the feathers. The female has more serious work to do."

"How does that fit the blackbirds?" said Mr. Ormsby.

"Every rule," said Mother, "has an exception."

There was no denying the fact that the older Mother got the more distinguished she appeared. As for himself, what he saw in the mirror looked very much like the Roger Ormsby that had married Violet Ames twenty years ago. As the top of his head got hard the bottom tended to get a little soft, but otherwise there wasn't much change. But it was hard to believe that Mother was the pretty little pop-eyed girl—he had thought it was her corset that popped them—whose nipples had been like buttons on her dress. Any other girl would have looked like a you-know—but there wasn't a man in Media County, or anywhere else, who ever mentioned it. A man could think what he would think, but he was the only man who really knew what Mother was like. And how little she was like *that*.

"Three-seven-four East One-One-Six," said Mother.

That was the way her mind worked, all over the place on one cup of coffee—birds one moment, Mrs. Dinardo the next.

He got up from the table and went after Mrs. Dinardo's letter—Mother seldom had time to read them unless he read them to her. Returning, he divided the rest of the coffee between them, unequally: three-quarters for Mother, a swallow of grounds for himself. He waited a moment, wiping his glasses, while Mother looked through the window at another blackbird. "Cow bird," she said, "*Molothrus ater.*"

"'Dear Mrs. Ormsby,'" Mr. Ormsby began. Then he stopped to scan the page, as Mrs. Dinardo had a strange style and was not much given to writing letters. "'Dear Mrs. Ormsby,'" he repeated, "'I received your letter and I Sure was glad to know that you are both well and I know you often think of me I often think of you too—'" He paused to get his breath—Mrs. Dinardo's style was not much for pauses—and to look at Mother. But Mother was still with the cowbird. "'Well, Mrs. Ormsby,'" he continued, "'I haven't a thing in a room that I know of the people that will be away from the room will be only a week next month. But come to See me I may have Something if you don't get Something.'" Mrs. Dinardo, for some reason, always capitalized the letter S which along with everything else didn't make it easier to read. "'We are both well and he is Still in the Navy Yard. My I do wish the war was over it is So long. We are So tired of it do come and See us when you give them the boat. Wouldn't a Street be better than a boat? If you are going to name Something why not a Street? Here in my hand is news of a boat Sunk what is wrong with Ormsby on a Street? Well 116 is about the Same we have the river and its nice. If you don't find Something See me I may have Something. Best Love, Mrs. Myrtle Dinardo.'"

It was quite a letter to get from a woman that Mother had known, known Mother, that is, for nearly eighteen years. Brought in to nurse the boy—he could never understand why a woman like Mother, with her figure—but anyhow, Mrs. Dinardo was brought in. Something in her milk, Dr. Paige said, when it was as plain as the nose on your face it was nothing in the milk, but something in the boy. He just refused, plain refused, to nurse with Mother. The way the little rascal would look at her, but not a sound out of him but gurgling when Mrs. Dinardo would scoop him up and go upstairs to their room—the only woman—other woman, that is, that Mother ever let step inside of it. She had answered an ad that Mother had run, on Dr. Paige's suggestion, and they had been like that from the first time he saw them together.

"I'll telephone," said Mother.

On the slightest provocation Mother would call Mrs. Dinardo by long distance—she had to come down four flights of stairs to answer—and tell her she was going to broadcast over the radio or something. Although Mrs. Dinardo hardly knew one kind of bird from another, Mother sent her printed copies of every single one of her bird-lore lectures. She also sent her hand-pressed flowers from the garden.

"I'll telephone," repeated Mother.

"My own opinion—" began Mr. Ormsby, but stopped when Mother picked up her egg cup, made a pile of her plates, and started toward the sink. "I'll take care of that," he said. "Now you run along and telephone." But Mother walked right by him and took her stand at the sink. With one hand—with the other she held her kimono close about her—she let the water run into a large dish pan. Mr. Ormsby had hoped to avoid this; now he would have to first rinse, then dry, every piece of silver and every dish they had used. As Mother could only use one hand it would be even slower than usual.

"We don't want to miss our local," he said. "You better run along and let me do it."

"Cold water," she said, "for the eggs." He had long ago learned not to argue with Mother about the fine points of washing pots, pans, or dishes with bits of egg. He stood at the sink with the towel while she went about trying to make suds with a piece of stale soap in a little wire cage. As Mother refused to use a fresh piece of soap, nothing remotely like suds ever appeared. For this purpose, he kept a box of Gold Dust Twins concealed beneath the sink, and when Mother turned her back he slipped some in.

"There now," Mother said, and placed the rest of the dishes in the water, rinsed her fingers under the tap, paused to sniff at them.

"My own opinion—" Mr. Ormsby began, but stopped when Mother raised her finger, the index finger with the scar from the wart she once had. They stood quiet, and Mr. Ormsby listened to the water drip in the sink—the night before he had come down in his bare feet to shut it off. All of the taps dripped now and there was just nothing to do about it but put a rag or something beneath it to break the ping.

"Thrush!" said Mother. "Next to the nightingale the most popular of European songbirds."

"Very pretty," he said, although he simply couldn't hear a thing. Mother walked to the window, folding the collar of her kimono over her bosom and drawing the tails into a hammock beneath her behind. Mr. Ormsby modestly turned away. He quick-dipped one hand into the Gold Dust—drawing it out as he slipped it into the dishpan and worked up a suds.

As he finished wiping the dishes she came in with a bouquet for Mrs. Dinardo and arranged it for the moment, in a tall glass.

"According to her letter," Mrs. Ormsby said, "she isn't too sure of having something—Roger!" she said. "You're dripping."

Mr. Ormsby put his hands over the sink and said, "If we're going to be met right at the station I don't see where you're going to see Mrs. Dinardo. You're going to be met at the station and then you're going to sponsor the boat. My own opinion is that after the boat we come on home."

"I know that street of hers," said Mother. "There isn't a wild-flower on it!"

On the wall above the icebox was a pad of paper and a blue pencil hanging by a string. As Mother started to write the point broke off, fell behind the icebox.

"Mother," he said, "you ever see my knife?"

"Milkman," said Mother. "If we're staying overnight we won't need milk in the morning."

In jovial tones Mr. Ormsby said, "I'll bet we're right back here before dark." That was all, that was all he said. He had merely meant to call her attention to the fact that Mrs. Dinardo said—all but said—that she didn't have a room for them. But when Mother turned he saw that her mustache was showing, a sure sign that she was mad.

"Well—now," Mother said and lifting the skirt of her kimono swished around the cabinet, and then he heard her on the stairs. From the landing at the top of the stairs she said, "In that case I'm sure there's no need for my going. I'm sure the Navy would just as soon have you. After all," she said, "it's your name on the boat!"

"Now, Mother," he said, just as she closed the door, not slammed it, just closed it as quiet and nice as you'd please. Although he had been through this a thousand times it seemed he was never ready for it, never knew when it would happen, never felt anything but nearly sick. He went into the front room and sad down on the chair near the piano—then got up to arrange the doily at the back of his head. Ordinarily he could leave the house and after three or four days it would blow over, but in all his life—their life—there had been nothing like this. The government of the United States—he got up again and called, "OHHhhh, Mother!"

No answer.

He could hear her moving around upstairs, but as she often went back to bed after a spat, just moving around didn't mean much of anything. He came back into the front room and sat down on the milk stool near the fireplace. It was the only seat in the room not protected with newspapers. The only thing the boy ever sat on when he had to sit on something. Somehow, thinking about that made him stand up. He could sit in the lawn swing, in the front yard, if Mother hadn't told everybody in town why it was that he, Roger Ormsby, would have to take the day off—not to sit in the lawn swing, not by a long shot. Everybody knew—Captain Sudcliffe's nice letter had appeared on the first page of the *Graphic*, under a picture of Mother leading a bird-lore hike in the Poconos. This picture bore the title LOCAL WOMAN HEADS DAWN BUSTERS, and marked Mother's appearance on the national bird-lore scene. But it was not one of her best pictures—it dated from way back in the twenties and those hipless dresses and round, bucket hats were not Mother's type. Until they saw that picture, and the letter beneath it, some people had forgotten that Virgil was missing, and most of them seemed to think it was a good idea to swap him for a boat. The U.S.S. *Ormsby* was a permanent sort of thing. Although he was born and raised in the town hardly anybody knew very much about Virgil, but they all were pretty familiar with his boat. "How's that boat of yours coming along?" they would say, but in more than twenty years nobody had ever asked him about *his* boy. Whose boy? Well, that was just the point. Everyone agreed Ormsby was a fine name for a boat.

It would be impossible to explain to Mother, maybe to anybody for that matter, what this U.S.S. *Ormsby* business meant to him. "The" boy and "the" *Ormsby*—it was a pretty strange thing that they had both had the definite article, and gave him the feeling he was facing a monument.

"Oh Rog-gerrr!" Mother called.

"Coming," he said, and made for the stairs.

From the bedroom Mother said, "However I might feel personally, I do have my *own* name to think of. I am not one of these people who can do as they please—Roger, are you listening?"

"Yes, Mother," he said.

"—with their life."

As he went around the corner he found a note pinned to the door.

Bathroom window up
Cellar door down
Is it blue or brown for Navy?

He stopped on the landing and looked up the stairs.

"Did you say something?" she asked.

"No, Mother—" he said, then he added, "it's blue. For the Navy, Mother, it's blue."

The Question of Privacy

Once upon a time, for artists, writers, and photographers, there were restricted areas. Signs were posted on trees, fences, doorways, panes of frosted glass, etc., warning the public to KEEP OUT, touching on the sentiment of No Trespassing. The line to be drawn, if possible, was that between the public domain and the private: the nature or condition of being private. Did the boy come with the pants or the pants with the boy? In the fullness of time this would lead to ineffable distinctions between bare-faced and bare-assed people, between photographs to which we are accustomed and those to which we are less accustomed—those it is agreed we are shocked by. There may be a dozen or so words, give or take a few gestures, to define a decent, respectable *image*, but a picture that is judged *indecent* may require several pages of scrupulous copy and involve large negotiable sums of money. Money and privacy share a bottom line. Has privacy become a genre of photography?

Not long ago—perhaps not long enough—both writers and photographers thought they knew "where to draw the line." The line itself seemed clear and unquestioned: the point of interest where to draw it. I first saw this line clearly, sharp as a crack in a mirror, on the ground glass of a camera I had set up in the bedroom of a farmhouse. The iron frame of the bed, with the

Bed with Night Pot, Home Place, 1947. Photograph by Wright Morris. Collections Center for Creative Photography, University of Arizona. © Arizona Board of Regents.

deep impressions the sleepers had left in the mattress, the string that dangled from an unshaded light bulb to where a groping hand might reach it, and beneath the bed, in the strong north light of an uncurtained window, a nightpot polished with the use of a lifetime.

I had come back to this farmhouse, after a lapse of thirty years, to a farm I had known as a boy, to document the lives of a man and his wife who had homesteaded the plains in the 1890s. At that time, among other distinctions, a remarkably clear line was drawn between the public and the private. That May morning I perceived, as I had not before, that this somewhat blurred and indistinct line was there on the floor before me, like a ray of sunlight, and that the camera eye had overstepped it. My eyes were wide open. How had that been possible? I had been given "right of passage" by the woman of the house, a model for all that is inviolably *private*, to take those pictures that would speak for the pioneer lives she and her family had led—of which I had one summer been a part. What had led me to take it? An extravagant respect for what we describe as the *facts of life*. My own early respect, as a native, had been confirmed and enhanced by a lyrical passage from Thoreau's *Walden*, spoken to me, as a writer, in private. In the privacy of the darkroom, however, as this image emerged from the developer, I felt remarkably ambivalent about it. A fact it was—but on the scales of value it was all exposure, and little revelation. Both of these facts were very much in the American grain. Thoreau's lyrical cry—"if we are really dying, let us hear the rattle in our throat and feel the cold in our extremities: if we are alive, let us go about our business."

And how is our "business"? Is it still business as usual? That Thoreau should have judged the weight and value of the world appropriate to the conclusion of such a passage, speaks to how profoundly the American grain is fractured on this subject. If it's a matter of business, is it still business as usual?

Bed, Ed's Place, near Norfolk, Nebraska, 1947. Photograph by Wright Morris. Collections Center for Creative Photography, University of Arizona. © Arizona Board of Regents.

This pioneer fact—a nightpot polished by use, under a bed sagging with invisible sleepers—did not appear in *The Home Place*, published in 1948, but would find its place in *God's Country and My People*, published twenty years later. My own ambivalence testifies to what is a matter of "custom" in the blurred gap between revelation and exposure. When in doubt, and the revelation seems thin, exposure can be relied on to clarify the distinction between fact and fiction.

A few weeks ago, in a local newspaper, I read that men were not lacking to "model their penises" for an upcoming film. Why not? Surely this male "member" constitutes a fact? In the stimulating area of "What is New?"—the photographer would appear to be a groundbreaker, previous uses of the penis largely limited to envy. But that's just an opinion: it's not an area where I can claim to be well exposed.

More than forty years ago, as I crossed a cornfield toward a barn I hoped to photograph, the owner of the barn fired a singing hail of buckshot over my head. This gesture was not unusual in the rural South. The crack of a gun—in Georgia and Alabama—was something to which I had become accustomed. On this, and other occasions, the gunman had missed me, but scored a bull's-eye on the target of privacy.

Has it been left to photography, more than avant-garde art or the modern novel, to bring clearly to focus the abstract-seeming issue of privacy? On the ground glass of a camera, or in the dim light of a darkroom, esthetic dilemmas pop into sharp focus. The writer, at the front of the novel, confuses the issue in this manner:

The characters in this story are wholly imaginary, and have no reference to actual people, living or dead.

This disclaimer, like Confederate money, is no longer negotiable. Implicit in it, however, was the admission that a person's *own* person was private property, but as everybody who is anybody knows, it is the *private* person the hunter is after. The writer wants, and will have, the photographer needs and will get the picture, nothing less than the whole enchilada. Ways of serving up the whole enchilada are what is new.

If it is still desirable—and it is, it is—to rope off areas of privacy, photographers will prove to have a vested interest in precisely what is roped off.

The Sound Tape

I lived across from the Porters most of my life. During the twenties, when it was fashionable to open developments that closed in the thirties, they built a chalet-type mansion across the road from my place. It was said to resemble something Mrs. Porter saw in France. We were not neighbors, however, as the Porter chalet was the first house in the new development, and mine was the last in what is charitably called the old. The road between us, I suppose, is a kind of Mason-Dixon line.

Although we lived in separate worlds, every morning Mr. Porter and I joined forces and rode into town on the same commuters' local, and in the late afternoon we rode home again. On occasion I found him walking home from the station and gave him a lift. I observed that he chain-smoked my brand of cigarettes, traded in his Ford coupé every second year, and checked the arrival and departure of the trains by glancing at his watch. Along with everybody else I made the observation that he led an orderly, careful life and that Mrs. Porter led a careless, somewhat disorderly one. Not that it mattered, except for the little problem of keys. When Mrs. Porter left her purse in the seat of some car or on some department-store counter, she also left, with certain unimportant matters, the keys to her house. As she did this five or six times a year, some thirty sets of keys were in distribution before Mr. Porter had the locks changed on all the doors. The distribution of the new keys, of course, promptly began. At this point Mr. Porter washed his hands of the matter—he rubbed his palms briskly together as he told me—it was *her* house, and she could do with it as she liked. Mrs. Porter solved the problem, as usual, by letting nature take its course, losing the last set of keys and entering the house through the garage. I could tell when she came home by the thump of the heavy overhead doors.

When they first moved in, I used to speculate about Mr. Porter's line. He seemed to have money, but I told myself that he worked for it. He kept the same monotonous schedule that I kept myself. He took the 8:04 in the morning, the 4:48 in the afternoon, with only Saturdays and national holidays off. It was nearly ten years before I discovered that Mr. Porter had no line—or rather that his only line was how to pass the time. But he went about it, as he did everything else, in a competent, businesslike way. He put in his eight-hour day at the club, where he applied himself to his growing tax problems and a wide range of anti-Roosevelt literature. He was the most informed man on obscure subjects I have ever known. A certain pride of class, I suppose, as one of the surviving unearned-increment boys, forbade him to apply himself to anything useful. But nothing prevented him from putting his mind to work. It was a good mind, and he worked it around the clock.

He preferred to sit alone, while commuting, but there were times when he found himself compelled to stand in the aisle or take the seat beside me. As he had paid for this seat, he always took it. Without troubling to open the discussion or indicating that he know who it was that sat beside him, he would share some of the strange lore he had stored away: the air distances between the capitals of the world, the reason for the smallness of French equestrian armor, or the meaning of the serial numbers to be found on the sides of freight cars. He spoke on all these matters with an air of authority, knowing that his listener would be poorly informed, which led most people to think that he was merely a kind of cybernetic marvel full of facts and figures, waiting to be tapped. I found it hard to explain the touch of covert sympathy I felt for him.

My knowledge of Mrs. Porter is of a different sort. What I choose to call my knowledge began on a fine summer dawn, just twenty years ago, when I saw her out padding around in her garden in what she called a shift. An abundant woman, built along the lines of the concrete goddesses that brooded in her garden, she sometimes fancied herself a suburban Diana with a pack of sleek hounds. Draped in her shift and armed with a pair of garden shears in case some urban interloper might stop to marvel, she loved to pad around her acres with the spreadlegged gait of a big circus cat. That summer morning, as I remember, she went along making tracks in the dewy grass, stopping now and then to lift the shift and gaze at her well-turned calves. Like many big women, she was vain of her shapely ankles and small feet.

Later in the morning, a wrapper over the shift, and holding aloft a few wilted flowers, she would cross the road to my seedy lawn and call on me. Would I like a few flowers? She knew that I didn't grow my own. So we would start with the flowers, which she would drop, sometimes head down, in the highball glasses, and then we would get around to the latest pet in her house. It had usually run off, flown off, or simply rolled over and died. She had tried, over the years, nearly everything: exotic imported birds, which I could hear in the summer when the windows were open, and pedigreed dogs which I could hear whether the windows were open or not. Sooner or later the birds stopped singing, the dogs stopped whining and barking, and the cats I had seen at the windows disappeared. Our discussion usually centered on what sort of creature she should try next.

This problem puzzled me, as Mrs. Porter had a friendly, sympathetic nature, and while the pets were alive she often carried them around in her arms. "Baby," she would say—I was not that type, but she liked to believe she had that type around her—"Baby, isn't he a lover?" and scoop her dachshund, Himmel, into her arms. But there was always more than the usual melancholy in Himmel's eyes. He had learned, much quicker than I did, that when Mrs. Porter put him back on the ground, she had also put him, for the time being, out of her mind. She might forget for a day or two that she owned a dog. There were times when she forgot what the name or breed of her latest dog was.

"Did that boxer, the lover, leave me, baby?" she would ask, and it was sometimes quite a while before she found out. Missing cats were often found trapped in her enormous closets, and some of the smaller dogs were hard to hear at the back of the house. But not to smell. In the summer Mr. Porter soon found them out. I would hear him going through the house from wing to wing, opening and closing doors.

It was by slow stages, I suppose, that Mrs. Porter moved from pets to goldfish, from fish to flower, and from flowers to the house. The house was always there. When a door was left open it did not run off. Something of the concern she felt for her pets, when they began to act distracted, now crept into her voice when she spoke of the house. As she had once said, "Baby, isn't he a lover?" and held up something for me to pet, she now called my attention to her house. From my porch we had a fine view of it. While I was getting her a drink she would move her chair around so that she faced the house. I'm not sure just when I came to know that the place across the road was something more than a house, or when she first noticed the change in its personality. She was the one to point out to me that its character had changed. She spoke of it as of a friend who had lost some endearing faculty.

"Baby," she would say, "what am I going to do about my house?" As a man would say, "what am I going to do about my wife?" I never knew. From where I sat it looked about the same. Every spring the same handyman painted the fence, whitewashed the concrete urns that flanked the doorway and repaired the holes that Mr. Porter's chains made each winter in the drive. Nor had she changed. She still left on my porch whatever she had brought along with the wilting flowers: sometimes her shoes, as she liked to cross the lawn without them; sometimes her squashed pack of menthol cigarettes. "I can't stand menthol, baby," she would say, "so I don't smoke much."

But she smoked more and more that summer, and if she left a squashed pack on my porch, she went off with my fresh pack tucked into the pocket of her gown. In August she spent a month at the shore, but when she returned it was not to my porch, and she no longer crossed the road to ask me what I thought of her house. There were also other changes; and when it was clear that Mrs. Amory Porter would soon be a mother, it was assumed that Mr. Porter had little to do with it. He had fathered the child, so to speak, by a legal transmission of the pollen, but in every matter that counted, the flower would be hers. Mr. Porter more or less said so himself. He was the first to joke about the matter; and when talk got around to the child, he would make that characteristic washing gesture with his hands, rubbing the dry palms together as if he stood before a fire. I didn't see Mrs. Porter that winter, but every day I drove past the house I felt that I observed a change in it. As a last resort, it amused me to think, Mrs. Porter had got around to changing her house by altering—insofar as possible—the inhabitants.

Eloise—as the child was named—was born in March. On the balcony, when the weather was pleasant, I sometimes saw the nurse with the hooded carriage, and I read in the paper that Mrs. Porter had returned to life—her name appeared on the usual committees and her voice was heard at the usual parties.

Mr. Porter no longer came home on the 4:48. He went in as usual, but came home at one o'clock. Early in May I came home early myself, as there were things to do around the house, and when I reached the Porter house I saw him wheeling something up the drive—a baby carriage, the perambulator I had seen on the balcony. When I stopped—I think I stopped to ask him what was the trouble—he wheeled it up so I could peer into it from the car. Eloise, at that time, was about ten weeks old. But the connection between the child in the carriage and the man who was pushing it was more than a resemblance—I felt I was looking at Porter himself. As if time, right there before my eyes, had unraveled the old man who stood before me, layer by layer, until nothing remained but the Porter seed itself in swaddling clothes; the Porter essence there in the perambulator. Porter knew this—he had wheeled the carriage up, so to speak, in order to prove it; and all the proof he needed he found on my face. Without waiting for me to speak or to recover, he wheeled her off.

For a year or more I saw very little of him. He had taken over, as he told those who asked him, the education of his child. But the following summer when I dropped into the big market where I did my shopping, Mr. Porter and Eloise were often there. In the spacious air-cooled market, full of soothing music and educational commercials, Mr. Porter, as well as Eloise, felt right at home. In the second year, as if to meet his needs, the new shopping cart made its appearance, and he would hustle down the aisles with Eloise propped up between the handlebars. Before she could talk, and long before there was reason to believe that she understood, he described to her the contents of the cans he purchased. He pointed out the label and other important details. It was a great comfort to him to find that this child of his old age—he was then in his late fifties—had a mind that was very much like his own. Curious, precise and absolutely disinterested.

When she was five or six—and when Mr. Porter was not at home—Eloise, like one of Singer's Midgets, would sometimes cross the road and enlighten me. All of my opinions, as she knew them through her father, were woefully misinformed. The correct opinion was the one she brought along. Her great field, as was his, was politics. From Eloise I learned, in the course of several summers, more about the workings of the Administration than I would ever have mastered by myself. I have no mind for figures; Eloise had no mind for anything else. Very early we discovered—or rather Eloise discovered—the fatal flaw, the Achilles' heel, in nearly every statement I put forth. Invariably I fell back on the word *feel*.

"Now don't you feel, Eloise," I would say, whereupon she would shriek and jump up and down. Like her father, she would rub her hands together.

"You just *feel*," she would reply, "Daddy *thinks*."

That, of course, was early, in the beginning, for later there was no particular need to tell me what Daddy did—or anybody else. At seven and one-half Eloise could do it for herself.

"You're always just feeling, Mr. Brady," she would say. "I *think*."

She was right. I was always feeling, but she could think. She would come to my porch—that side of the porch where the grass and the robins had taken over—with her little head, like a worming robin's, cocked to one side, ready to pounce on the first wormy feeling I let slip out.

A thin, sober-faced little girl, with the oversized clothes her father bought for her, she seemed to be a woman without ever having been a child. As she stood there reciting, I seemed to hear many small fine wheels going around.

She went to school, but she was not popular. Neither boys nor other little girls seemed to interest her. She would do her lessons many months in advance and, using the books of the girls ahead of her, master the subjects she would be having the next year. She had the time. There was nothing else that she cared to do. On weekends she might walk across to tell me where macaroni was made or to name the city with the largest smelting works. She knew. And she never seemed to forget. If I happened to meet Porter at the A&P or coming home on the local, I could tell by the nature of his lecture what subject Eloise was now on at school. They read the same books, went over the questions carefully.

Mr. Porter would pick her up at school, and I would often find them, an hour or so later, sitting in the front seat of the car that was parked in front of his house. Winter afternoons, when the days were short, the overhead light in the car would be on, and I would see Mr. Porter's head bent over some book, or the head of Eloise, nodding briskly, as she talked to him. At their backs was the empty house, a pale light burning behind the blind in Mrs. Porter's room.

In this manner he instructed her in fractions, learned something about algebra himself, and brushed up on the French he had not used for many years. In the A&P, around the frozen food locker, I would sometimes hear an excited exchange, as if a pair of expensive imported servants were debating in French the merits of stringless or French-style cut beans. Their arguments were full of a kind of heat lightning, intended to sharpen the faculties and illuminate the subject, and he would sometimes turn his back on her to conceal the pleasure on his face.

That was the fall that Harry Truman was a doomed, nearly pitiful man. Mr. Porter had never been in better spirits, and sometimes two or three times a week Eloise would come over, ring my doorbell and recite a bon mot. But just before the election I saw little of her. Then on Halloween, early in the evening, somebody rang my bell. When I opened the door, there stood Eloise. She carried a pumpkin lantern, made of orange and black paper, and on her small sober head sat a pointed witch's cap. The black sateen lining of one of Mr. Porter's coats covered her like a sheet. The effect was that of a dummy that had been dolled up. I failed to notice for the moment that her hand, the palm up, was extended toward me.

"That's a wonderful costume, Eloise," I said, carefully screening my language.

"You're supposed to give me something," she said.

"Oh," I said. "What would you like? How about a piece of cake?"

"I'd rather have money," she said, "if you don't mind."

That set me back a bit but I said, "Is it customary to ask for money?"

"Father says if *he's* elected, we'll all be begging," she said.

"Well, there isn't much chance of that," I said. "Is there?"

We stood there while she thought. I could see that she thought there was not much chance but that she had been impressed by what she had heard.

"Father says if *he's* elected, he's just going to give up."

"If he's elected, Eloise," I said, sounding quite a bit like her father, "it means that most of the people in the country voted for him. It means he may not be *your* man, but now he's *our* president." When she didn't reply to that I said, "Well, how do *you* feel about it?" It was out before I knew it.

"What reason is there to go on in a world like that?" she said.

Was that her father? I wasn't sure it was. I put my hand into my pocket, took out some change, then said, "Well, here's twenty-five cents if you spend it right away," which was pretty sharp, but she settled for it. I held out the quarter and placed it in the hand with the long fingers and the small palm that snapped shut like a trap when the coin touched it. She turned without another word and walked off. Her small feet made a tapping sound on my brick walk. When she had first faced me I had thought how little like a Halloween witch she was, but as she walked off, her witch's head bowed, I wasn't so sure. It crossed my mind—just faintly, that is—that my grown-up idea of witches was silly, but her idea of a witch was one that meant business. Not foolishness.

I forgot about Eloise until four days later when I sat in my room listening to the returns. A little after midnight I stepped out in the yard to smoke a cigarette. It was a sharp but very pleasant night. The Porter house was dark, without a light burning, but out in front was the Porter car with the parking lights on. The front window was down and I could hear the radio. The voice was announcing what appeared to be a surprising trend.

That left a certain impression on me but I didn't think too much about it until the next morning, about eight o'clock. The phone rang just as I was getting ready to leave the house. It was Mrs. Porter. I could hear the bathwater spilling into the tub behind her and the blurred nasal noise from her radio.

"This you, baby?"

"This is me," I said.

"Is my little sound tape over there, honey?"

"Your sound tape—" I said, and turned to look around the room. I knew that they were making and selling such things.

"You're cute as cotton, baby," she said. "You know what I mean, *his* little sound tape. She isn't here. Is she over there?"

"Oh," I said. "Oh no. No, she's isn't over here."

"Is *he* over there?"

"No, he isn't either," I said.

As there was no reply to that, I said, "I suppose you know they've elected Truman."

"*They* did?" she said.

"I mean the people did," I said.

"You think they went to an all-night movie?"

"I've no idea, Mrs. Porter," I said. "And right now I've got to run for the train."

She didn't answer.

"Well, I've got to run—" I said, and did. With the single exception of Mr. Porter, I'm usually the first car out in the morning, and I sometimes pass him on the highway where he waits for the school bus. When the weather is cold, he and Eloise sit there in the car. He was there ahead of me as usual, and through the glass at the back of the car I could see their heads leaning together bent over some book. Some lesson or problem that she had to puzzle out. When I pulled alongside, I gave a tap on the horn as I usually do when I pass them, but this time he didn't toot back. In the rear-view mirror I glanced back at them. Eloise, her head lolling to the side, was asleep on his arm. Mr. Porter's chin was resting on his chest. At that point it occurred to me that they had been up all night. They had probably sat right there in the car taking in the returns. Eloise was wearing her new school cap with the bright school colors, and the yellow tassel dangled where the sunlight streamed through the glass. I was relieved that my toot on the horn hadn't waked them. That was something I could leave to the school bus.

In the evening on my walk through the station I took particular trouble to steer clear of Mr. Porter's usual route. The election might be too much for him. I bought a paper for the late returns, went down and took my seat in the smoker, then opened the paper and stared at Porter's face—a photograph taken, I would say, thirty years ago. What struck me was how much he looked like Eloise. Mr. Porter had been found, the report said, with his only child, Eloise, in their car parked in the neighborhood in which they lived. They had died apparently sometime during the night. A faulty heater had flooded the car with poisonous gas.

Very little was said openly, but under the talk that got around to me was the feeling that Porter had acted deliberately; had persuaded his impressionable child to go along with him. This came from people who had known him very well, who now referred to him as "poor Amory" and sometimes crossed my lawn to ask if I had any insight into the case. I said I hadn't really known Mr. Porter at all. We usually agreed that he had been a hard man to figure out.

Now that he is gone, I find he is often in my mind. I seldom board the local or back out my car without thinking for a moment of Mr. Porter, though I doubt that we ever exchanged a personal remark. Mrs. Porter, they tell me, now spends her time in France. The house across the road is empty, but not long ago a prospective tenant who had got wind of its history stepped over to ask me what it was all about. He had heard, he said, about the Porter case. He couldn't believe that a man would treat his only child like that. It made me think of that night when I had opened the door of my house, and Eloise Porter in her witch's costume had confronted me.

"It's not a matter of feeling, Mr. Brady," she said, "it's what you think."

As usual, Eloise was right. So far as I know she was never wrong.

Excerpt from *The Deep Sleep*

Katherine

Her mother closed the screen, hooked it, and said, "If she thought I would give it to her, she would take it."

"Well, if you're not going to wear it, Mother."

"She is a shrewd customer," her mother said. "If *she* looks at a hat, the hat is coming back." Crossing the room her mother stopped to pick up a piece of Kleenex, but she stayed down there. "Chocolate," she said, "who's been eating chocolate?"

"Did this Muriel get her divorce, Mother?"

"I'm afraid I don't keep track of such things."

"Well, I've never seen a woman work on a married man any harder. If we had a place for her upstairs I think she'd have fainted just to let him carry her somewhere. *Doct-tah Bahhhh* — honestly, do they talk like that at Smith?"

Her mother picked up two glasses and said, "I suppose you noticed Mrs. Crowell didn't finish."

"She probably wasn't thirsty, Mother. I didn't finish mine either."

"I don't think she approved of the color of the glasses," her mother said. "If a Crowell approves, they never fail to mention it."

"Right now I don't care whether she approves or not," Katherine said.

Holding the glasses in her hand, her mother stood there listening.

"That ticking—" she said, then, "Who do you suppose has been eating chocolate?"

"Mother, it's after midnight. I'm going to bed."

"If you would listen to her talk," her mother said, "you would suppose she never touched chocolate. But mention Toll House cookies and watch her eyes roll." Her mother put the two glasses on the tray, and then carried the tray into the kitchen. Katherine put the chairs back in place, turned off the lights under the shades, then turned to hear the water running into the sink.

"Mother!" she said.

No answer.

"Mother, we are going to do that tomorrow morning. We are not going to stay up and do it now."

Didn't she hear? Katherine could hear the silver rattling in the pan. She went out into the kitchen where her mother stood leaning on the sink, her hands in the water, working up a suds with a piece of Fels Naptha soap. Behind her the day's plates were stacked, and in a tray at her side was the silver.

"Those new suds are not for me," her mother said.

"Mother, I am not going to argue. I am going to bed."

When the suds appeared her mother said, "Your Grandmother washed and rinsed her dishes. It won't hurt you to listen to what your Grandmother says."

"I am going to be perfectly selfish," said Katherine, "and say that I am the one who is tired. I am the one who wants to go to bed. I've just got to get some sleep for tomorrow. I'm completely worn out."

"I suppose that's where he went," her mother said.

"I don't know or care where he went, Mother, but I know where I am going. But it will do no good if you're going to stay up and wash. You can't sleep in a house where somebody is rattling dishes around."

"Your father and I," her mother replied, "can not sleep in a house where the dishes are dirty. There has not been a dirty dish in this house in thirty-seven years."

Katherine did not reply. She placed her hands on the sink board, and her knuckles turned white from the way she tried to grasp it, but neither the sink, nor her mother, said anything. At the top of the stairs, in the room where the Grandmother now lay sleeping, Katherine had spent most of her childhood lying awake. Lying awake in the morning listening to father squeeze the orange juice and make the coffee, and lying awake at night listening to them wash the day's dishes. After the guests had gone, and the children had been put to bed. Then the dishpans that had been hung up the night before would be taken from the hooks and refilled with water, and the dishes that had been rinsed and stacked would be washed again. The silver that had been rinsed, scalded again. Every dish soaked in the soapy water, scrubbed down with the small raddled mop, then dropped into a dishpan of warm water, from where her father picked it up. Every dish, every piece of silver, every piece of glassware, every pot and every pan, passed through this treatment, passed through her hands, then through his. Every faded pink plate with the Willow pattern was carried into the front room and put in its place, and every piece of silver was returned to the silver drawer. Every pot was hung under the sink, or put in the lower shelf of the oven, or placed over the pilot light so it would dry out. And every single piece of it had its own sound, every piece of glassware had its own tinkle, in and out of the water, and every pot had its own rocking motion on the shelf or the wall. Without ever being there, Katherine lived through it all. And all of it without a word, without a human sound, as talk or speech was thought to wake them, and the ten thousand noises were supposed to put them to sleep. She never missed a one. She hung on to the last sleepy squeeze of the rag. She could hear the slushy whisper as it made a final pass over everything. Over the top of the stove, over the bread board, over the sink board, over the table, and then the wet flap as her mother hung it up to dry. Spread it out, like a fishnet, between the handles of the faucets, where it gave off an odor like a clogged drain. Then her father would come up the stairs first, carrying his shoes so as not to wake them, and some time later her mother would pad around the house. Trying all the doors, checking all the windows, opening or closing the radiators, and then, but not till then, turning off the lights. And then, but not till then, Katherine would hear the sound of her brother's breathing and the dragging of the weights in the clock that once stood at the foot of the stairs. With her father's snoring, with her mother's silence, she would go to sleep.

"Thirty-seven years and twelve days to be exact," her mother said.

If she went to bed she would lie there awake, just as she had thirty years ago, feeling sorry for her parents, and feeling ashamed of herself. She would lie there awake, curled up in the hole she had lived in most of her childhood, listening to the sounds that came to her from the mouth of the cave. She would sift every sound, every fumbling movement, through her mind. She would sort it all out, like the stuff in a drawer, looking for the key. She would live all of it over, she would bring it up to date for the last twenty years, and then she would be right back again where she started from. There was no key, there was no explanation, there was no solution to the game in the kitchen, to the rules of the house, or to the laws of her mother's world. But they were there. The laws and the rules had not changed. While in the house the only solution was to follow them.

"Where are the dish towels, Mother?" she said.

"Right where they always were," her mother replied.

Why had she asked? To make conversation. To break the spell. Something might be said, just *might* be said, that might explain something. She walked around the table to where the morning dish towel was spread on the radiator, and the lunch towel was fanned out on the rack. It was dry, as today there had been no lunch. Her mother took her hands from the pan of suds, placed her knuckles on her hips and said, "Why, over in Hershey—" she pointed, "the entire plumbing system was endangered by the use of detergents in one day's wash." She paused there, then said, "Pedlars left it on the porches, I suppose."

Hershey, Katherine knew, had not suffered from detergents, from some new soap or some new gadget, but from the collapse of moral fibre from within. An un-American shrinking from an honest Fels Naptha wash. A bombing attack that they were unable to resist. Her mother returned her hands to the suds, giving them a stir that made them fizzle, then carefully, as if for a baptism, she dipped the first glass. When Katherine picked it up her mother said—

"Does that have the stamp on the bottom?"

"Yes, Mother—"

"Your Grandmother's jelly glass," she said.

That glass went into the cupboard across the kitchen, where there were five other such glasses, and Katherine and her brother had drunk their milk and orange juice from them. They were cheap brittle glasses, water too hot or too cold might break them, but after seventy years six of them were still there.

"I won't have her thinking we don't take care of her things," her mother said.

In the glass door of the cupboard Katherine could see the light over the sink, and her mother's gray head, her rounded shoulders, bent over the pan. She was worn out. There were dark circles under her eyes. But there was no indication whatsoever that what she was doing was a tiresome chore, or that she merely did it to get it done. There was every indication—if Katherine could believe her eyes—that her mother's hands, elbow deep in the suds, were where they belonged. That every washing motion had a meaning, and accomplished something. After a long day of nothing done, nothing really done, just a day that slipped beneath her, she could come to grips with something solid every night. What had been dirtied during the day could be cleaned up. Another day, if and when it came, could be started afresh.

One cup at a time, one glass at a time, one spoon, one fork, and one knife at a time, were just so many necessary worthwhile accomplishments. Had it been possible, Katherine wondered, that for more than thirty years her mother had *enjoyed* what Katherine had believed to be the bane of her life? The ten o'clock till midnight daily wash? A time when everything in the house that had been sullied—including the lives of the inhabitants—could be put through three cleansing waters and made pure again. Had she pitied her mother for one of the real joys of her life? Running the water, stirring up the suds, dipping and rinsing the assorted objects, each one of which had some special meaning for her. The Grandmother's jelly glasses, the Willow Ware from the shop in Surrey, the bone-handled knives from the store in Munich, operated by a man named Rautzen, and the family silver that would always lack the bouillon spoons.

"Your father and I," her mother said, washing the can the ripe olives had come in, "always found the time to run our own house."

Her mother, God knows, understood nothing, neither her husband, her son, nor her daughter, but perhaps it was not beyond reason to understand her. Perhaps *that* was just what her husband had done. Perhaps that explained what could not be explained about him.

"What do you do with your extra fat these days?" her mother said.

"We just throw it out, Mother. Nobody seems to want it."

"Well, I will *not* throw it out," she said. She turned to gaze at the Crisco can on the stove, the lid tipped back so the fat could be poured into it. "The people who are pouring it out will be crying for it next," she said.

"That's human nature, Mother."

"It is not *my* nature," her mother replied, and Katherine, a tumbler in her hand, felt it slide down the towel then strike the radiator. The pieces dropped and scattered on the floor.

"One of the amber?" her mother asked.

"I'm awfully sorry, Mother—"

Her mother turned from the sink, stooped to reach beneath it, and came up with a brush and a dust pan. "I am almost positive," she said, "that Mrs. Crowell didn't care much for them."

"Let me, Mother."

"No, I *know* that radiator." She let her mother slip by, and watched her sweep up the glass. "It gets around the leg. It chews up the linoleum." Her mother swept it up, carefully, then seeing other spots of dirt around her, she went over the general area with her brush. "You see that corner?" she said, and Katherine bent over to look at it. "He comes in and just stands there. He's worse than your father on a piece of rug."

"Mr. Parsons—?" she said.

"If I ask him to sit down, why, then he'll just sit till I ask him to leave."

"I don't know what we would have done without him," Katherine said.

"Your mother would have done whatever she was able," she replied. With the dust pan and the brush, she pushed through the screen to the rear porch. She emptied the broken glass into the waste can, firmly put on the lid, then stood there looking across the yard at the summer night. Katherine could hear her deeply breathing the cool night air. Absently, as if fingering her hair, she removed the sheet of towel paper from the clothesline, and slipped the plastic pin into the pocket of her dress. The summer night was very lovely, and her mother, while her hands were busy, seemed to be listening to the music of the spheres.

"I don't know what I'd do," her mother said, "if other people didn't go to bed."

Katherine waited a moment, then said, "Is it all right if I go now, Mother?"

"Your father would go to bed, but he never slept until I was there."

"Good night, Mother," Katherine said, and when her mother didn't answer she started for the stairs.

"Which one is Orion?" her mother said.

"I'm afraid I've forgotten it all, Mother."

"I'm going to miss your father," her mother said, and Katherine turned, her hand on the stair rail, as if another person, not her mother, had spoken. A voice, perhaps, from one of the letters she never mailed. Katherine wanted to speak, but now that this voice had spoken to her, broken the long silence, she could hardly believe what she heard. She went on up the stairs, entered her room, then closed the door before she remembered, before she noticed, that Paul wasn't there. Still, she would have called to him except for the fact that she had no voice, her throat ached, and he had been the one who had cried that this was a house without tears.

Mrs. Porter

The cool of the evening came to Mrs. Porter from the Poconos, from Valley Forge, from the slopes where Washington's men were quartered, to where she lay in the dark on the cot on the screened-in porch. At her feet was Conshohocken, at her head Bryn Mawr, on her left was Paoli and on her right was Mannyunk. On the bed at her feet was what she had taken off, and on the chair at her side was what she would put on.

Black straw hat with grosgrain ribbon, spider veil
Dark two piece shantung suit
Black faille purse
Black mesh gloves
Black kid pumps, medium heels
In bowl on sideboard pearl necklace, matching earrings.

Her body at rest, her mind at ease, her day in the hands of Clough & Bayard, she closed her eyes, she stopped resisting, but she did not sleep. Above the sawing of the crickets she could hear it, Tick-tick-tick. *Mrs. Porter, your hearing is very remarkable,* Dr. Lloyd had said. Anyone might hear the ticking in the house, the ticking in the cupboard, the ticking in a pocket, but who could hear the ticking in the woods? Would you believe it, Dr. Lloyd? she had said. I am prepared to believe anything you tell me, Dr. Lloyd said.

A safe place. He had put it, he said, in a safe place. In the quiet she could hear it very plainly, tick-tick-tick. There was no tick in the electric clock, there was sometimes a tick in the shade of the lamp, and there was once a tick in the horseshoe crab that Katherine brought from the Cape. *Tick-tick-tick* he had said, so they had thrown him out. She had observed Mr. Parsons take him out of the barrel and go off with him.

All around her, like the sound of dripping, tick-tick-tick. She arose from the cot, took from the drawer of the sideboard the candles that were there in case of power failure, and the matches that were there in case the gas went off. The house was dark, but she did not scratch a match. Through the window of the living room she could see the light beside the bed of Rosa Erskine, where she lay reading the back issues of fashion magazines—and from where she could see, if she raised her eyes, a match flare in the Porter house.

With the candle in her hand, but out, Mrs. Porter crossed the living room rug to where Mr. Erskine had left his iced tea glass on the floor. He had hidden it under the skirt of the floral print on the chair. As she passed his chair Mrs. Porter kicked the glass, then she stepped into the water, into the tea and on the slice of lemon, before she heard the glass roll across the tile floor and thump on the door. It struck the woodwork, it struck the lamp, then it rocked back and forth, like a saucer, until she got down on her knees in the water and felt around for it. The glasses were no good for color, but after all of that it hadn't chipped or broken, and she made a mental note to call Mrs. Crowell and point that out. With the candle in the glass she went up the stairs to the second floor.

Webb

When the rolling tumbler struck the door Webb opened his eyes, tried to move, and thought for a moment that he had been buried alive. In the cave of the attic there was not a crack of light. One arm had gone to sleep, and in the grip of the cot he felt paralyzed. He closed his eyes. He waited for the trouble to go away. Webb had often seen his cats try that, and sometimes it worked. While in this condition, his eyes closed, he heard the faintest creaking in the room below him, and the soft cat-like padding of bare feet. On the attic rafters, when he opened his eyes, was a flickering light. It waved about on the ceiling directly over the ventilator grill, which Webb had left open when he dropped Parsons the liver pills. He did not move, he watched the light flicker and blow on the ceiling, like smoke, until he detected the unmistakable smell of fire. That got him up. On his hands and knees he crossed the floor. With his face pressed flat to the grill he saw Mrs. Porter, in her nightgown, peering around the room like Lady Macbeth. In her right hand, like a lantern, she held an iced tea glass which contained a smoking candle. Her eyes were wide, there was nothing in her face but the shifting light of the candle, and Webb was sure she was walking in her sleep. That she had returned, in this fashion, to the scene of the crime.

With her back to him, she crossed the room and opened the top drawer of the dresser, rummaging her hand into the back corners, where she found more socks. She then drew it out, as he had, and pushed her hand into the drawer beneath it, rising on her toes to increase the length of her reach. The same with the next drawer, then the next, whereupon she turned as if Webb had spoken and crossed the room to a large bowl on the sewing machine. She put her hand into the bowl, felt around, and drew out a round flat object, which she held near the candle to watch the three bee-bees moving around. She played the game for a minute, perhaps, then she put it away. In the left top drawer of the sewing machine, she found a bronze baby shoe. Webb thought that might be what she wanted, as she kept it, grasped tight in her hand, and crossed the room into the hall, but there she put it down, like a paper weight, on the memo pad. Gazing back into the room she saw the beds, and stepped in far enough to poke around at the mattress, fluff the pillow, and look beneath the pottery lamp on the nightlight stand. There she found four or five sugar-covered horehound drops. She took them along with her, into the hallway, and as she started down the stairs her shadow swelled and filled the landing at the top.

That was all, nothing there but the shadow, but the sight had made the hair on Webb's neck rise, and if there had been blood left in his veins it would have run cold. As it had once before, as it did the winter morning that he had broken into the house, and with Dr. Barr right at his heels he had run up the stairs. Up to the landing, up to the point where the specter appeared from the Judge's doorway—appeared then disappeared without a word or a gesture—and Webb had been swept with both pity and terror for this man and his wife. Pity for the man, but terror for the power that made itself known in the woman as she passed before them, flesh and specter, down the hall.

Had it been the sight of death, or the sight of life, that had terrified the Judge? The powers that had shaped whatever it was that he had lived? And the terror he had felt, the terror he had known, that he might live the same life over, and the powers that had made and broken him once, would make and break him again. This might look like pity to Webb, but it would look like something else to the man who could see himself stretched, who could see himself broken, on the same wheel of life.

The shadow was still there, filling the hallway, when the door to the guest room opened, and Webb caught a glimpse of his wife's distracted face. She followed her mother down the stairs, and a moment later, in the rooms below, he could hear the sound of drawers being opened and closed, as if Mrs. Porter had forgotten what time of night it was. It made it easier for Webb to leave the attic, to get the trapdoor down and then get it up, and when he stepped into the hall it was empty. Katherine was not there. He made his way slowly down to the landing, and from there he could see, at the far end of the room, Mrs. Porter with the sputtering candle in her hand. She was removing certain books from the fireplace shelves. Webb could see that she was somewhere in the Harvard Classics, and the opening she had made, in the brick wall at the back, the latched door to a secret chamber of some kind. She drew up a chair to stand on before she opened it. The door stuck, she had to strain, and then it suddenly opened with the sound of a cork, and a cloud of dirt and soot, sucked in by the draft, filled that end of the room. For a moment Webb thought that the candle had been snuffed out. In the darkness he could hear Mrs. Porter coughing, then the cloud seemed to pass, and he could see her fanning at the streamers of soot with one of the books. As the air began to clear, she carefully returned the books to the shelves. They were all in place, it seemed to Webb, when she discovered the order of their arrangement, and then she rearranged them, properly, on the shelves. She was not impatient. He could hear her muttering the alphabet. One book falling open, she paused to read the passage, her lips carefully forming the words, and her head nodding in agreement to what she read. To *know* that book, to mark that place, she crossed the room to her memo pad, tore off the top sheet, and filed it with an inch showing at the top. But on that inch she had written something, and reading it over she said aloud—

"Clorox, Air-Wick, digitalis—"

"Mother—" said Katherine, softly, "Mother—are you all right?"

Mrs. Porter did not raise her head. She was not alarmed. Stepping from the kitchen door Katherine said, "You want to scare a person silly, Mother?"

"I think that must be an old one," Mrs. Porter said.

Katherine walked into the living room beside her, and when her mother did not turn, or seem to hear her, she stepped forward and lifted a slipping scrap on her mother's nightgown. In the dim light of the room, the sputtering candle behind them, the gesture struck Webb as very familiar, and he realized that it was just what Mrs. Porter would have done. First things first. First, last and all the time. The Harvard Classic still in her hand, but closed firmly on what she had marked, Mrs. Porter observed that her daughter's long tight braids were down.

"You don't comb them out?" she said.

"I was just too tired to bother," Katherine replied.

Mrs. Porter reflected that that might be so, studied her daughter's face for a moment, and then, as if Webb had spoken, turned to look at him. Not at him, but in his direction, at the oval shaped basket in the piano corner, where Webb had dropped, several hours before, the cheap dollar watch. Without speaking, Mrs. Porter crossed the room, dipped her hand into the basket, scrounged it around beneath the paper, and came up with the watch.

"I knew I heard a ticking," she said soberly.

"Honestly—" said Katherine, "is everybody crazy? Who in the world's watch is it?"

"Your father's," she said, simply. Then, "Nine twenty something—can that be right?"

"Mother," said Katherine, "it's after two thirty."

"Your father loses them," Mrs. Porter said, "your mother finds them."

"I have had all I can stand, Mother," said Katherine, "and I am not going to leave this room until you do. Nobody can sleep while you are up padding around the house."

"I just knew I heard the ticking," Mrs. Porter said.

"Mother," said Katherine, "give me that watch," and she walked up to her mother, took the watch from her. "Now I've got it, and there will be no ticking if you go up and sleep in your own room. I'm going to sleep down here whether there's any more ticking or not."

She took her mother by the arm, and as they came toward the stairs Webb stepped from the landing into the kitchen, and standing there in the dark he saw them make the turn, slowly go up. At the top of the stairs Mrs. Porter said, "A safe place. That's where he said he put it."

"Put what, Mother?"

"The Golden Swiss Ticker," Mrs. Porter said, and then she stepped into the bedroom, padding softly across the floor directly over his head. A moment later, the springs creaking, she got into bed.

Webb remained in the kitchen until he was sure she would not come down again. Then he groped through the house to the screened-in porch, felt his way around the chair hung with her clothes, and lay out on the cot from where she had just got up. He smoked the last crushed cigarette in the pack, and when the light appeared in the eastern sky he watched the Porter bats, as Parsons called them, winging back through the broken windows of the garage. He remembered, before he fell asleep, to do one more thing. The Golden Swiss Ticker, in its morocco case, he put into the sideboard, behind the chest of silver, not a very safe place but one where Mrs. Porter might come upon it. If she didn't he would stumble on it himself.

"Mother," he would say, "what in the world is this?" and he would stand there, with the case open, until she came toward him and looked at the watch.

That was quite a picture, one that pleased him, and whether he heard the ticking or not, something kept him awake until he heard the Grandmother coming down the stairs.

The Character of the Lover

This story, originally published in American Mercury *in 1951, anticipates the novel* What a Way to Go.

For no other purpose, it would seem, than to accommodate Dr. Emil Hodler, the drug store in his neighborhood put in a large table of bargain books. Publishers' reminders, as they were called. There was no clerk assigned to this table, but the young man who worked behind the notions counter would come forward and take Dr. Hodler's twenty-nine cents. It was usually for one of Dr. Hodler's books. On the jacket of the book there would be a picture of Dr. Hodler, looking like Franz Werfel, but the shock of recognition never crossed the young man's face.

"You like it wrapped?" he would say, and there was never anything in his manner to indicate that he was speaking to the author himself. He was either not very bright, or he didn't seem to care.

This young man was called Robert by the other clerks. Dr. Hodler was familiar with the type, and there had been a time, not too long ago, when he thought all of these idle, handsome young men were snobbish customers. Free to roam through the better class men's stores more or less as they pleased. He still found it hard to believe that these casual creatures were clerks. If Robert differed from these strange young men it was largely due to the notions department, the counter piled high with electric fans, irons, and heating pads. The quality of his deliberation was also harder to define. Dr. Hodler simply felt addle-pated and foolish when he talked with him.

In something more than the clinical sense, Robert began to interest Dr. Hodler when he found that the young man took a certain interest in the world of books. In particular, those that Dr. Hodler picked out. He often asked just what such and such a book was about. With this in mind, Dr. Holder was careful to buy only those books that would tend to develop a young man's taste. His own, for example, when they turned up, otherwise the more familiar classics.

It soon reached a point, however, where Dr. Hodler was sorely pressed to find on the bargain table something that he could recommend. In this extremity he settled for a doubtful book of his own. Doubtful, considering Robert's inexperience. The hero in *Blast*—a man somewhat taller, but otherwise not unlike Dr. Hodler—was hamstrung and helpless because of his basic sense of decency. Respect for his fellow man hampered him at every point. Like Hamlet, he was crippled by hours of fruitless analysis. Seeking to understand, to fathom, he had lost the will to act. As this would be quite a dose for Robert, Dr. Hodler let several days pass, nearly a week, before going back for a report.

"Well, how did you get along?" he inquired, which was the way Robert himself would have put it. Robert deliberated even less than usual.

"The character of the lover is not my type," Robert said.

This was not much, certainly, in the way of classic criticism, but it summed up the difference between the characters accurately.

"Ah so—" Dr. Hodler said, being somewhat at a loss for words, and looked at Robert with an eye as to what type of lover he might be. He found it hard to say. By and large he would be the silent type.

"No, he's not my type—" Robert said, and then disappeared behind the notions counter, where he wrapped a heating pad for a lady customer.

On the bargain table, that afternoon, were several reprint copies of a book that Dr. Hodler had been careful not to recommend. A book of romantic nonsense that belonged to another, now dead world. A book that the author ironically called *This Side of Paradise*. But in the light of Robert's opinion, Dr. Hodler felt just perverse enough to pick this book from the table and offer it to him.

"Is it more my type?" said Robert.

"You let me know," Dr. Hodler said, and went off. That was not at all like him, not a bit. But he was a man who expected too much from books. He expected them to mean as much to others, for instance, as they had meant to him. The feeling that Robert was rather hopeless led him to stay away for more than a week, and he even thought of buying his remainders somewhere else. But a habit is a habit, so he wandered back. Even as he entered the store he could see that something had happened to Robert, as he waved—he beckoned to him, that is. Dr. Hodler dallied with the heating pads before idling up.

"There you are," said Robert, "where have you been?"

"I've been pretty busy—" Dr. Hodler began, implying that some people he knew were not, but Robert was not listening to him.

"I've read them—" he said.

"You've read what?" said Dr. Hodler.

"I'm in love with her too," said Robert. "I know exactly how he feels."

"Who is this—?" Said Dr. Hodler.

"Daisy," Robert said. As Dr. Hodler looked blank, Robert added, "You know, Gatsby's Daisy."

Now Dr. Hodler had once, long ago, looked into the Gatsby book. He had read it in France, in a pirated edition featuring a profile snapshot of the author, and appropriately titled, *Gatsby, Le Magnifique*. It hadn't impressed him much.

"You liked it?" Dr. Hodler asked.

"He's my type," Robert said.

"He's a little old-fashioned—" Dr. Hodler began.

"You knew him?" said Robert.

"I saw him once," said Dr. Hodler, as indeed he had, and he cleared his throat to describe that strange affair. He started—then he stopped, as it suddenly crossed his mind that Robert meant the character, not the author, of the book.

"What was he like?" Robert said, and rose to his full height, waiting for Dr. Hodler to comment on the resemblance. When he didn't, Robert said, "Will you have lunch with me?"

It startled both of them.

"I'd be glad to," Dr. Hodler said, "but as I was saying, right now I'm pretty busy."

"I'm right around the corner," Robert said, "we'll have it in my apartment," and he took from his pocket a small pigskin card case, removed one card, passed it to Dr. Hodler. *Robert Gollen*, it said, and gave his address on Park Avenue. "So we can talk," said Robert, "we can't talk here." Then he took the card from Dr. Hodler's hand and wrote a few words on the back of it, *Tuesday, the 17th, at 12:00*, returned the card to him, and disappeared behind the notions counter. What Robert had to say, it was clear, would have to wait for the proper time.

That Tuesday was a warm day for the season, and Dr. Hodler carried his coat as he walked in the sun on Park Avenue. The address on the card, a brownstone mansion with a reconverted schizoid air, had boards over the stairs while a few stone steps were being repaired. As he started up the stairs, he heard somebody call his name. Directly overhead, about three floors up, Robert had his head through a narrow window.

"Would you please use the door at the side?" he said, and waved his arm to indicate which one. Dr. Hodler went back to the street and around to a small door clearly labeled Service Entrance, which had been propped open with a soiled copy of *Blast*. As he stepped inside he could hear the voice of Robert. "I'm here on three," he called.

Up on the third Dr. Hodler entered a hallway, and looking small in the doorway, was Robert. On the tile floor in the hallway Dr. Hodler's shoes made quite a stir. Robert stepped to one side to let him in, then closed the door at his back, and Dr. Hodler turned to face, on a low platform, an enormous rose-colored bathtub. He has seen such a tub—he had been in it—in a Victorian tourist mansion in Mexico City, and along with the tub there had been an arboretum and a pair of chained birds. At the far end of the room, like a faint blue lantern, a narrow ventilating window opened on an airwell, letting in the hushed roar of the traffic on Park Avenue. As Dr. Hodler had friends who sometimes specialized in bizarre entrances to their apartments, he thought this was merely one more of them. Or that the young man thought he might like to use the facilities. He waited, as the room was dim and he couldn't make out the other doorway, when Robert said, "You like to look over my books?"

Dr. Hodler was so sure that was meant to be funny, that he turned with a smile on his face, ready to grin at another American joke. But there before him, at the foot of the tub, was a shelf of books. Dr. Hodler stood there, facing these books while Robert went off to prepare the lunch—that is to say, that he walked to the other end of the room. Dr. Hodler could hear the sound of the silver, the pat-pat of the paper plates, and the pop of the cork as a bottle was opened.

"I hope you like shrimp salad," Robert said, and Dr. Hodler turned to say that he simply loved shrimp, and see that a card table had been placed over one end of the tub. As the tub curved in at that end, there was room for two folding chairs with stainless steel frames, and soft leather backs and seats. Dr. Hodler had seen them in a window at Abercrombie & Fitch. Over the table Robert had spread a cloth with monogrammed napkins to mark their places, and at each place was a Danish silver knife and fork. Paper spoons stood up in a piece of Steuben glass. "Well, I guess we're all ready," Robert said, and as Dr. Hodler drew up his chair, Robert smiled and made, so to speak, just a passing remark—"I do without it," he said, "until I can buy the best."

The shrimps—as Dr. Hodler remembered later—were very good. They were served with a sauce of his own concoction and a bottle of Semmelweiss Sauterne, an inexpensive native wine that he found, as he said, fairly tolerable. The rest of the luncheon came out of cartons as Robert simply didn't have the time, with an hour off for lunch, to prepare everything. They had strong black coffee from a Thermos, and at the bottom of his cup, when he tipped it up, Dr. Hodler observed the label of Black, Starr & Frost.

While they ate, Robert talked. Dr. Hodler missed some of the details as his interest was divided, but Robert had a way of making his points.

"You know, my name is not Gollen," he said, in a manner that got Dr. Hodler's attention; then he added, "Like Gatsby, I just picked it up. Does it matter?" he continued, when he saw the look on Dr. Hodler's face.

"Not intrinsically—" began Dr. Hodler, "but—"

"I just didn't like it," Robert said, "and now I wonder what I saw in Gollen?" He deliberated for a moment, then said, "The name I like is Nick—but that's your name."

"My name?" said Dr. Hodler.

"You know—" said Robert, "Gatsby and Nick," and Dr. Hodler, a little vaguely, remembered. It had been Nick who told Gatsby's story, so to speak. Dr. Hodler smiled, then stopped as Robert leaned forward and said, "Would you like to hear something of my story now, Nick?"

With the napkin Dr. Hodler wiped his face, then nodded his head.

Well, it was quite a little story, Robert said, as first of all his mother was an actress, and they had been on the go all of the time, on the continent. Living in Paris, Biarritz, Algiers, Monte Carlo, and places like that. He had shuffled in and out of expensive private schools. It had left its mark. His grounding in the classics was very poor. Then his mother married a Spanish count, old family with nothing but honor, and in no time at all their small inheritance was wiped out. To make a long story short, the count soon died, after several years of mourning his mother died, and Robert had drifted aimlessly about on different tramp steamers. Picking up experience, but little else. Nothing that would help him very much in his professional life. However, he had plans—nationwide plans to distribute ten-cent books through drug stores—but he needed someone he could trust with the literary end of it. Someone like Nick, who could fill in where his own background fell short.

He stopped there—it was where he had planned to stop. He excused himself, rose from the table, and left Dr. Hodler to puzzle out for himself if what he had heard was Gatsby, was Gollen, or was merely applesauce. A good deal of it had a familiar ring. At the far end of the room Dr. Hodler could see a large steamer trunk, well pasted with labels, and Robert appeared to be inside of it. He was looking for a key to a small drawer in the compartment section. Dr. Hodler remained at the table, sipping his black coffee and gazing at the half dozen pairs of shoes, in shoe trees, under the tub. In the tub, extending its length, was a narrow foam rubber mattress with the bed clothes folded neatly over the drain.

Coming back to the table, Robert extended to Dr. Hodler a tooled morocco folder, which he opened on a large glossy photograph. It showed Robert, wearing a tourist cap with the flaps tied with a bow at the crown, standing in the midst of quantities of small luggage, several steamer trunks. Every piece of the luggage was stamped with the exotic labels of the world. Directly behind was a painted screen, meant to represent a departing steamer, from the deck of which many kisses were thrown, and others waved small flags. The photograph was a joke, one of those things country boys mailed home after a weekend in the city, but the young man in the tourist cap, the plus fours, and the rubber-soled shoes for deck tennis, gazed from the luggage with deliberate serenity. It was not funny. And Dr. Hodler did not laugh.

"Back from the West Indies," Robert said, and took the folder from Dr. Hodler, walked back to the end of the room, and placed it in the trunk. Then he closed the trunk with a snap, and turned to ask Dr. Hodler if he would mind passing him the silver, the knives first. Dr. Hodler was glad to, and Robert rinsed the silver under the faucet in the basin, then rinsed the glasses, placing them on a paper towel to dry. The silver Robert returned to a non-tarnish flannel case. Looking at his watch he announced that it was now one o'clock, and faced the mirror on the bathroom door to comb his hair. Then they went back down the stairs that Dr. Hodler had come up, and at the foot of the stairs, soberly, Robert shook his hand. It was clear to Dr. Hodler that he had made some kind of pact. He stood there, in the Service Entrance, watching Robert go down the street shoulder to shoulder with the men who set the style. But with a little more shoulder, and a little more style, than the rest of them.

As he was very busy, he didn't get around again for several weeks. Robert was not in the store the next time he dropped in. He had his own day off, of course, and Dr. Hodler didn't think anything about it until the next time, when an elderly man was there.

"Is Mr. Gollen on vacation?" Dr. Hodler inquired.

"Who?" said the clerk. "Oh him. No, he got fired."

"Robert left?" Dr. Hodler said, as a pact, after all, had been made.

"Nope, he was fired," said the old man. "Guess he slapped one of the customers."

"He what?" said Dr. Hodler.

"I didn't see it," said the clerk, "but Mr. Prewitt, the boss, saw him slap him." Dr. Hodler waited, and the old man said, "Guess it was one of these anti-Jewish books, and this fellow Gollen just refused to sell it to him. Said if he wanted stuff like that he'd have to buy it somewhere else. Now you can't treat the public like that," the old man said.

"You say he slapped him?" said Dr. Hodler, as the lover in Dr. Hodler's book, in the continental manner, slapped the Nazi thug who then shot him.

"I guess this customer got a little peeved and made some anti-Jewish remark himself, and then this Gollen asked him to please step outside. Right out there in the street, right there on the curb, he slapped him in the face."

Dr. Hodler closed his eyes. He tried to picture it.

"He was wearin' the company jacket," said the old man, "with the name right there on the jacket." He reflected, then said, "If he'd just hit him, it wouldn't have been so bad."

Dr. Hodler thanked him, and as he said so many times in his own books, went for a walk with his thoughts. He went up Park Avenue, but he found the Service Entrance was locked. No copy of *Blast* now held open the door. Dr. Hodler felt responsible, somehow, as if had it not been for himself, and his bookish habits, the boy would still have his job. He felt like going back to the drug store and explaining to Mr. Prewitt that this strange act had been committed by somebody else. That the youth they had hired, Robert Gollen by name, had little to do with it. But he didn't. Perhaps he wasn't too sure of it himself. Instead, he sat down and wrote a letter, addressing himself to *My dear Gatsby*, and saying that the plan he had spoken of interested him very much. He suggested the date for another luncheon, and then signed the note, *Yours, Nick.*

Ten days later, unopened, the letter came back. Across the left-hand corner, in pencil, someone had scribbled: "R. *Gatsby Gollen gone to* NAVY.

That was all. That was all the news of Gatsby that he ever had. But when the war broke out, a few months later, Dr. Hodler found himself giving special attention to all the casualty lists. The lists of heroes, especially. One of these days, he knew, R. Gatsby Gollen would turn up.

Excerpt from *The Huge Season*

The Captivity: I

They tell me that my father, a Latin teacher, would place his silver watch, with the Phi Beta key dangling, on the right-hand corner of the desk in his Vergil class. When he was not lecturing, the students would hear the loud tick. The watch had been given to him by his father when he became a Cum Laude Latin scholar, and the inscription *Incipit Vita Nova* had been engraved on the back. A very punctual man, my father wound the watch when he heard the first bell ring in the morning, then he would place it, with the fob dangling, on the corner of his desk. Time, for my father, seemed to be contained in the watch. It did not skip a beat, fly away, or merely vanish, as it does for me. So long as he remembered to wind the watch Time would not run out. There was no indication that he found his subject a dead or dying language, or the times, for a man of his temperament, out of joint. He died the winter of the flu epidemic during the First World War.

I never heard my father lecture, but I have his silver watch here in my pocket, still keeping very good time. It is his watch, but my own Phi Beta key now dangles from it. I have the habit of looking at the watch without seeing the time. I teach, among other things, my father's subject, but it seems to me the times *are* out of joint, and that the language is not merely dying, but dead. It was still alive—or I was more alive—when my father, for cultural reasons, spoke it at the table more than thirty years ago. The dining room was always dark, even in the morning, and the Latin my father passed to me with the toast seemed as good a language to start the day with as anything else. Our house was on Byron Street, in Chicago, just a five-minute walk, as my father timed it, from his room on the third floor of the Lakewood High School. That part of Chicago, even today, might be in Terre Haute, Des Moines, or Ann Arbor, or any other town with a fairly large residential area. It is why I feel at home, as we say, in any town where the houses have lawns and front porches, and something of a stranger where the living has moved around to the back.

We had a brown frame house, more or less like the neighbors', with the gable at the front and the back, the front porch open, but the porch at the rear closed in with screens. A piece of sagging wire went around the small patch of grass at the front. In the spring my father would put in a little grass, then tie strips of rag, like ribbons, to the wire, so the neighbors' kids would not trip on it in the dark. A broad flight of steps led up to the porch, where my mother, between supper and the dishes, would sit in the swing behind the wire baskets of fern. She would sit there because her kitchen apron was still on. My father would sit on the fourth step from the bottom, sprinkling the grass. The best stand of grass was there near the steps, where the water dripped from the leaky nozzle, and the third step from the bottom had warped so badly it had worked loose. It was one of the things my father always intended to fix. My mother had warned him that some member of the family was sure to break his neck. But my father died in bed of the flu, and my mother, for reasons of her own, preferred to go up and down the rickety stairs at the back of the house. I lived in it long enough to go off to college, and some years later the house was sold. The loose step was still there when I walked past the house eight or nine years ago.

My room was at the front of the house, under the gable, where the ceiling sloped down over my bed and the window at the foot of the bed opened out on the roof of the porch. The street light came through that window, and in the spring and summer the sounds of the street. A block to the west, then a block north, the Ashland Avenue cars reached the end of their run, and when the trolley was switched there would be a white flash, like lightning, on the sky. Both summer and winter this white flash would light up my room. Where the ceiling sloped down over my head I once wrote out the declensions of my Latin verbs, and on the warm summer nights I would lie there on my back, memorizing them. I would wait for the flash of the trolley wire to check on what I had learned. Later I began to pin up certain pictures—Bebe Daniels was there at one time, beside Sappho—and, for all I know, a picture of Charles Lindbergh may still be there. It showed him in the cockpit of the *Spirit of St. Louis*, about to take off. It was a picture you have probably seen, but I doubt if you ever saw, or heard of, Charles Lawrence, the tennis player. I took his picture down when we moved, and I still have it somewhere.

Lawrence was quite a tennis player at one time, and the picture I have, although it is faded, gives you some idea of his tennis form. His back is to the camera, and he is about to serve the ball. You can see the ball at the top left corner, you can even read the label stamped on it. All the other details in the picture tend to be a little blurred: the wire screen at the back, the row of white bleacher faces with deep eye shadows so that they look like pansies, and the racket itself a blurred current of air approaching the ball. It is not, by modern standards, a good photograph. They do that sort of thing much better these days. They don't play better tennis, however, and the one thing that comes out clear in the print, blurred though it is, is the way the player goes after the ball. You can see that he takes the game seriously. I do not mean that he takes it professionally. A stranger to the game might feel that this was not the picture of a game at all, or that the blurred figure was preparing to strike nothing more than a ball. That kind of seriousness—I almost said deadly seriousness—has gone out of it. On the other hand, the stranger might not notice it at all. It might strike him as not much more than a poor photograph. If you think that great champions are made by eating Wheaties, that great songs can be written on commission, you will be inclined to feel that I am reading something into this photograph. In that sense you will be right, as I am reading into it most of my life.

My mother believed that true breeding, like crime, would sooner or later appear on the surface, but she was thinking of the Nielsons, the Vikings whose course she had charted for nine generations, across continents and oceans, to a grand anticlimax in me. Of my father's country breeding she did not speak. A self-made scholar, born in South Dakota long before true breeding or my mother got there, my father could give me little, she believed, beyond parenthood. His Greek translations rather than his Irish background appealed to her. At Oberlin, happily, he met my mother, which assured me the breeding I might have lacked, and an eye on the future as well as the past. From Oberlin my father went to Colton in California, where he was known as something of a classics scholar, but my mother didn't think there was much of a future for the classics in the West. They came back to Chicago, and while they waited for an opening that would open into the future, the war came along, and near the end of the war, the flu.

I was not quite nine years old when my father died. As I had been when he lived, I was sent to bed early, where I studied the verbs I had written on the ceiling, with the understanding that one day I would take my father's place. Lying there on the bed, summer and winter, I relied on my ears more than my eyes, and put great store in all the neighborhood noises. On summer afternoons I could hear the crowd roar over at Wrigley Field. Later I would read that Hack Wilson had hit a home run. In the winter

I could hear the boom and the crack of the ice on the lake. Many years later, in France, where I should have been homesick, I felt more or less at home because the grass below my window was cut with a mower that had been made in South Bend. I knew the sound, even though it was cutting French grass.

Our house was like a tunnel in some respects, the daylight glowing at the front and back, but the blinds drawn at the dark windows on both sides. Our neighbors, in my mother's opinion, were too neighborly. In the summer, when these windows were open, we could smell what the Millers were cooking, and hear how well they liked it when they sat down to eat. After the meal the Miller boy would run the player rolls through the piano backwards, or the Miller girl, Arlene, would turn up the radio so she could hear Guy Lombardo while she sat out in front of the house with her date. He was, as I remember, almost a young man, with cuts on his face to indicate he was shaving, and a Scripps-Booth roadster with Northwestern pennants on the windshield. I saw only his face, for he never got out of the car. I remember the ah-oooga of his horn, and the glow, after it was dark, of the red and green gems in the nickel-plated dashboard light. Later he took her to dances when Wayne King was over at the Aragon. Arlene was nearsighted without her glasses and thought she was dancing under the stars—the boy didn't tell her that the clouds were on the ceiling rather than the sky. But that is not so unusual. He might not have noticed it himself.

I didn't have the time for girls, but I took in a movie on Saturday night. They were featuring some pretty good bands, at the time, on the stage. The band leader acted as a sort of master of ceremonies. I usually went early, if the show was in the Loop; it gave me time to maneuver from a seat at the back to one nearer the front. During the intermission the organ played, rising out of the pit like a car for a grease job, and we all sang the songs the projector flashed on the screen. There often was a glowworm hopping from word to word. I didn't sing, not having much of a voice, but after the show I would walk along the river, where the Wrigley Tower was reflected in the water, and hum to myself the tunes I particularly liked. "If I Could Be with You One Hour Tonight" was one of my favorites. I first heard "Yes Sir, That's My Baby" at the State, where they had a fiddle player no bigger than his bass fiddle, and he could hardly be seen until he started thumping it.

My mother was usually out on the porch when I got home. We had a radio of our own, but the dry-cell batteries were usually dead, so my mother would listen to whatever was on the Miller set. The Millers usually watered their lawn in the evening, when the water pressure was up, and Mr. Miller liked to water the lower limbs of the trees. Long after he had stopped, the leaves dripped water on the walk. The night would be quiet, with the groan gone from the hydrant, except when the motorman, over on Ashland, walked through his car, turning over the seats for the trip back. We could hear the Miller dog skid on the kitchen linoleum. Mr. Miller usually commented that now he had sprinkled it would probably rain, and Mrs. Miller would ask him to bring in the chair cushions from the porch. When it was finally quiet my mother would offer me a penny for my thoughts.

At the end of the war, to make a little money, my mother decided to take in a roomer, a Mrs. Josephare who taught History of Art, Spanish, and French. We spoke nothing but Spanish and French at our meals. One summer Mrs. Josephare went to Seville, but as she was going just for the summer she left her books and box of wide-brimmed hats in my father's room. She never came back, and we never heard from her. My mother kept the box of hats in the attic; Mrs. Josephare, who was very frugal, had often complained, in both Spanish and French, about the things Americans threw away.

I was brought up with the understanding that I would go to Oberlin, like my parents, and I had my father's Oberlin pennants on the walls of my room. I spent a weekend on the campus to pick up impressions, and I was impressed. But my mother, in order to avoid putting all my educational eggs in one basket, also applied for a scholarship in California, where my father had taught. Thanks to his reputation, I received a four-year scholarship. That was two years better than the Oberlin offer, and my mother reasoned that the thing for me to do was start at Colton and finish at Oberlin. That way my education would be accounted for. The turning point in my life, if it had one, lay in the decision to go to Colton first, for it was there I met Charles Lawrence, the tennis player. He was there because one member of his family had endowed the school. The endowment would help fill certain unusual gaps in his scholarship. We were both freshman, and we shared a suite of rooms with two other freshman, Jesse Proctor and Ed Lundgren, so that Lawrence had his captive public right from the start. I remember thinking, at the time, that we were like the iron filings in the field of a magnet that Lundgren liked to play with at his desk. But that was not it. Or rather, it was more than that. All that does is give a name to the magnet—it doesn't explain the lines of force, or why it was that Lawrence, who was the magnet, became a captive himself. So there we were, the four of us, in a strange captivity.

Peter Foley: 1

Early morning, the 5th of May, 1952.

The man in the bed, a professor named Foley, lay listening to the mournful cawing of the crows. They cruised directly overhead, or hovered like vultures in the tulip trees. Cawing at the house, the cat in the house, and the man in the bed. Blackbirds hammered at the seedpods in the gutters, starlings strutted in the grass beneath his window, and on the chicken wire spread across the top of the chimney a robin built her nest. Now and then a rain of soot or a sprinkling of twigs, pipe cleaners, and string dropped down the chimney, spattering the yellow pages of a manuscript lying in the fireplace. Thrown there to be burned by the author himself, the man in the bed.

The manuscript was entitled "The Strange Captivity." The author had worked at the book, off and on, for fifteen years. He knew everything about it, that is, but how to finish it. Now he knew that, but the knowledge had come too late. You couldn't call a man a captive who had lost all interest in his escape.

The morning of the day before, the 4th of May, the professor had got up to let out his cat and found the Sunday paper lying on the porch. The name of Mrs. Hermann Schurz, his landlady, was scrawled across the top left corner. Foley picked the paper up, glanced at the headlines. They were not happy. He returned the paper to the porch. Then he stooped over, propped on his knees, to examine a head that looked familiar—the back of the head, for that was all that showed in the photograph. This man sat at a table, facing the microphones, and the questioner faced him and the cameras. Beneath the picture the caption read:

UNMASKS VOICE OF AMERICA

"Well, I'll be goddamned!" Foley said aloud, as if unmasked himself. He knew the head of this man, even without the face. He knew the unmasked voice as well as he knew his own. Better, perhaps. Eyes closed, he heard this voice say, "There's a bull in this story, Foley. But he's a nice bull. He don't shit in the bullring."

There was always a bull in one of Proctor's stories, and this one, Foley felt, would be no exception. He grinned. With good-humored admiration he wagged his head. Then he stooped over, smiling, to read the article.

The last-named witness, J. Lasky Proctor, created a stir at the proceedings with the frankness with which he collaborated with the senators. Asked if he had once been a member of the Party he replied, Well, in a sense—

What did he mean, "in a sense"?

Back at that time, he replied, he had been a very good American. A good American had to believe in something good. The Party had been it. It had been something in which a man could believe.

Did he mean to say he was no longer a good American?

If he was, he answered, he wouldn't be here.

In Russia, perhaps?

No, just in jail, he had replied.

And everybody had laughed. Foley also laughed, thinking to himself how much it sounded like Proctor, and how little, in more than twenty years, he seemed to have changed. It was twelve years since Foley had spoken to him; in the city—in New York, that is—bending over one of the toothbrush bowls in the lavatory of the YMCA's Sloane House, the grape-colored bruise still showing on the foot where he had shot himself.

"I'll be goddamned!" Foley repeated and, still smiling, entered the house. He walked to where the percolator rocked on the stove, poured himself a cup of coffee but did not drink it. Unsmiling, he stood at the window, smoking cigarettes. The morning breeze was strong with the scent of the rotting ginko pods. He faced it, he hardly remarked it, for the mist was rising from the pond, revealing what Mrs. Hermann Schurz described as a sight for sore eyes. A small flock, a covey of white birds, unidentified. Ducks of some kind, looking like freshly painted decoys. A sight that Mrs. Schurz loved, but she never ceased fearing for their lives. They were innocent ducks, like Peter Foley, J. Lasky Proctor, and other birds of that type. Sitting ducks, seemingly unaware of the facts of life. The patriotic marksmen of the penny arcade would soon pop them off. And that book, that thing Foley was writing, what was it but the "Sitting Duck Hunter's Manual"—a guide to the look, the diet, and the habitat of all sitting ducks? Dead ducks as of Sunday, the 4th of May, 1952.

Foley had walked down the hall to his study, scooped the pile of yellow sheets from the canned-milk carton, crossed the room to the fireplace, and thrown them into the grate. He had stooped to scratch a match on the hearth, but in the quiet, his head in the fireplace, he could hear the birds nesting at the top of the chimney. The match had burned down, and he had gone back to bed.

Everything in Foley's life dated from something—his father's watch, his mother's death, the characters and events of his first two years in college—but his real life dated from J. Lasky Proctor, and they both dated from Lawrence. Charles Gans Lawrence, heir to the barbed-wire empire, once well known for his tennis game without ground strokes, his bullfighting without sword strokes, and now remembered, if at all, for his early death in the afternoon. Known to the world as Lawrence; to Proctor as the man in whom the sun rose and set. They had all risen with it, perhaps, but they dated, like fashions, from the moment it set. The 5th of May, 1929. Other suns had set that particular year, few of them in a blaze of glory, but with the passing of Lawrence a constellation had blacked out. Gone. One seldom, if ever, heard from such bright suns as Proctor and Lou Baker, such satellites as Lundgren, Livingston, and Peter Foley himself. Snuffed out, leaving no trace, casting no light, emitting no radiation, no blaze of worlds in collision, but still circling in their orbits, in their appointed places, after twenty-three years.

On the 3rd of May—the date was certain in his mind as he had kept the stubs of two lottery tickets—on the 3rd he had spent his first night in Paris, kissed his first girl, and all but had his tongue bitten out of his mouth. Near the Etoile. In the shelter of a bus stop on the avenue Hoche. Girl known as Montana—Montana Lou Baker—and the morning of the 5th she woke him up to tell him that Charles Lawrence, the man in whom the sun rose, had shot himself.

That had been the end—but not officially. Officially, the survivors had gone on to die off piecemeal, as playboys or professors, or reappear as fossils, taken alive, on the nationwide patriotic TV programs featuring the good, as well as the bad, Americans. The good brought forward, like a painless extraction, to smile at the world through all-American bridgework and speak with the filtered, uncontaminated voice of America.

That had made it official. That made it clear the jig was up. What had taken more than twenty years to die was now dead. The Lone Eagles were now a covey of Sitting Ducks. Dead, or good as dead, like the striking resemblance that Peter Nielson Foley once bore to Charles A. Lindbergh, another fossil from the great Age of Flight. The lemming-like un-American drive of young Americans to be somewhere else.

"Foley," Proctor had once said, "you self-effacing bastard, who the hell are you?"

Well, who the hell was he?

From the mirror that he faced, twenty-five years later, there came no reply. The blue eyes were now gray, the cleft chin was now double, the sandy hair had receded, the nose and ears protruded, but the self, that fossil-haunted self, was still effaced. Name being withheld until kith and kin had been notified. Remains bore close resemblance to Nordic (maternal) side of the family, strongly given to notion that the Vikings found, then lost, America. Bachelor, professor of languages of no practical value, well known on quiet calcified campus for lifelike impersonations of Buster Keaton and a record of Hoagy Carmichael singing "Hong Kong Blues."

"A penny," his mother used to say, "a penny for your thoughts."

God knows why. He really never had thoughts. But that was how his mother had faced the problem of silence, and when Lou Baker had been snuggled in his lap, before she had bitten him, such a silence had to be faced.

So he had said to Montana Lou Baker, "A penny for your thoughts."

A mistake. One of the turning points in his life. For Montana Lou Baker, Bryn Mawr '27, had thoughts—but not her own.

"Give me a penny," she had said, and he had fished out a small French coin. She grabbed it, raised her head, and intoned, "There's more crap talked about this town than any other goddam place in the world."

"Is that *your* thought?" he asked knowing that it wasn't.

"It's his," she said, "but I agree with it."

"'Crap' doesn't sound much like him," he said.

"He didn't say crap," she said, "he said bullshit," and when the word came out, although he had been prepared, he recoiled.

"Didums nasty word hurtums?" Lou Baker said.

"I guess I don't like to hear a woman swear," he replied.

"You know the three ages of man?" she asked, and he neither did, nor did he want to, but she sat up straight, her fingers spread, to count them off. "There's the age of stone, when you throw rocks at each other; then there's the age of steel, when you throw that at each other; then there's the age of bullshit, when you throw—" and he clamped his hand over her mouth. He held it there till she squirmed, then he removed it, and she said, "My mother used to wash my mouth out with Fels-Naptha. She made me bite it. You want to wash my mouth out?" and then she turned and stuck her red tongue right in his face. He almost got it, but she was too quick for him. She slipped off his lap, where she had been curled up in the ankle-length camel's hair coat she was wearing, and ran down the street to the *pension* where she lived. But her coat was heavy, and he soon caught up with her. He grabbed the belt across the back, swung her around, took a grip on her short hair as they did in the movies, and with her head tipped back he kissed her on the mouth. She returned it—then clamped down on his tongue. The pain was so bad his eyes filled with tears, and he covered his mouth. She ran down the street, laughing and hooting, the flat-soled huaraches slapping on the pavement, and before he could catch her she had got the door open, then closed again. From an upper-floor window she pelted him with pennies, as if he were an organ grinder.

He had walked three or four miles, through the Paris night. Above the trees along the Champs Elysées the morning sky was reflected in the curtained windows, and the gray stone buildings had a bluish cast, as if dipped in the sky. When a taxi driver hailed him he would signal that he wanted to walk. He was ashamed to try to speak any French with his swollen tongue. From the corner of the Tuileries, looking back, he watched the sun rise on the Eiffel Tower, come down the tower, that is, like a lift making all the stops.

Foley's life—such life as he possessed—seemed to have begun with one Jesse Proctor and to have ended when that Proctor had given up. The Laureate of the Age of Bullshit, as Proctor had prophesied himself, had survived the stone and steel, but the manure had been too much for him. The single shot that killed Lawrence had crippled all of them. That shot had been fired on a warm spring morning, like the one Foley could see from his bathroom window, a mist over the pond as there had been over the Seine. When Foley had crossed the Pont des Arts a bum of some sort had been seated right beneath it, rubbing a thick, soapy lather into the curls of a high-bred dog. The dog's fine collar and leash, with a clean towel for drying, lay at his side. Twenty-four hours later Lawrence was dead, and almost twenty-three years later, to the day, one J. Lasky Proctor was burning at the stake. One manuscript, ready for burning, lay in the grate.

On his lidded eyes Foley rested a forefinger, a thumb. Like a bouncing ball, or the glowworm hopping from word to word, he saw the legendary headlines, exploding like fireworks:

LINDBERGH LANDS IN PARIS
EDERLE SWIMS CHANNEL
LOEB & LEOPOLD CONVICTED
RUTH MAKES IT SIXTY

And larger still, like a backdrop against which the fireworks were displayed, the mural-size photograph of a tennis player serving the ball. This photograph was printed on the cover of a book, with the player's signature at the bottom, and across the top the Spanish word

QUERENCIA

Querencia? That part of the ring, the bullring, where the bull felt at home. The book was a novel about a tennis player who, when injured, had made himself a great bullfighter. The author's name appeared on neither the cover nor the title page. It was in the book, rather than on it, turning up in the dedication, which read:

For
JESSE PROCTOR
Without whom this book
Would not have been
Written

A hoax, the neatest trick of the decade; published without its concluding chapter, the author's name unmentioned except on the dedication. The morning it was published, May 5th, Peter Foley was awakened by Montana Lou Baker, who told him that Charles Lawrence, the subject of the book, had shot himself.

Only one man knew whether Lawrence had ever set eyes on the book. Richard Livingston the III, the practical joker, the man who had published the book in ten copies, knew that, of course, but nobody knew Richard Livingston. Not that well. Not after Lawrence had shot himself. But whether Lawrence had seen it or not he was dead; Jesse Proctor, the novelist, had been blighted; and Peter Foley, the witness, still had an unfinished book on his hands. Not to mention Lou Baker, the haunted siren, with a blighted masterpiece of her own that filled to overflowing two

Campbell-soup cartons. It was Foley who had kept her at work on it. Knowing all the time it would never be finished—no more than his own. Unfinished, these books gave purpose and direction to their lives. There was always a page, a scene, or a chapter to be modified. New material or new light on old material, was always turning up. Now there was more of it. A chapter on J. Lasky Proctor, ex-novelist, salvage expert, and importer of Jews.

Montana Lou Baker had been a little haggard, a bony, legend-haunted Garbo, the last time Foley had seen her in New York. They had gone over to Chumley's, where the walls were lined with the jackets of books other people had written, a few people had read, and everybody had forgotten—except Lou Baker. She knew the authors. She had read and remembered the books. She lived a life as bygone, and as dated, as the characters. In the Chumley museum of jackets and blurbs she was at home. La Grande Baker, in her turtleneck sweater, a few stringy wisps of hair stuck to her forehead, forever picking the crumbs of badly rolled cigarettes from her lips.

"Oh, Christ, Foley," she had said, and after a while he had put in, "A penny for your thoughts." He *would*. He had blurted it right out.

And Lou Baker, naturally, had said, "There's the age of stone, when you throw rocks at each other; then the age of steel, when you throw that at each other; and then—"

Then came the age they were living in now. The age of—the blighted Laureate. Jesse Proctor become J. Lasky, the suspect Voice of America. In twenty-three years Foley had spoken to him just once.

Year of the Fair—the World's Fair out in Flushing. Foley had gone into town, taken a room at Sloane House for the night. Slept late, and had the barracks-size bathroom almost to himself. He stropped his razor, lathered his face, then noticed—reflected in the mirror—the legs of the man at the toothbrush bowl at his back. Had a towel around his waist, head bent over the bowl, and very fine legs. Foley knew them, both legs and feet, in particular the foot with the bruise on it, about the size and color of a smoky Concord grape. That was where Jesse L. Proctor had shot himself. Shot himself with a Colt .38 or whatever, while crossing the Mojave in the seat of Lawrence's sports coupe. It had put him on crutches for at least eight months. Up until that moment he had been a quarter-miler, and not much else. But after shooting himself it had been necessary for him to take stock, as the saying goes, and while his foot had healed he had begun to write stuff that was pretty good. He had never run again. From that point on he had done nothing but write.

So Foley turned, his face lathered, and said—no, he didn't say it, it was not necessary, for Proctor turned from the toothbrush bowl and said, "How are you, old man?"

Just the same? Almost, but not quite. The blue-edged barbed-wire scar was still like a bone in Proctor's face. And the face was more—well, it was more Jewish, whatever that was. Head thrust forward, cocked a bit to the right. Foley finished shaving, and Proctor led him back to the room he shared with two other fellows, but they were gone all day, so it was like an office, he said, all to himself. There he showed Foley letters, at least five of them, on the letterheads of important business houses, giving him large orders for a new, patented World's Fair cane. It was not at all new, and not yet patented, but it was designed to wholesale for three cents, and was stained and grooved to resemble a piece of rustic wood. With a banner and a tin-plate tip on the point, it would cost five. The cane would retail at the Fair for fifteen or a quarter, and in the letters on hand Proctor said he had requests for two hundred fifty to around three hundred twenty thousand canes. His cut, per cane, would run about one-half cent, but if he could place orders for two hundred thousand with a firm he knew in South Carolina the cost would be reduced and his profit would run a good full cent. When you figured in the hundred thousands, that added up.

Then Foley took him to Childs for breakfast, since Proctor was a little short on cash at the moment, although his credit, not to mention his prospects, was extremely good.

"I'll give you a blast, old man!" he said, rushing off to a sales appointment, and Foley noticed that he still had his limp.

Hearing the cries of the birds, hearing them coming nearer, Foley closed the slats of the venetian blinds, stood with his back to the window as the cat, with his escort, passed. Routine maneuver. No crisis, as yet. Peace did not reign, but it was being observed in the northeast corner of God's half acre. Mrs. Hermann Schurz, in bed over Foley's head, would have her ear to it.

He left the bathroom, took a seat on the bed, put on his socks. He put a shoe on, then slipped it off, thinking now was the time for his narrow-cuff flannels. French seat, English flannel, dating from the spring that Ivar Kreuger, the match king, shot himself in Paris, and Bruno Richard Hauptmann, paroled ex-convict, kidnapped Charles Augustus Lindbergh, Jr. No one would ever believe he wore a pair of pants that old. Or that his gabardine jacket, trimmed with chamois, dated from the contract negotiations, successfully concluded, for a prospective Foley book. Book now lying in grate of fireplace, jacket now hanging on imported hanger. Would have looked good on Lawrence, man from whom Foley took his cues. Lawrence had been the model, but it had taken Foley, on what was described as his salary, all of twenty years to assemble the parts. And in those twenty years the world had gone on to other things. Leaving Foley with a style, an air of distinction, that he otherwise might not have had. He seemed to represent the finer things of a better day. In the twenties the rich spent their money on feathers and established standards that were hard to follow, but in the forties the rich made the old cars do and wore the old clothes. Foley was not rich, but he had something of the patina. In the lobby of a building on Fifty-seventh Street, on his way to somebody's water-color show, he had been stopped by a woman, a woman of breeding, with the well-preserved sheen of good saddle leather, and she had wanted to know, she simply had to know, where he had got his shoes. The shoes on Foley's feet that day were more than twelve years old. They might well have been the last pair of such shoes in the world. Foley couldn't tell her that, or that he had bought the shoes back when she might have been in college, but he could tell her that he had bought them in Vienna, he had forgotten just where. He didn't tell her this was way back before Herr Dollfuss was Chancellor. The style had come back, in the last few years, but not the men who patented it. In such shoes there were feet, but not those of Proctor, and in such jackets there were arms but not those of Lawrence. With the exception of Foley. He still wore the same shoes, the same pants, the same coat. But he was not, of course, the same man himself. Not after twenty-two years, three hundred and sixty-four days. The night Montana Lou Baker had bit him a waiter at the Café des Deux Magots had congratulated her on being with such a handsome young man. Foley made him think of Le Grand Charles Lindbergh, he had said. Lou Baker had smiled. She had resembled Le Grande Garbo that night herself.

A dull thud, characteristic and familiar, communicated to Foley through the boards in the floor, announced that the cat had come in the pantry window. In with a bird, that is. If he had no bird he was willing to use the door. With bird, however, he used the pantry window, dropping from the high shelf with a thud, then depositing the bird either in, or on, the sack of Bermuda onions in the vegetable bin. If in, it might not be discovered for some time.

That made it three birds in five days, and Foley sat quiet, his eyes lidded, listening for the telltale scrunch of the onion bag. It came. It seemed to come with the draft from the fireplace. Foley opened one eye—closed it when he saw the pages of the manuscript. Relief. Almost sickening sense of relief. What would he do, in God's name what *would* he do, without his own captivity?

As if it mattered if these captive ducks were dead. *His* ducks. Dead or alive, what mattered was that they were *his*. Foley's lifelike decoys. He would make them look so real nobody would know it—not even the ducks.

He crossed the room to take the sheets from the grate, but as he kneeled on the hearth something splattered on the top sheet. Bird dung. Asterisk indicating the chapter left out. "Always let it dry, old man," Proctor had said, "then chip it off."

He left it there to dry, finished dressing, checked his pockets for money, keys, and Lou Baker's phone numbers, leaped the gap in the hallway the rug did not cover, and let the door slam behind him, rattling the bottles with the note that said "No milk until tomorrow," and under a cloud of cat-yawping birds he began to run. Across God's half-acre, around the edge of the pond to where the two strange birds, unidentified, were napping, but suddenly arose, water dripping from their feet, and flapped away. There he turned and looked back, glanced rather, for in the window directly over his study he could see the figure, massive and yet suspended, of Mrs. Schurz in a cloud of gray flannel, made by herself when she learned that ladies' nightwear, in her size, came only in pink.

He walked on, across the empty pike as strange as the vacant morning aisles of Macy's, then cut around the supermarket, the entranceway full of bucking broncos, jet-propelled rockets, and cans of Miracle-Gro plant food, across the acre or more of black-top staked out with posts, and diagramed for parking, then up the flight of steps to the local platform and down the tracks to the east. As he went along the platform he passed an old man stretched out on a bench. A hat was tipped on his face, and his head rested on an overcoat tied up with a rope. A man of fifty-five, maybe sixty, an old-style tramp rather than a bum. Foley had seen him around the neighborhood for five or six years. The old man often used the gents' facilities in the college dormitories. He attended the spring track meets, the home ballgames, lolled at his ease on the slopes around the pond, and was sometimes observed listening to the long Field Day speeches with a critical air. Foley had seen him as far as Paoli down the line. Always walking. He never hailed anybody for a ride. In the summer he was often seated on the big sandboxes of the Highway Department, swinging his feet like a kid and whistling softly as he watched the Main Line traffic flow by. He recognized Foley, for they exchanged greetings from time to time. The old man puzzled Foley because he hardly seemed aware that he was a bum. He might have passed as any local character, somewhat seedy, who pushed a mop in the diners or swept out the drugstores, if he had just given up carrying his winter coat tied up in a rope. That troubled Foley. The man seemed to have no pride. Otherwise he seemed to have what he needed—enough money for the food he ate out of paper bags, and paper cartons of milk that, when empty, he carefully deposited in the bins for trash. He did not smoke, was not known to drink, and chewed on nothing more offensive than the row of toothpicks he kept in the band of his hat.

One day Foley saw him in the gay deck chair of the new laundromat that had opened near the college, watching most of his clothes swill around behind the glass of the machine he faced. He had taken off his shirt, socks, and underwear, but not his pants and coat. He sat at his ease, a toothpick in his mouth, watching the clever, almost-human machine wash, rinse, and spin-dry his clothes. A ladies' wrestling match on a TV screen couldn't have absorbed him more. It was clear that he was pleased, but not overly impressed. He seemed to be, like his rope-tied bundle, nearly self-contained. Fussing all round him were a dozen rattled women, their eyes scanning some page, their fingers plucking at their hair, but even the pitiless stare of their spoiled children failed to penetrate him. For one spring, and all of one summer, Foley had hated the old man's guts, but now he walked in an arc, at the edge of the gravel, to keep from troubling his sleep. The sweat-stained felt hat with the toothpicks in the band remained flat on his face.

Looking south, beyond the pike and the market, Foley could see the green, parklike gap of the campus and the tops of the drooping willows that surrounded the pond. An island. Not a piece of the main. The world passed it by like the stream of traffic on the pike. One morning, from where he now stood, he had watched the blue heron that summered on the pond appear above the trees, the great wings flapping, water dripping from the feet like wet and trailing kite tails, and cruise over his head like some unnamed bird from the lost world behind the trees. A symbol of the college. A symbol of Foley himself. But the heron could fly, Foley could not, and the heron had other, wilder rendezvous, where the world along the pike was as passing strange as a crazed bat's dream.

The tramp sleeping in the station, the heron on the pond, and Foley teaching Pindar to the Quaker freshmen were three examples of the prehistoric present, the persistence of the past. But the heron and the tramp had the better of it. The past that persisted in them had less compromise. Compared with the heron and the apple-cheeked tramp, Peter Foley was as ancient as the coelacanth, that steel-blue fish, long reputed dead, that had somehow refused to give up, and shared with J. Lasky Proctor the news spotlight and the Committee nets.

Foley stepped back from the edge of the platform as the local pulled in. He started up the steps, backed down, as a passenger, the image of his father, and a Latin teacher at a boy's school near the campus, was getting off.

"Morning, Peter," he said, raised his gobbler's neck from the raddled rim of his collar, and passed, with a glance, judgment on Peter Foley, playing hookey from his academic duties.

"Morning, Allen," Foley muttered, let the old man get off, then walked through the empty train to the smoker. He dropped down in a seat where a morning paper had been left. A New York paper, with a two-column photo on the front page. The Senator from Wisconsin, his back to the camera, was wagging his finger at a man with a saintly, that is, almost silly, smile on his face. A bone-white scar showed in the dark beard along his chin. His hair was clipped like that of a monk, and though he faced the inquisitor his gaze was like that of the marble heads in Foley's Latin books. The stone eyes open wide, polished and smoothed, but not drilled for the pupils, so that the vacant, dreamy gaze was turned inward rather than out. Very much like the gaze of a tennis player well known in the twenties, and a flyer whose picture Foley had pinned to the ceiling of his room. But this was J. Lasky Proctor, unmasked Voice of America. Foley recognized the scar, and perhaps the gaze was due in part to the flashbulbs that were popping—or was it also due, in part, to the persistence of the past? Jesse L. Proctor, of Brooklyn, Avenue J, shown wearing the expression popular in the twenties, once worn by Lindbergh, by Lawrence, and known as the Lone Eagle gaze.

"Christ!" Foley said aloud, which was what he had exclaimed when he had bumped into Proctor, or Proctor into him, in the Hoffritz lobby near Forty-third Street.

"Sorry, old man," Proctor had replied, "not Him, just one of His humble servants," then he had turned and limped off, still favoring that foot where he had shot himself.

Made in U.S.A.

Time has complicated rather than simplified Crèvecoeur's disquieting and perennial question, What is an American? This problem has engaged, in one fashion or another, both the distinguished native and the curious alien, minds of such different fiber and range as Henry James and D. H. Lawrence. At the moment, the world at large is seeking to arrive at a sensible opinion on this very subject. Is it Elvis Presley or Richard Nixon? Is it Stan, the Man, Musial, or Marilyn, the Chick, Monroe? Is it Harry Truman or Dwight Eisenhower—not to mention that often evoked but seldom pinned down shadowless figure called the man in the street? Not merely the world at large, but we, too, are seeking an answer. We are all curious. Nothing interests us quite so much as ourselves.

One might say that the writer, above all others, takes a vested interest in this topic, since he, in his fashion, is largely responsible for its existence. Character, as I never tire of saying, is primarily an imaginative act, a fiction, to which the flesh is incurably responsive. It is the fiction that shapes the fact. In a crude but instructive way it is no accident that the world's fairest morsels, as of this moment, are disturbingly alike. It is little more than a question of measurements. Mademoiselle Bardot, curved on the cinerama, is less a morsel created by God—although He certainly did His bit—than a somewhat fashionable fiction out of Hollywood. So it is only right and proper we should take her measure on the silver screen.

But with Americans, millions of them, all around us, how can our character be such a puzzle? Have we no eyes? Do we never gaze into our mirrors? We are faced with the paradox that the observant stranger may know more about us than we shall ever know about ourselves. With the exception of Henry James, it is the alien who gives us the durable world—and James, of course, had the vantage point of his exile. If length of stay were important to the grasp of national character, every citizen who reaches sixty years of age would be able to put De Tocqueville to shame. The opposite extreme is nearer the truth. A single hour in New York City will serve the traveler better than a stay of several years. His greatest vantage is to be free of our own clichés. He comes, of course, with his own, as every season of books bears witness, and we read that life must be different, indeed, in Rome, in Siam and in the hills of San Francisco. But in terms of what we seek to know about ourselves, the peculiar savor of our uniqueness, a few observant days will saturate the senses, and a week or two more might destroy the bloom of it. The rest is data to be gathered by machines that often bear a striking likeness to human beings.

The traveler who has crossed what we call a border, from France to Germany, from Austria to Italy, from Mexico to the United States, is freshly exposed, for one brief moment, to the climate of character. It comprehends the widest differences. A Harvard man, for example, in his attaché suit, would seem to have little in common with a Basin Street hepcat, but if chance or the Army should throw them together in a bar in Rangoon, or a pillbox in Korea, they will recognize each other on sight as one of a kind. This is one of life's most appalling revelations. It is the layer of bedrock that lies below the veneer of personality. That very person you cannot bear as a neighbor will prove to be, in alien waters, the one man alone who can read your smile, or recognize in your shrug commitments too profound to articulate.

This knowledge, happily, came to me quite young. I was on winter loan to an uncle in Texas, where I was exposed, as part of my education, to several hundred little Haldeman-Julius Blue Books and a day at the bottom of the Carlsbad Caverns. We arrived before dawn in order to see the sky darken with clouds of bats. It seemed to me they would leave little room for the tourists, but there proved to be room, lots of it, and after several haunted hours of subterranean life we assembled on a spot called the Rock of Ages. There a hymn was sung, and at its conclusion a gentleman with the voice of Zeus read off a roll call of all the states present. At that time I called Chicago my home, and hearing him call out "Illinois," I cried out "Here!" As I did, another voice blended with mine. Across the rock, his shadow looming like a monster, I saw this figure coming toward me, a flesh and blood creature from the very same state I was from myself. You can picture for yourself our embrace. It evades my powers of description. Even my uncle, a skeptical man, fell under the spell of this mystical union and invited the stranger to share our lunch. Our parting, at the cave's dark mouth, was something of a strain. I took his address, he took mine, and a month or so later, from Bloomington, Illinois, I received a letter on his business stationery. He was a dealer in cars, Used Cars, and he just wanted to tell me and my uncle that if we should ever want a good used car he would see that we got the bargain of our lives.

It seems to me this incident is saturated with *American* character. That chronic sense of aloneness, of not belonging—thanks to our uninhibited powers of destruction—breeds a passionate need to pin something down, or join something up. My used car salesman had come to the Carlsbad Caverns in order to find, and embrace, one of his own kind. Our mania for joining—book clubs, record clubs, health clubs, muscle clubs, golf clubs, clubs against joining clubs—is a feeble effort to slow up the flux that is the genius of the culture to promote. As we talk about the Good Old Days, we can hardly wait to "modernize" the business, the kitchen and the basement, turn in last year's car on a new one, and play those dear old noisy records on the latest hi-fi outfit. But the old standards, to put it charitably, are not relevant. It is here that De Tocqueville was right and James was wrong. The culture that both dismays and amazes the world is something more than a diversion from Continental models—it is a new experience in human resources, in human energy. Destruction, rather than construction, seems to generate the climate of its character: it is not just today that the new is already obsolete. Here is De Tocqueville:

I accost an American sailor and inquire why the ships of his country are built so as to last but for a short time; he answers . . . that the art of navigation is every day making such progress, that the finest vessel would become almost useless if it lasted beyond a few years. In these words, which fell accidentally . . . from an uninstructed man, I recognize the general and systematic idea upon which a great people direct all their concerns.

What is instructive here is not only the observation, but the way the observer accepts it as a fact. He does not use it as a basis for moralizing clichés. He has found, and accepts, a new facet in many-faceted man. This is what we must try to do ourselves, putting to pasture for the moment our beloved opinions, and attempting to gaze, "right fronting and center," at the facts themselves. For this, too, as Thoreau reminds us, is in the grain of our character.

On the rim of the Grand Canyon last spring, I waited in line for a seat in the Grill as I used to wait to see Douglas Fairbanks or Greta Garbo. A place was found for me near the window, where a white-haired, gently befuddled lady, her hands full of postcards and curios for the children, returned to the table to leave her tip.

She had fifteen cents clutched between two fingers, but seeing me there she upped it another dime. What might I think if she had left only fifteen cents?

This gentle creature was the spit and image of one of my fictions, and I would not have been surprised if she had paused to pick the lint off my sleeve. Skeptical concern for the wandering male child gleamed in her eye. Her hands, her tired feet, the glimpse I caught of her handbag, revealed a woman who had come into leisure after years of hard work; a woman who had made it, that is, the hard way, and who could very likely tell you a thing or two about the nature of life. Life, yes, but not leisure—leisure would be her undoing, leaving her to drift upon the shoals and reefs of tipping finance. In the vast, becalmed sea of leisure she was rudderless. Bits of rock for the children, greeting cards for the elders, get-well or consolation cards for the sick or bereaved, kept her—as her nieces would say—occupied. And here she was, amiably mindless, at the south rim of the Grand Canyon, with a collection of technicolor postcards that almost had her out of her mind.

I judged her old enough to be my mother, but I was the one who felt like the parent. Affection, shame and concern troubled me. I felt—indeed, I knew I was—responsible. In the family of American character I consider aunts and uncles my peculiar province—I take them in, like umbrellas, and after a few repairs put them back into service. On occasion I make up one from scratch. There on the rim of the Canyon, of all places, I ran into my own handiwork, as she had run into moccasins, blankets, beads and gifts for the child who is tired of everything. For her innocent fatuity I felt personally responsible. What would she do next? It seemed to me that I knew better than she did. If I put my mind to it, she would do it. It was as simple as that. Such character has its origin not in fact, but in fiction. Very likely it is a fiction that the character has not read. Untold thousands of young men who never set eyes on a book by Hemingway are pure and unadulterated Hemingway characters. It is a matter of style. It is style that sets the cliché.

But we must go even further. Character is revealed cliché. Both are, at their best and worst, inflexible. Both are appallingly predictable. The personality is styled in such a mold that its actions conform to a pattern, whether the pattern is virtuous, as we see it in a *man of character*—or delinquent, as we see it in a teen-ager of the beat generation. Both are American characters. An American fiction has shaped the flesh. A corset of inflexible characteristics gives them support. Just as crusty old characters now ornament the inns and byways of New England, taciturn Indians and soft-spoken Kee-*ow*boys ornament the corner drugstores of the West. They represent the great power, and the abuse, of the cliché. Our first problem, surgically speaking, is to remove the encrusted cliché from the subject. In the beginning was the word, and the word was made flesh. American character emerges from the American language, as the language emerges from the shaping imagination. These are bold words. To what extent do they account for the facts?

Is this not tantamount to saying that before Shakespeare, Cervantes and Melville, there were no Hamlets, Don Quixotes or White Whales? It is. In the precise sense that we recognize the type—the unique shock of this recognition—the Hamlets, Mournful Knights and White Whales follow on, rather than precede, the imaginative act. Those men so much like Hamlet and Quixote, and those White Whales so much like Moby Dick, were necessary to germinate the fiction that bred the type as we know it. But all those early Hamlets were obliged to lack the essential ingredient that Shakespeare added. The boy who casts himself as Jesse James or Marlon Brando, the girl who casts herself as Jayne Mansfield or Greta Garbo, are those who bear witness to the cliché. We are left with a product rather than a process—a coonskin hat rather than Davy Crockett. The child who wants to be Superman—but no more super, mind you, than his playmates—testifies to the power of a new conception, and its dissolution. It is the cliché, not the process, that proves to be contagious.

But every cliché once had its moment of truth. At the moment of conception it was a new and wonderful thing. That first joker to stop you cold with "Hey—straw's cheaper" put his finger into the formation of your character. So did that first cowboy you saw in the ads or on the silver screen, and that tattooed he-man who has lately taken to smoking filter-tip cigarettes.

Of the pantheon of characters available to us, from the hotrod hepcat to the cool chick, it is the cowboy that I find the most instructive. Now that he is all but gone, in fact, it appears that he is here to stay, in fiction. As every young man must know, and countless young women, he is currently pushing tattoos and filter-tips. What else he finds the time to do is not clear. The filter-tip is *new*, with its miraculous fibers, but the cigarette itself began with the cowboy, a pack of tissue-thin paper and strong tobacco in a Bull Durham sack. Perhaps the scene already arranges itself. We see him on horseback, a sea of cattle stretched behind him, but he has paused in the day's occupations to roll, with the skill of a magician, his immortal cigarette. The pouch dangles at his chin, we see the noose between his strong white teeth. He taps a few grains of the weed into the paper, his light-creased eyes scanning the horizon, and then, quicker than the eye, with a cunning sleight of hand it is rolled, and the tip of his tongue supplies the timeless seal. A flick of his thumbnail lights the match, we see the flame cupped in his lean brown hands, and as he inhales we taste the heavenly smoke with him. In our nostrils is a blend of sage, saddle leather and cattle-scented air. "Heigh-ho, Silver!" says a voice deep within us, and we are off.

It is no ordinary mortal we watch riding away. Style has made him a symbol, and what he smokes is an immortal weed. It will never pass—on the evidence—into nothingness. It will be brought back, like the "Venus de Milo," to sell strapless bras to less endowed charmers, or filter-tips to those mindful of their lungs. But our concern is with the use, rather than the abuse, of this conception. He is that hero with a thousand faces cut down to our size. He is that archetype, the self-sufficient man, reduced to his wits, his guts and his horse, who takes on single-handed the forces of evil in a world he never made.

There is some evidence to support the assumption that the only new man of the brave new world is the plains cowboy. No cliché has proved so durable, both at home and abroad, as that of the fast-shooting Lone Ranger, the truly good badman, mounted on his faithful horse. A unique product of the high plains environment, he was bred both so true, and so fine, that with the passing of the cattle kingdom he has passed with it. He has exchanged his mortal life for an immortal one. The newsstands of the world, from Omaha to Timbuktu, proclaim the durable charms of this conception—just as the small fry of the world, year in and year out, keep his memory green.

What we are faced with is less a man than a style, a fact transformed into a fiction not by one imagination but out of the folk mind of the tribe. No writer or painter—although there have been many—has set his seal on this conception. William S. Hart, Tom Mix, Hoot Gibson, Harry Carey, Gary Cooper, all have in turn loaned out their talents in its service, but the figure is mythic, and most easily apprehended when masked. Language and gesture, sign and symbol, the expressive ornament and the bone-clean essential, have seldom been combined with such casual perfection as in this lean figure on horseback. The saddle itself, like a coat of arms, is both heraldic escutcheon and portable empire, and I can think of no figure except the Indian in which form follows function so smoothly. The six-shooter, that portable arsenal, was the key to the cowboy's triumph over the Indian, and in turn over the imagination of men.

I have dwelt on this figure as one of the essentials in the

formation of American character—gesture rather than speech, action rather than talk, with an indifference mindless as the wind to those aspects of life that come under the rubric of thought. Anti-eggheadism is deep in American character. Such ideas and intuitions as we find congenial have been sheared of their breeding through *style*. Hemingway turning a phrase, the cowboy rolling a cigarette, the gunman slipping on or off a glove—for these things we have a painter's eye and a writer's ear. But let's have none of this long-haired talk about it, son. Just another slice of pie.

The Bryn Mawr girl I used to know—one of the first to wear dark glasses in the dark—left the seat of my Model A roadster strewn with the tobacco she lost while rolling her own. Was it the money she saved? The aroma of the weed? No, it was the charm of the style. It currently puts levis on many pretty bottoms, and tattooed anchors on many pale hands. Clichés, bless them, both destroy life—and make it possible. Otherwise we would all, like that student from the progressive school, find the willful blowing of the nose impossible.

The contagious elements in style evade formulation. They are creations, rather than fashions, and arise out of organic impulses and hungers. In the cowboy I choose to see not only a unique contribution to style, but the key, in his fashion, to our many-faceted character. Of all of our improvisations he is perhaps the most perfect. And this has been his ruin. It has made him, in the flesh, inflexible. He was as doomed, on his conception, as the dinosaur. But in the treeless ranges of the mind, where he now does his roaming, this has proved to be the source of his charm. He resists, that is, our mania for tampering. Sombrero, chaps, shooting irons, coil of rope, the boots that make him walk like a cripple, these are things that do not give way, for long, to anything else. And this is rare, I hardly need tell you, in America. In a technical sense, the flair to improvise is the green light to leave nothing, good or bad, alone. We tamper with cars, radios and, above all, with our lives. That celebrated American know-how (subject to unpredicted Russian lunar eclipses) is a by-product of the curiosity that finds the attic full of irons, vacuum sweepers, record players and velocipedes that Father—when he finds the time—hopes to fix himself. Hi-fi apparatus will be there next—if anyone still has an attic—along with certain novels on the beat generation and an assortment of coonskin hats. I have a friend who has just moved his records into the attic to make room for more hi-fi equipment. The only records he needs now are those of oboes, clashing cymbals and trains leaving Grand Central. Lowering the needle to the platter he will say, "Now listen to this!"—and we do for thirty seconds. Then we skip a few grooves and listen to the rain falling on the roof.

This is a little maddening—but it is straight-grained American character. And it brings us, by circumambulation, to the center of our subject. If improvising is the key, there should be an art of improvisation. And we have it. It is what we call jazz. We not only have it, but it has proved to be, along with the cowboy, the most virulently contagious of all of our exports. It is not only politics that makes the world rock and roll. Wherever music can be heard, one hears jazz. And what is new in jazz is that improvisation—in the past a gift, or flair, of the jazz musician—has been raised to the level of an art. The man who improvises, who achieves more than a form of musical doodling, creatively produces something new out of something that was old. In part he destroys what was hallowed and familiar—it is here we hear the cries of distress and anguish—for the old beloved tune can hardly, as we say, be recognized. That, indeed, is the musician's intention. *Make it new* is precisely his challenge. Often he muffs it. Even in jazz, such talent is rare. But today he knows what he is about, and the American mania to tamper is slowly emerging into an American form of art. With or without our compliance it will charm us. In the harmonious sounds of jazz blend the discords of our nature. From the tweeter in the hi-fi speaker comes the word—*improvise!*

The attractive aspects of improvisation are obvious: we see and hear it daily in speech and gesture; it blows a fresh breeze into corners of staleness; the commonplace routines—cutting the grass or cutting the rug—will have a touch of this audacity. The gifts of youth take precedence over the skills of age. The high style is *Easy does it* and *Look ma, no hands!*

The debit side is less dramatic, but more disquieting. As a way of life the improvising flair lacks staying power. Almost anything but greatness can be pulled from its hat. The long pull, the lifetime effort, is against this grain, not with it. It believes with almost superstitious reverence in something called luck. This will serve the man at the gaming table, but in the exercise of will and imagination that generates great art, the improvising flair is a tool, but not an end. It is an amateur's gift and must be trained to do professional work. This does not often happen. We instinctively look for the short cut, the easy way.

On the evidence, which is impressive, improvisation is capable of singular achievements, especially of a collaborative nature, but that extended effort we recognize as greatness is not one of its characteristics. We have more men with greatness thrust upon them than we have men who achieve it. Only one thing has appeared to take the place of the mythic log cabin and the rise from rags to riches. This is the jackpot. First you need all the breaks; then you need all the luck.

And to improvise, however well, is to breed a form of incoherence, since everything must remain in a state of flux. The Indian clubs are in the air all at one time. It is virtually impossible to describe the *state* of things. A thing is no sooner made than we modify it; a street no sooner laid than torn up; a house no sooner built than torn down; a reputation no sooner created than exploited. Anyone who has looked for the house where he was born, the empty lot where he played, the porch where he wooed his sweetheart, will know the singular paralysis that grips the heart to find these landmarks gone.

It is here that the question arises, Without a sense of the past is it possible to have a culture? Or to put it more bluntly,

Without a sense of the past do we have *people*? What else—we can hear Henry James ask—what else is human culture? But of this essential ingredient we have only its aftertaste, nostalgia. The past itself we daily destroy before our eyes. The great city of New York rings with the hammers of salvage, and hamlets that late gave birth to men of distinction are wiped off the map to make room for superhighways.

It gives pause. Is this a way of life, or a way of self-destruction? Perhaps the finest mind we have produced saw this with his customary penetration, but it proved to be one observation with which this restless analyst would not come to terms. The destructive elements in all this construction brought the mind of James to a standstill. What was it but a monster that fed on its own brood?

No, since I accept your ravage, what strikes me is the long list of the arrears of your undone; and so constantly, right and left, that your pretended message of civilization is but a colossal recipe for the creation of arrears, and of such as can but remain forever out of hand.

This would seem to be a conclusive indictment. It expresses my own disquiet and apprehension. But it is now fifty years since it was made, and the culture of arrears is still very much in business. From the point of view of history, of the conservation of resources, we seem to be dealing with a flaw in nature, but our responsibility in this discussion is not merely to indict it, but to confront it. The destructive element is not the last word. However repellent it seems to the mind, however inadmissible it is as an aspect of culture, we are obliged to admit that a principle of waste can generate and sustain a great civilization. Perhaps not forever, but no principle has met this test.

On the evidence, which is impressive, the vitality of such tireless improvisation proves to be contagious on a world-wide scale. The stranger admits to not liking what we are—but to coveting, incurably, what we have. This distinction is naïve. What we are is what we have. And when he has it—which will be soon enough—he will be the same.

It lies beyond the range of this discussion to speculate on the nature of such energy, except where we seem to see it, or feel it, in the formation of American character. It is here that the word "improvise" provides a link. Energy that appears primarily destructive has its constructive elements, and in what we call jazz the constructive element is now paramount. Sound and fury that all too often appear to signify nothing are more disposed for human use than James was able to acknowledge. On this point it is James, himself, who sets us straight.

From the moment that the critic finds himself sighing . . . that the cluster of appearances can have no sense, from that moment he begins, and quite consciously, to go to pieces; it being the prime business and high honor of the painter of life always to make sense—and to make it most in proportion as the immediate aspects are loose or confused. The last thing decently permitted of him is to recognize incoherence—to recognize it, that is, as baffling; though of course he may present and portray it, in all richness, for incoherence.

If we are, indeed, so richly incoherent, the fault would seem to lie with the fiction—as it does. It is bad fiction that governs our lives. I wish we could say that all bad fiction goes where the critics would like to put it, but we cannot: it goes into the too, too solid flesh. It is what we see, if we can bear to look, walking the streets. Like the dead with their green complexions that Strabo saw and complained of, they are full of such vitality that the living run for their lives. The good prevails, if at all, by the skin of its teeth; but the bad would seem to be the very stuff that life feeds on, so let us be dutifully thankful for so much of it. In this gross pasture the wild flowers smell the best.

But if we ask ourselves why American life, with its incoherence, so captivates the stranger, the answer does not lie in our department store basements, where we usually look. It lies in the imaginative nature of life, in the fact that nature imitates art. Nowhere else in the world, and at no other time, has a culture so massive remained as a *process*, changing its shape, and its nature, daily, before the world's eyes. It is this that proves to be contagious in our jazz, our literature and our movies. Life is captivated by the sight of life. The daily ruin that we make, and yet somehow survive, is not unlike that of the conceptual process. This is what the imagination must do with the diet of outworn clichés. This is what Americans must do with their loose and confused lives. Make it new. Never mind what it costs. In our language what we call slang, in our music what we call jazz, and in almost all of what we call fiction, this destructive-constructive improvising is the key. As it is part, indeed, of every truly creative act. "Every genius," Malraux observes, "leads a revolt against a previous form of possession . . . it is the fact that he alone, amongst all those whom these works of art delight, should seek, by the same token, to destroy them."

Something commensurate with our capacity for wonder draws Americans to the rim of the canyon, to the brink of the abyss, and to the gadget department of the local dime store. There we see what both man and God hath wrought. Neither spectacle leaves us gratified. Out of the cloudless sky a voice whispers—*improvise!*

The Grand Canyon, so far, has resisted, but I wouldn't lay bets on it. I found the white-haired lady who had upped her tip a dime seated where the view was the most expansive. In her lap she had peanuts for the chipmunks and a newspaper. The headlines reported that another rocket had been shot into space, and there was a picture of it. Without turning her gaze from the Canyon she said, "*What* will they do next?" And knowing her better than she knew herself, I did not reply. She not only knew; she was preparing herself for it.

Excerpts from *In Orbit*

This boy comes riding with his arms high and wide, his head
dipped low, his ass light in the saddle, as if about to be shot
into orbit from a forked sling. He wears a white crash helmet,
a plastic visor of the color they tint car windshields, half-boots
with stirrup heels, a black horsehide jacket with zippers on the
pockets and tassels on the zippers, levis so tight in the crotch
the zipper on the fly is often snagged with hair. Wind puffs his
sleeves, plucks the strings of his arms, fills the back of his jacket
like a wineskin, ripples the soot-smeared portrait of J. S. Bach
on his chest. His face is black as the bottom-side of a stove lid,
except for his nose, which is pewter-colored. He has the sniffles,
and often gives it a buff with his sleeve. He is like a diver just
before he hits the water, he is like a Moslem prayer-borne toward
Mecca, he is like a cowpoke hanging to the steer's horns, or a
highschool dropout fleeing the draft. If he resembles this the
least it is understandable: it is what he is.

All of this can be taken in at a glance, but the important detail
might escape you. He is in motion. Now you see him, now you
don't. If you pin him down in time, he is lost in space. Between
where he is from and where he is going he wheels in an unpredictable orbit. To that extent he is free. Any moment it might
cost him his life. As he rides he sings "I Got You, Babe"—but

he has no babe, worse he has no voice. The words of his song string out behind him like the tail of a kite. The fresh smear of road oil scents the air and his visor is smoked with road film. Underfoot hisses the adhesive rip of soft tar. The line down the center of the road is the zipper, and he is the zip. Yet he is doing no more than what comes naturally, if you'll admit that it takes talent. This he has. The supernatural is his natural way of life.

That's the picture. You might want to add a few details of your own. A few ribbons to the helmet, trailing like a jet's stream, or the boot tops worn with the suède side outside, or a windscreen smeared with the wings of gnats and honey-freighted bees. Across the back of the jacket might be studs of nickel, or gems that gleam in the lights like a road sign. The hair should be long, the levis short, the cuffs raggedly scissored and preferably frayed. But natural or supernatural the boy needs food, and the bike needs gas. Topping the rise he climbs, propeller-type banners twirl between the gas pumps of the One-Stop Diner. The woman hosing down the cinders glances up to watch him go by. She knows the type. She is puzzled why this one doesn't stop. They come from miles around to stop at the One-Stop Diner, not to whoosh past. From the handlebars of motorbikes parked at the side dangle the tails of coons sold in auto-parts stores. They stopped to eat, they stopped for gas, they stopped to splatter ketchup on a plate of her French fries, to play the jukebox, to use the can and run a comb through their duck's ass hair-dos, their wind-glazed bloodshot eyes like those of beached fish. They stopped to stop. Having stopped made it possible to go. Pauline Bergdahl, safe between her gas pumps, wearing unlaced tennis sneakers and a surplus pea jacket, takes it all in, and then some, at a glance. Does she note something more than a favoring wind at his back? Something more than the usual spring in his legs? To the trained eye there's a difference between a boy on the go and one on the run. As he passes she flicks him with a spray from her hose, and the boom of his sound wave twirls the banners and presses the dangling bib of her apron between her lean thighs.

To the trained eye there's a difference between a boy on the go, and a boy on the run. Pauline Bergdahl admits as much to Curt Hodler when she gets to the phone and calls him.

"Mr. Hodler," she says, "he'd've stopped if he hadn't."

"Hadn't what?" says Hodler.

"Swiped it, Mr. Hodler. Some find it just too much trouble to lock it." Hodler makes no comment, so she adds, "Just remember they ain't a mean bunch, Mr. Hodler. Whatever else you can say, they ain't a mean bunch."

Whatever else Hodler can say, he has said many times. He is silent until the buzzing sound tells him that she has hung up. Thanks to her, however, it cannot be said that Hodler is a stranger to the type. They go by him on the highways, snorting like gas saws, they occupy the cushioned booths in the One-Stop Diner, they cluster like hoods around the phone booth and block the mirror in the lavatory, the air scented with their reefers, hair pomade, and saddle soap. Hodler has been in the war, and he would choose it again to facing them alone in a movie lobby. If they ain't a mean bunch, he is a simple coward at heart. He is also editor of the *Pickett Courier*, and will pay cash money for hot news tip-offs. Many of them come from Pauline Bergdahl, who knows the type. If the tip is a hot one Hodler will pay ten dollars. If it is a cold one he will pay five. In Pauline Bergdahl's case the issue is not so simple since her cold tips often prove to be hot ones. He can save five dollars by taking it cold. In her case, it is less a question of temperature than talent. Only Pauline Bergdahl would report, in passing, that a motorbike was squeaky new. If Hodler doesn't have the talent, over the years he has learned to have a little patience. With a little time Pauline Bergdahl's tips often proved to be hot.

Her specialties are fires and highschool dropouts, but she sometimes calls Hodler on neighborly matters. One is Holly Stohrmeyer. A neighbor of Pauline's, Miss Holly is a gentle, childlike woman, and like a child she loves to wander. She's not young, but no one can think of her as old. On a warm spring day she might just slip off and be gone for hours. It's the wandering that has led to problems, and why her people, when alive, moved into the country. It helped, of course, but it didn't stop it. As a rule one of her neighbors finds her dawdling along the road. The dogs love her, so she never goes far unchaperoned. On a warm springy day like this one she might make it all the way to Bergdahl's Corners, where Pauline would give her a glass of buttermilk or a cup of tea. Pauline has stopped giving her ice because of the way she sits and chews or sucks it. If Mr. Bergdahl is around he will drive her back home, or Pauline will call Hodler, or her guardian, Sanford Avery. She usually calls Hodler because Sanford Avery is not her type. He has more or less implied that Miss Holly wouldn't wander if people didn't reward her with so many free drinks.

There was a time, of course—and not so far back—when gentle simple-minded people like Holly Stohrmeyer found their proper place in a town like Pickett. The men could always help with the mail glut at Christmas, cut lawns and rake leaves, run the necessary errands: the women could help with the ironing and sewing, help with the chores. Even today a simple fellow called Charlie shines most of the gentlemen's shoes in Pickett. Not the ladies', however. They are disturbed by his jokes, and the time it takes him to make change. At one time Miss Holly, too, had her place, and was in some demand as a babysitter. But these babies grew up, and she was not quite so good with the babies of the postwar generation. Perhaps they were smarter. Perhaps she had got a little less smart herself.

Since the war Hodler did his little bit to help settle, he has been the editor of the *Pickett Courier*. He works hard. He does not cheat or gamble but he relies heavily on what is known as luck. The vague nature of this word is a solace to Hodler because he chooses most of his words with care. No one has ever heard him say, "As luck would have it"—but as luck would have it, he hears it all the time. Mrs. Bergdahl, for example, can seldom make her point without it. "As luck would have it, Mr. Hodler," she says, "I was there between the gas pumps, hosin' down the cinders, when—" Hodler knows better than argue the point. Nothing is less a matter of luck than the weather, but Hodler admits to the frailty of language. The forecast for today, for example, reads:

Friday, May 17th
Chance for rain 80%

As luck would have it the chances for rain, this time of year, are often better. But the forecast is less important than the date, May 17th. The date, strange to say, is more important in the long run than anything in the paper. Day in and day out the news is pretty much the same. All of it bad. Most of it soon forgotten. It is the date that gives it meaning. It makes more sense out of the news than Hodler can make. If, as luck would have it, anything of interest happens on this sultry May morning, Hodler will end up remembering the date. If a paper loses its dateline it loses its mind. The purpose of the forecast is to pin down the day, whether it rains or not.

Of Swiss ancestry, Hodler's big-knuckled hands are like bared roots, or grape stumps after pruning. He has never plucked a grape, or bared a root, but if you are *echt* Swiss you are born with such hands. If you are Hodler, you will never, no never, really train them to type. Nevertheless, he has managed to both write and type a book about the Swiss who shaped American culture. But little consolation it gives him. What, if any, *shape* has it? On Hodler's troubled mind's eye it seems a mindless force, like the dipping, dancing funnel of the twister, the top spread wide to spew into space all that it has sucked up. It is like nothing so much as the dreams of men on the launching pad. Or those boys who come riding, nameless as elemental forces, their arms spread wide and with coiled springs in their asses, ticking off the countdown they hope will blast them out of this world. A crippled, clod-footed species when not mounted on something, their legs bowed to fit their mechanical ponies, idle, loutish, but not—on one authority—a mean bunch at heart. Hardly a day passes, if Hodler is on the highway, he isn't hooted or buzzed by one of these phantoms, whooshing past him like a rocket about to take off. When they go by him everything is flapping, a penumbra of light vibrates around them. Where are they going? Even worse, where have they been? As luck would have it, Pauline Bergdahl often claims to know.

But on a morning like this one Hodler's first thought, hearing Pauline's voice, was of Miss Holly. He almost suggested he might stop by, and take her home. But Pauline had merely called to say that in her opinion it was twister weather, and while hosing down her cinders she had seen, just in passing, this boy on the swiped motorbike.

"Pauline," Hodler had said, "how you know he *swiped* it?"

"Mr. Hodler," she replied, "he'd've stopped if he hadn't."

That was half an hour ago. The wisdom of it still weighs on Hodler's mind. When the phone rings again he is almost certain he knows who it is, and says, "Pauline?"

But it is not Pauline. The hoarse voice brays, "Nope, this Avery. You alone, Hodler?"

Hodler is always alone, but out of habit he says, "How's Miss Holly, Avery?"

"Who the hell'd know that!" he croaks. Sanford Avery is Hodler's local weather beagle, an authority on early and late frosts, long dry spells, long wet spells, long hot and cold spells: if it's long on something it's Avery's. Hodler says, "What's the dope?"

"Can you get out here quick?"

That he sounds hoarse with panic does not disturb Hodler. Avery panics easily. He lives alone on a chicken farm with a woman who would tax any man's patience. "I'm callin' you before the Sheriff," he says. "How soon can you make it?"

"Miss Holly—?"

"She's been—attacked."

Hodler thinks of Bluestone's big police dog, Hank, he thinks of bees (the house is a hive) and he thinks of snakes. "By what?"

"Ah-tacked. Ah-*tacked!*" Avery whispers hoarsely to keep from shouting. "Ah-*tacked*, Hodler. She's been raped."

Hodler doesn't believe that for a moment. "It isn't something she thinks? Something she's just dreamed up?" The sound Avery makes is characteristic. A cross between a snorting neigh and a whinny. "Look—" Hodler says, "you've got to be sure. With something like this *we've* got to be sure."

"She tried to ward him off! She cut him. She cut herself."

Hodler knows the house: he can see Avery standing just left of the kitchen stove, facing the wall phone. His voice is like that of an old hound.

"You're sure?" Once more Avery whinnies. "I'll be right out, you hear me? Don't call *anybody* till I get there, you hear me?"

"She slashed him! There's blood on the knife!"

Hodler puts the phone in the cradle gently. If he doesn't hear the click Avery will go on talking, assuming that Hodler sits there listening. Living with a child has made him garrulous. It has finally made him mad. This does not come as a surprise to Hodler, but the manner of its coming is surprising. Miss Holly raped. Miss Holly slashing at somebody with a knife. What a light that cast into the darker corners of Avery's mind! Hodler shakes two aspirin from the bottle on his desk and rises to walk to the water cooler. His pants peel like a Band-Aid from the hardwood seat of his chair. The morning is already warm and sultry. May days that began like this often ended up in a blow. Pauline Bergdahl had already said so. An opinion that Sanford Avery would second. He would have said so himself if he had not lost what little mind he had.

Miss Holly *raped?* Hodler sees her always in the same velvet dress, the green beige faded to the color of a train seat, smooth as the stroked pelt of a cat on the seat and the lap. It went well with the upholstery on platform rockers and helped to hold her to chairs with slippery covers. Her dangling ankles would be crossed: the corset propped her erect. The parents of very small or nursing children often had the problem that Miss Holly's velvet bust, so pneumatically ample, might be strewn with straight pins and needles that dangled a teasing length of thread. These hazards never troubled Miss Holly, but they often punctured the younger children. They did it deliberately, since it was known that she would kiss anything that bleeds or hurts.

When Hodler came to Pickett he would often see her, trailing a two-wheeled cart, doing the Stohrmeyer shopping. She had a list. She often did the shopping for people who were busy, like Curt Hodler. She bought his aspirin, his razor blades, and the Red Cross cough drops he ate like candy. She was good with money. In the moist palm of her hand even old dirty coins looked new. Hodler was not one of the first, however, to learn of Miss Holly's problem. She was shoplifting. Someone phoned it in as a hot news tip.

Along with all those goodies she would put into her cart, there were countless others she slipped into her pockets. Without exception they came in small tins and bottles: they were little things. She seemed to find anything that was small enough hard to resist. That included pills, perfumes, and cosmetics, bottles of saccharine, deodorants, vanilla extract. Pills and vanilla extract soon run into money. But there were ways to deal with the money angle. What proved impossible to handle was Miss Holly's passion to give it all to children. Aspirin, Band-Aids, dental floss, nail polish, and especially a wide selection of lipsticks. Lipsticks were things most small fry could appreciate. Hodler often saw them, painted like Indians, holding a powwow in the playground, their mouths stuffed with Miss Holly's free packets of Feenamint or chlorophyll gum.

From Hodler's window she might be mistaken for one of them. Her face is round and smooth, she has a child's serene unblinking gaze. She is pretty as a child. The freckled nose has not emerged from her face. Someone has likened her to a doll with a real wig. From the rear, however, and down on her own level, she resembles a cello in a snug velvet case. Her hair is worn in the long tight braids that occupy her hands most of the morning. These small hands, pudgy as a child's, absent-mindedly move across her gaze for wisps of hair that cling to her lips, or comb the vacant air near her face for invisible strands. This gesture suggests a child's long, long thoughts. There is nothing, no nothing, to suggest the woman somebody will rape. Hodler's pity for her is compounded of pity for himself. If the needle hadn't skipped in the making of Miss Holly—a stitch somewhere dropped, or perhaps one knotted—it is probable, if not likely, that Hodler would not now be a bachelor. Nor Miss Holly Storhmeyer, if Avery proved to be right, assaulted and raped. Wouldn't it be Hodler, of all people, to inquire, "And how is Miss Holly?"

For more than twenty years Avery's cynical answer had been the same. *Who the hell would know that?* Now thanks to some snooping idler, or passing stranger, that was no longer an idle question. Somebody finally knew. It is a torment to Hodler that this essential knowledge is what he once desired for himself. How *was* Miss Holly. Some idle lecher, some wandering pervert, some bored delinquent, some loyal friend or guardian, envied but unknown to Hodler, and still at large, finally knew.

§

Hodler sleeps. He is hardly a man of pent-up emotions, but after any bad storm he sleeps like a baby. The worse the storm, the better he sleeps. Something in his nature, as well as in nature, seems to find release. His landlady is under orders to wake him at seven, but this clear, cool morning she lets him sleep. One shoe dries in the kitchen. His wet clothes hang where they can drip in the tub.

It is always Haffner's luck to sleep through the twisters, then wake up safe and sound and read about it in the papers. This morning there are no pictures in the *Pickett Courier*, but a note to the effect that the prediction proved accurate. *Twister weather, chances for rain 80%.* One of Hodler's checks will go off to Pauline Bergdahl in the early mail.

Kashperl daydreams. His nurse, Miss Boyle, has opened the blinds so he can see for himself that the town is still there. Not all of it, however. The historic elm is gone, but a wedge is on display in the Pickett Inn. Personalized wedges, bearing the college seal, are available on order from the alumnae secretary. In Miss Boyle's frank opinion many people will buy one to remember the twister, rather than the college, or the day the juvenile delinquent was on the loose. Little is known about him beyond the fact that he is juvenile.

While Miss Boyle chatters Kashperl daydreams of unrelated matters. How once he crouched, like an egg in its cup, to scan the volumes in a basket priced at 10¢. As he browsed another man's feet appeared at his side. They were large, pavement-flattened city feet in a pair of battered, world-weary shoes. Ashes from a cigar occasionally dropped to the brim of Kashperl's hat. The floorboards creaked as the man shifted his weight. Kashperl remained crouched, like a thief in a cornfield, while this reader sampled volumes from the upper shelves. Like Kashperl he dipped into them at random. From one, without warning, he intoned—

Ah, what a dusty answer gets the soul
When hot for certainty in this our life.

Kashperl made no sign. The finger of God might have written this message on the wall of his mind. A dusty answer. Vintage pathos for Kashperl's soul. The man who spoke these words then creaked off ignorant of what he had done to Kashperl. Hot for certainties in this our life, Kashperl a collector of dusty answers. It was no accident the author remained anonymous.

The big wind has not disturbed the Stohrmeyer house but it departed with most of the leghorn chickens, not one of the sickly Plymouth Rocks. How explain it? Avery can hardly wait for Hodler to get to his office. TWISTER PICKS GOOD HENS FROM BAD ON STOHRMEYER FARM. Looking for the eggs, Avery has found an old hen with a brood of chicks. She follows him, the chirping brood trailing, across the pitted yard to where Miss Holly sits in her rocker coring apples. Not an apple was touched. Already bees hover over the peelings in her lap, and swarm in a cloud above the roofless porch.

Early this morning Emil Bergdahl, his nightshirt tucked into his pants, served coffee to a kid who had run out of gas. In Bergdahl's opinion his wife had done more damage than the wind. Through the windows she had smashed he could see the banners still waving between the gas pumps, and the coon tail dangling from the handlebars of one motorbike. Two others were gone. There's no accounting for a twist in the wind. The kid with the dented helmet paid for his coffee and two packets of chocolate cupcakes, but he left his guitar as deposit on four gallons of gas. He gets eighty to the gallon, if he first gets the gallon into the tank.

That's the picture: there are those who can take it in at a glance. This boy now goes riding with his arms sucked in, his tight-assed pants glued to the saddle. There is no longer much flex in his knees, much spring in his legs. The words of a song do not trail out behind him like the tail of a kite. The levis stretch and fade on the rack of his thighs and his flesh is the color of sun-dried laundry. If travel broadens, why is it everything else shrinks? The shark-toothed jaws of the zipper gleam at his open fly. On his chest J. S. Bach dries in a manner that enlarges his forehead, curves his lips in a smile. Is that for what looms up ahead, or lies behind? This boy is like a diver who has gone too deep and too long without air. If the army is no place for a growing boy, neither is the world. Bombed out are all of the bridges behind him, up ahead of him, treeless, loom the plains of China, the cops, LeRoy Cluett, and the sunrise on the windows of the Muncie Draft Board. There is no place to hide. But perhaps the important detail escapes you. He is in motion. Now you see him, now you don't. If you pin him down in time he is lost in space. Somewhere between where he is from and where he is going he wheels in an unpredictable orbit. He is as free, and as captive, as the wind in his face. In the crown of his helmet are the shoes of a dancer with one heel missing, one strap broken. Such things come naturally to knaves, dancers, lovers and twists of the wind. This cool spring morning the rain-scoured light gleams on his helmet, like a saucer in orbit, where the supernatural is just naturally a part of his life.

Wake Before Bomb

This story, originally published in Esquire *in 1959, is an early version of the novel* Ceremony at Lone Tree.

One afternoon in Acapulco, where he had gone to sulk, Conley had eaten a cup of the shaved ice doused with purple syrup from a hair-tonic bottle that he knew, with reasonable assurance, would make him sick. Within a few hours it did. He was living near the bay, in a tourist *posada*, and this stratagem got him the attention of a child named Quirina, one of the landlady's numberless offspring. Señora Mendoza, a brooding sow of a woman, doled her children out on a part-time basis to run errands, wave fans, or sit and chatter with bilingual tourists. Until he poisoned himself Conley lacked an excuse to keep the child around, where he could look at her, since Señora Mendoza naturally thought he had other interests. He didn't. What he wanted—after Miriam—was something in the nature of a disinterest. Something that a laying-on-of-hands would not destroy.

He had left Miriam at the airport in Mexico City—or rather she had left him. One of her goddam moody streaks: he thought it would pass. He gave it time to pass, then he had written her to say that he was near the end of his rope. He had a quick reply:

Which end? Here it is snowing. I am probably sicker than you are. For God's sake don't meet somebody who needs you. Thank God I don't.

Love, Miriam

That afternoon, with something like deliberation, he had paid a pimp, in a Buick roadster, to bring him a muchacha of Guadalajara, who had walked up the slope to his room under a parasol. She considered the Acapulco sun bad for her work. At night, when she did most of it, she might be taken for a black. He had asked her to take a bath under the oil can with the holes in the bottom, but she said no, it would take the curl out of her hair. Her mouth full of gum, she lay out on the bed, the scent of her hair oil on his pillow, as firm and unravishable as a bowl of wax fruit.

Then Quirina. She had, from God knows where, honey-colored hair that hung below her shoulders, and a downlike frost of it along the bony ridges of her spine. Her body was stick-like, it was so thin, the skin on her ribs transparent as vellum, the armpits as smooth as a marble faun. The head seemed so large he thought it might break off when she laughed. And when not with him, sitting there on his bed, she would stand, like a morning flower of evil, in the rubbish and filth that made up the yard. Where he could see her. Oh, she never lost sight of that. Puzzling at first, then disturbing, were the large limpid eyes of a kept woman—a well-kept woman—in the face of a child. A woman, that is, who both accepted corruption and savored it.

His hair was sometimes in his eyes, or plastered to his forehead, and she would sit, as if daydreaming, running her hands slowly through it, as if he were a pet. She seemed incredibly bright, quick to learn, curious about all the things that he told her, but a day or two later she had forgotten all he had said. Hours on end she seemed so bored that her idle hands explored her body, like a monkey, not for lice, but just as a way of passing the time. She was also very dirty, although a warm sea lapped the front of the house. Thinking it would please her, Conley had given her his shaving soap. The scent she liked, but not the lather, and would rub it dry on parts of her body. The delights Conley took in being ill began to wane; he was soon reasonably well.

He collected shells, driftwood, and postcard snapshots of himself. In these pictures, taken by boys with antique cameras, he looked for evidence of moral deterioration, but found none. He saw himself, sitting or standing on the jutting rocks or the salt-white sand, his body tanned darker than his shadow, looking much healthier than when he had arrived. In one, a scavenging vulture seemed to peer over his shoulder. The vulture looked evil indeed, but Conley did not. One of these cards he sent to Miriam, but received no reply.

At sunrise, a week or two later, he hired the boys who spent the day diving for coins to give his Plymouth a push. When it started he just kept it going. He went up the coast route, where it was warmer, sleeping on the beach at Mazatlán and going through his clothes for the last of the lice. The Gordons might not like that. Evelyn Gordon had never really changed. Conley could not complain about that, since it explained why their door was always open. "You just come when you want to, and stay as long as you like," she said. They had the room and the money. They liked to hear what he had been up—or down—to. He mailed a card from Guaymas warning them to expect him in two or three days.

The Gordons lived in Berkeley, and Conley traced on the map the shortest route for him to get there. It went up through Las Vegas to Reno, then across to the coast. He cranked a few of the slot machines in Las Vegas, then drove north, until the driving made him sleepy. He stopped at the edge of a place called Beatty, tried two of the tourist courts, but they were full up. What explained it? He asked the elderly woman who stood in the door if people came to Beatty for the gambling.

"Gambling?" she said, as if it had skipped her mind. "Oh, no, they come for the bomb."

The bomb? For a moment Conley had not replied. In Mexico he had forgotten about the bomb. It seemed strange to hear about it in a wilderness of slot machines, from a white-haired woman who twisted the apron tied at her waist. The radio at her back played old-time hymns. Pinned to her dress, like a brooch, she wore a metal-framed film about the size of a dogtag. Nothing was on it. Was that why Conley stared?

"Oh, that's to check the fall-out," she said. "Everyone who lives around here wears one. They come around and check it. That way they know if the place is safe to live in or not."

The way Conley gazed at her led her to feel he was not too bright. A motherly sort of person, she opened the screen, asked him to step in. If he didn't mind a room without a bath, and no TV, she might put him up.

Conley said no, he wouldn't mind, he wouldn't mind at all. She showed him the room, one used by her son, but he was away making good money helping dude ranchers look for uranium. Her head wagged as she thought what fools these mortals were. For herself, she would rather let the uranium lie. It didn't poison people in the rocks where they found it, or make the dust hot. But she hoped it was all for the best, and some people were certainly making money. As Conley signed the register she asked:

"Did you want to be up for the bomb?"

"For the bomb?" He saw that it was a routine question.

"Just before dawn," she replied. That was when the breeze died, if it was going to. When he didn't speak up she said that if he hadn't seen a bomb go off, he owed it to himself. Terrible as it was, it was also a marvelous sight. It rose over the mountain—she turned to wave her arm—which lay between them and the testing grounds, at Frenchman's Flats. There was this flash, then this pillar of fire went up and up, like a rabbit's ear.

Conley turned as if he saw it. The pillar of fire like a rabbit's ear. "You better be up for it," she said, and after his name in the register she added: WAKE BEFORE BOMB.

Conley had gone to bed soon enough, but not to sleep. Although several blocks away, the blinking neon signs at the gambling halls made patterns on the ceiling. He could hear gusts of jukebox music when the doors opened. On the eve of a noise that would be deafening, the stillness of the night seemed to keep him awake. Every half hour or so he glanced at his watch. After midnight the noise down the road seemed to get worse. People seemed to be having one hell of a time. Did the bomb help? Did they come here with that in mind?

It made him curious. He dressed, then walked down the slope to a building on the corner, a sign in the window reading BREAKFAST SERVED AT ALL HOURS. Inside there were ten or twelve people, but most of the racket seemed to come from the jukebox. Most of the coins seemed to come from a woman dressed in black. She wore a smart, sheath-type dress zippered up the back. Her hair was black and her face, or its make-up, almost dead white. A heavy purse dangled on its strap, the mouth gaping a loose pack of bills. Five dollar bills. She played five dollars a crack. She stood at the table with the others but all of her attention was focused on the dice. Was she alone? At the bar she bought her own drinks. In her left hand she held the tall glass, in which the ice melted, and in the other a cigarette. The ashes fell into the mouth of the bag, dusting the bills.

"She just got herself unhitched," said the bartender, by way of explanation.

"Ah, so," said Conley, and remembered this was Nevada.

"They get unhitched, then they go on a spree." He caught Conley's eye, added, "On the alimony."

"It's going to be a short spree," Conley put in, "the way she's going." The barman shrugged. What was a spree if it wasn't short? Something about the way she handled the money led him to feel she wanted to lose it. The words of an old tune came to Conley's mind: *Oh, she can dish it out, and I can take it.* He wondered if he could. He wondered, watching her, what it might be like.

She would come to the bar, hand the fellow her glass, then take the refill and go back to the table. In the mirror behind the bar her eye would give him a mechanical wink. Was it a male re-flex? She came and went in the impulsive way of very near-sighted people, not bothering to look, as if she had her own radar. A little after three o'clock in the morning she was playing alone. Con-ley had moved to the stool that stood beside her, and when her glass was empty he took it to the bar for a refill. She called him sweetheart, sugar daddy, baby doll, and when her feet began to hurt her she slipped off her shoes. A little after five she had run through the money, and Conley offered to buy her a breakfast. It proved to be no bargain. He sat watching her eat. On her third cup of coffee she leaned back and said:

"Sweet Jesus, I did it." She looked pleased.

"You like to lose?" said Conley.

"I like to lose *his* gaw-dam money."

"If you got stuff of your own—" began Conley.

"Me?" she said, and in that manner that fascinated him she clawed around in her bag. Down at the bottom she found a coin.

"*That's* mine!" she said. "Let's spend it!"

"What will it buy?" asked Conley.

She took off her glasses, and through slits in her eyelids peered around the room, Birdlike. The way she gambled. They settled on the jukebox where the lights were bubbling. "Let's have some music in the joint," she said, and went over to it, kicking up the loose sawdust. She bent low to read the song titles. "What you like, baby doll?"

"Something soft and sentimental," said Conley. She pushed several of the buttons, then waited. Conley recognized the tune as one called *Stardust*.

"That's sentimental," she said. "Is it soft?"

"Was when I was in college. We used to drive into the Co-coanut Grove to hear it."

"I don't dig that jazz."

"The old tunes?" he said.

"The gaw-dam good old days," she replied. "If they're gone, what's good about 'em?"

Before Conley answered she pushed another button, and as the record dropped she came back to the table, spread her arms like wings, and said, "Let's dance."

Conley got to his feet, buttoned his coat. Miriam was a tall, graceful dancer who liked a little of the saddle showing, as she put it. Conley took that stance, his back straight; she moved in and fastened to him. Like plaster. *Tight*, he thought. *The poor kid's tight.*

"You dig the elevator dance?" she said.

"What's that?"

"No steps," she replied, so he took a few. She was light on her feet. The floor beneath the sawdust was slick, and in one corner of the room, unwatched, the clinical eye of the TV flickered at them. She wedged her face between his chin and his shoulder, biting the lobe of his ear. When the music stopped she said:

"What a gaw-dam bore it is to get to know people. They're so much nicer when you don't know them, don't you think?"

Conley stood there as if reflecting, and she put her hands behind his head, the fingers laced, and drew his mouth down to her lips. Leisurely her tongue explored his mouth. Drawing away she said, "You believe in your luck?"

"Not in mine!" Conley replied.

"Then in mine," she said. "You believe in luck?"

She gazed at him as if his eyes were closed, removed her grease from his lips.

"I'd be hard put," Conley said, "to know what the hell I believed in."

"There's always life insurance," she said. "They got it all figured out. Irwin believed in it."

"That your husband?"

"Sweet Jesus!" she cried, grabbing his arms. "I got news for you, he's not my husband any longer!" She kissed him. "I'm a free woman; you a free man?"

"As of now, I am."

"Irwin's like you," she said. "The brainy type."

"You didn't like him?"

"How can you like life insurance? He was a gaw-dam computer. He computed his love-life. He had it all computed when it would be over. Sweet Jesus!" Conley said nothing and she added, "That's one thing I'm *not* computing, are you?"

"Not at my age," he replied.

"Sweet Jesus, you sound just like him. You think we meet the same person over and over?"

"Not me," Conley said. "This is a first time for me."

She gazed at him steadily. "Is it really?"

"I'm driving through to the coast," he said. "You want a ride?"

She found a cigarette, then clawed in her bag for a lighter. He realized she had not heard what he had said.

"What do you think about death?" she said, and fanned the cloud of smoke from his face, as if to see.

"I think it's pretty much lost its meaning," he replied.

"Sweet Jesus! What the hell gaw-dam meaning did it ever have? It scares the hell out of me, doesn't it you?"

"It wouldn't if life had any meaning," he replied.

"You sound so gaw-dam much like him I can't believe it. Your name isn't Irwin?"

"No, Gordon."

"You should meet him. You have so much in common. He's so gaw-dam scared of everything like you are."

"What makes you think I'm so gaw-dam scared?" said Conley. He hadn't meant to saw gaw-dam. It slipped out.

"Baby doll," she said, patting his arm. "I don't mind if you're scared. I'm no gaw-dam Joan of Arc." Her hand remained on his arm, two fingers drumming. They both noticed it, and she said, "Sweet Jesus! Let me get it off!" and began to tug at the ring on her finger.

"That finger's swollen," said Conley, taking her hand. "It won't come off till you calm down."

"If he was here, know what he'd say? That it had some gaw-dam mystic meaning. That it swelled just to keep us together. Some jazz like that."

"Sit down," said Conley, "and raise your hand over your head." She did as she was told. He turned to the bartender, said, "Got a piece of soap?" The bartender found a piece of soap in the sink in one corner, said: "Nice if all you needed to break the old knot was a piece of soap, eh?"

Conley moistened the soap, rubbed a bit of the lather on her finger. It looked tight. "Been on there a while, hasn't it?"

"Eleven long gaw-dam years."

"It's going to hurt a little," Conley said, squeezing, but it didn't. No; it slipped off fairly easy. He passed it to her and she said, "Sweet Jesus!"

"What you going to do with it?" said the barman.

"Do with it?" she said, turned in her chair, and before Conley could stop her she threw the ring across the room. It fell without a sound into the sawdust.

"Christ!" said Conley, and went over as if he might find it.

"Now that's a goddam woman for you," said the bartender. "Eleven years of a man's life—Pffffftttt!"

"Ha!" she cried. "You see! You're all a gaw-dam bunch of computers."

"Goddam heart of stone," said the bartender.

"You sentimental bastards!" she yelled. "It's the ring you want, not the woman. Every gaw-dam thing you do is a gaw-dam investment. The gaw-dam children. The gaw-dam life insurance."

"And why the hell not?" said Conley.

Like a woman keening, her eyes closed, she swayed a bit.

"Because it's death," she said. "You hear me, it's death! It's a gaw-dam living death once you start computing."

Winking at Conley, the bartender said, "Looks like she's tight as a witch's tit."

Did she hear? Conley noticed the beads of sweat on her lip,

coated with face powder. In the mirror behind the bar he watched the bartender take out his watch, then turn to check it with the clock on the wall.

"Twenty to six," he said. "Guess they called it off."

"Damn!" said Conley. "The bomb? You mean they didn't do it?"

"You'd have known it. Makes a big flash, the windows rattle."

Conley said, "Hell, I left word for that woman to wake me. Wonder if she did?"

"She's pretty punctual," replied the barman. "Means business, you know."

From beneath the saucer on the table Conley took the check and walked back to the counter. He slipped the glass top back and helped himself to two cigars. He lit one, twirling it slowly on his lips. Coming back to the table he said, "I'm driving to the coast, if you're going my way."

"I'm not going your way," she replied.

The tremor in his hand, not Conley, shook the ash from his cigar. "You mind my asking," he said, "which way you are going?"

"I've not the gaw-damnest notion in this gaw-dam world."

"Okay," said Conley. "That's fine. Okay. Instead of you going my way, let's say I'm going your way." He waited. She turned, with no sign that she had heard him, and looked slowly around the room. Her shoes. They were over in the sawdust near the jukebox. She left her bag on the table, still gaping, then crossed the room and picked up her shoes. Shaking out the sawdust, she slipped one on, said:

"He says when I got my shoes off I look like a Jeep with the springs broke."

"Irwin?" Conley said.

"You got a coin?" she called, and he went over, held out some change.

"One for my baby, and one for the road," she said, and then, as the music began to play, "Baby doll, let's dance."

Excerpt from *Plains Song: For Female Voices*

When Sharon had left the farm to live in Lincoln, she had emerged from an oppression so habitual she had hardly suspected its existence. On returning she sensed her submergence to that lower level of feeling. As if drowsy with ether, she observed their movements and listened to their voices. Did this partially conscious life offer comforts she would live to miss? Half consciously she sensed that. The physical presence of Madge, thick with another child, reduced Sharon's capacity to think, blurring the line between the young woman who recently departed and the one who had returned.

Each day of her visit Sharon put off till the next day asking Madge how she liked marriage. It seemed obvious. How imagine her in another context? Each day after lunch, they sat in the shade cast by the house, with Blanche in the wicker basket between them. The child never cried. She resigned herself to lying on her back rather than her tummy. She resigned herself to Madge's attentions; she resigned herself to Sharon's indifference. Sharon was not too fond of children, and Blanche had resigned herself to that.

"I suppose you like city living better?" Madge asked. A film of moisture gave a shine to her plump face. She had pinned up her hair to feel the coolness of the draft on her neck. It startled

Sharon to realize that she would like the city better if Madge lived in it. She could see her with Blanche on the grass in Lincoln Park, or on a bench at the zoo.

A doctor in Columbus had told Madge that she had too many teeth in her lower jaw. It amused Madge to learn that. It gave Sharon dull shooting pains in her teeth. When they had been little girls it was often Sharon who knew that Madge was sick before Madge did. There were veins like those in a leaf at the back of her knees.

There might still be light in the sky when Ned Kibbee went to bed. He would water the lawn while they washed and stacked the dishes, coming in with his shoes soaked by the wet grass. Sharon would hear the alarm go off at five-thirty, and the pad of Madge's feet as she walked to the kitchen. At night they might sit up, after stacking the dishes, and listen to John McCormack on Madge's new Victrola. Madge had sung for three years in the Battle Creek choir, and liked a good tenor voice. She did not have a musical gift herself, but she felt a gift for it ran in the family. It had turned up in Sharon. There was a touch of it in Fayrene. She came back from the Ozarks with her neck and arms tanned, but her face still a botch of pimples. Madge always hoped she would come back different than she went away. Fayrene was a slender, shy girl, with pigeon breasts so high they looked artificial. At the sight of Sharon she had been speechless. The boy sweet on her, Avery Dickel, had a good job in a creamery in the Ozarks. Fayrene was being encouraged to practice on the flute for the Battle Creek band.

There were spells when the two women said nothing they remembered, or were aware that they had said. Ned Kibbee helped himself to the food on the table that Sharon no longer took the trouble to offer. He didn't think it rude. He really preferred to help himself. Without interrupting what she was saying to Sharon, Madge would spoon-feed food into the mouth of Blanche, half of which she spat out. While eating she tightly clenched her little fists and banged them hard on the shelf of the highchair. Madge's comment was that like her daddy, she would make a good carpenter.

Ned took time from his work to drive them both to the station, where Madge refused to weigh herself on the waiting room scales. "It's no business but my own," she said to Ned. Ned weighed 179½. Sharon weighed 104, including one pound of homemade fudge. She would come to visit them again at Christmas, if she cared to, or if not at Christmas, early next summer. Hugging Sharon to her the best she could, Madge repeated, "It did Cora good to see you. You're like one of her own."

The long night of fitful sleep on the train Sharon felt herself in limbo, neither coming nor going, seized with a longing that had no object. What was it she wanted? Loneliness overwhelmed her. The lights of the villages flashing at the window, even the glow of lamps in solitary farmhouses, made a mockery of her independence. What was it in her nature that led her to choose a life alone? If the man across the aisle, graying at the temples, reminding her of Professor Grunlich of Dartmouth, wearing a Palm Beach suit with bits of grass in the pants cuffs, buckskin shoes with toes that were grass stained—if this man had spoken to Sharon, if he had suggested she join him for dinner in the diner, if he had sensed, as he surely would, the contradictory needs in her nature and had been free to administer to them, the Sharon Rose who boarded the train in Columbus might not have been the one who got off it in Chicago, and the book of her life might have been different. But he did not speak to her. When she awoke from a spell of napping he was gone.

During the Sunday service Madge studied with interest every married couple she could set her eyes on. There they sat. A few hours earlier, there they lay. Some on their sides, some on their backs, and a few on top of each other. She saw it only dimly, but as something she had experienced she could accept it. It strained her mind, however, it strained her very soul, to accept this fact for the others. The women corseted and solemn. The men sober as judges. Between and beside them the children that had to be made.

Madge would soon have been married for sixteen months. Was there a day of fifteen of those months she had not pondered her experience? Wanting children, she had been prepared for the worst, knowing that the worse had happened to Cora. It could be endured because it need not happen too many times. Madge had chosen Ned as a man she liked and had felt he might minimize the necessary torment. This proved to be true. It has startled her to find how such an easygoing man could become, on the instant, almost a different person, but this could as soon be said of herself. It more than startled her to admit it. She was humbled and bewildered to find that such a torment gave her pleasure.

What would her husband think if he knew that she enjoyed it? Her pains to deceive him relaxed when it seemed clear that it hardly mattered. She had assumed it would end with her pregnancy and was part of a new bride's remarkable sensations, but with the child born she had felt desire for her husband. That she concealed, of course, scarcely admitting it to herself. She had no way of knowing if Ned was aware of her reluctant-willing collaboration. She feared what might happen if she took the initiative. Now that she was pregnant again he turned on his side and was usually snoring while she brushed her hair. She liked his snoring. What would it be like to have a man who lay snoreless and awake?

Madge had hoped that Sharon had come back to say that she had met a man and planned to get married. Only when this had happened would Madge be free to hint that she found Ned different than she had expected. In what way? Sharon would ask. Madge could not touch on it until Sharon had had the experience. The two girls were open and frank with each other, but they had seldom discussed men and boys. They had never discussed boys and girls. Sharon had blurted out her opinion of marriage on hearing that Madge was engaged to Ned, but Madge felt that this was in part her anger at losing her friend. Sharon was such a pretty thing, like a beautiful doll, Madge found it hard to see her sleeping with a man. She was like a child. How did such little women mate with grown men and have babies? Madge was curious. She felt in Sharon no curiosity on the subject. Madge had had a baby. It might have been brought by the stork.

That this baby was a female, the image of Cora, the fifth girl child in a family of females, might have discouraged a man like Ned from the prospect of a large family. Of Mrs. Kibbee's five children, three were sons. The two girls, who came third and fifth, had the advantage of a likeness to their mother, a handsome Scotswoman with almost orange-colored hair and a complexion she had to keep out of the sun. The two daughters were married off before the sons, one to a station agent in Fremont. Mrs. Kibbee felt that children blessed a marriage, but not if they ran exclusively to girls men did not consider attractive. Mrs. Kibbee spoke to Madge, feeling that the woman had the final say in such matters, and Madge was grateful for the advice, knowing that it was so well intended and being in agreement that a family of girls you couldn't marry off was hardly a blessing to a marriage. Madge didn't say so, of course, but to have borne Cora's child as her first one had led her to look forward to the second, her first child being, in everything but name, Cora Atkins's second. Anybody could see it. Nor was it Madge's nature to deceive herself. Some weeks before Mrs. Kibbee discussed the matter with her, Madge was two months pregnant with her second child, not a word on the subject of children having been exchanged with her husband. Need there have been? He would have left it to her. He was like Emerson in the way he would walk and stand at the screen if she had a problem, and hear what she had to say while he gazed at the sky and picked at his teeth.

"You do as you see fit," he'd say, and push the screen open to close the discussion. With a hammer, a saw, and some nails he could build a house, he could measure, consider, and come to decisions, but all matters that he couldn't hammer, saw, and measure he left to her. She was flattered.

"Ned takes care of the outside," she said to Sharon. "He leaves the inside to me." Weeks after Sharon had left she found herself pondering what she had said. It did not please her that Cora might have said the same thing.

"She looks like her father," Cora said of Madge, "but she's not at all like him. She likes to work."

She was slow, and she took her work easy, as she had to, but she liked it. She differed from Cora. Unfinished work weighed so on Cora's mind she might get up at night, or from a nap, to do it. Told to rest, she would reply, "I can't rest while there's work to be done." In that very fact Madge took pleasure. Leaving off at night, or resting during the day, she thought of the unfinished ironing and mending and fruit canning. That it remained to be done reassured her. That it was endless did not depress her. She got up pleased in the knowledge there was work to be done. Ned had bought her a motor-driven washing machine that spared her the drudgery of tub-washing sheets and diapers, but she reserved his shirts and socks for the pleasure it gave her to use the washboard. She liked the sound of it. She liked the feel of it under her knuckles. A new bar of Fels-Naphtha soap seemed as fragrant to her as bread from the oven. She liked to slice it as she did butter. The smell of soap on her hands was not unpleasant. The laundry chore to which she looked eagerly forward was hanging out the wash: the blue-whiteness of sheets stretched on the line, and their sun-dried sweetness when she took them by the armful and squeezed the fragrance into her face. They smelled to her like freshly kneaded dough, or cooling bread. Ironing she kept for evenings, when it was cooler, her board set up in the draft from the back to the front, her skirts pinned up so that it would blow cool on her legs. In the winter, the side blinds drawn, she would take off her dress and iron in her slip, her backside warmed by the hot air from the floor radiator. The glide of the iron, the silken feel of the cloth, the sight and smell of a new scorched patch on the pad (reminding her of Cora) were overlapping pleasures so satisfying she delayed work that she might have finished. While ironing she reviewed the day's events, or lack of events, reflections that might come to her mind at a time when she was not in a position to enjoy them. The scorched odor of the pad was attractive to her, and the strokes of the iron, her mind would pass over and over the wrinkle in her thought till she had smoothed it out. Tilting the iron on its end often signaled a resolution, and the slap of her moistened fingers on its bottom, testing its heat, indicated a fresh beginning. Her own swelling body had its scent which puffed from the dress she stretched on a hanger. She liked to iron without her slippers, enjoying the coolness of the linoleum floor in the summer, and the warmth in the winter, the pipes of the hot-air furnace passing beneath. Ned browsed in the catalogues while she ironed, comparing Ward and Sears Roebuck prices, smearing the heel of his hand with the order forms he had made out with his indelible pencil. She was a help to him in working letters of complaint.

Cooking was a chore that had to be done, but it gave Madge little satisfaction, eating being a chore necessary in the performance of duty. Ned ate without comment, his head over his plate, glancing up to look for something that proved missing: Madge read these glances and handed him the salt, the sugar, the syrup, the butter. She had her own breakfast later, when her hands were free. He was fond of his pancakes hot from the griddle, two at a time. She liked to watch him eat. Watching him eat she first saw his long tangled eyelashes. As well as she knew him she wouldn't think of mentioning it. Every man she knew smoked, or chewed, or both, but Ned did neither. "How come you don't smoke or chew?" she had asked him, the first thing she had liked about him. "I guess I never started up," he replied. As a carpenter he needed his mouth free to hold nails. He hammered one thumbnail so many times it surprised her it wasn't black. She said to him, "Ned, you got just one pair of hands. You go on like this and you'll have just a half pair." He startled her by replying, "Which half you like me to pinch you with?" Actually, it wasn't so unlike him to pinch her, but it was not at all like him to say so. If he caught her stooping he might give her rump a slap, or give a flip to her skirts as she passed the table. "Ned Kibbee!" she would say. "What if your mother saw you?" "She prob'ly did," he replied. "She don't miss much." Most people were ignorant of the playful side to his nature. Sunday afternoons he would lie on the floor and let Blanche crawl over him looking for his head. He could hide it so well the child would get worried. Playing with her father was the only time she smiled. He could give her the hiccups by lowering his head and blowing his hot breath on her belly. "What's she going to think if you keep that up?" Madge joshed him. "She's going to like boys more than girls," he replied.

Nothing more than that was ever said between them on a subject that went unmentioned. Until Ned had made the comment, Madge had had no idea that he was aware she might have options. Did he know what they were? How had he concealed from her such thoughts as he had? She knew so well what he would say before he spoke up this other Ned Kibbee aroused and disturbed her. What might he be thinking? Did he think about all of the things that she did? The way they slept together was acceptable to Madge because it took place in the dark, and required no discussion, but her very consciousness quivered to think that he thought about it in the light of day. When he lifted his eyes to glance at her, might it be on his mind? This alerted her to feeling that she possessed, at the root of her nature, something that she should not surrender, and it was a lucky thing for them both that she felt this the keenest when seven months pregnant. So there was no occasion for her to show reluctance where she had been such a willing accomplice.

Farmhouse near McCook, Nebraska, 1940. Photograph by Wright Morris.
Collections Center for Creative Photography, University of Arizona.
© Arizona Board of Regents.

Source Acknowledgments

All excerpts by Wright Morris are reprinted by permission of the University
of Nebraska Press.

"A Man of Caliber" originally appeared in *Kenyon Review* 11 (Winter 1949):
101–7.

"The Character of the Lover" originally appeared in *American Mercury* 73
(August 1951): 43–49.

The Deep Sleep published by the University of Nebraska Press in 1975.

"Glimpse into Another Country" originally appeared in the *New Yorker*, September 26, 1983.

The Huge Season published by the University of Nebraska Press in 1975.

The Inhabitants published by Scribner, 1946.

In Orbit published by the University of Nebraska Press in 1976.

"Letter to a Young Critic" originally appeared in the *Massachusetts Review* 6,
no. 1 (Autumn 1964): 93–100.

Love Among the Cannibals published by the University of Nebraska Press,
1977.

"Made in U.S.A." originally appeared in *The American Scholar* 29 (Autumn
1960): 483–94.

My Uncle Dudley published by the University of Nebraska Press in 1975.

One Day published by the University of Nebraska Press in 1976.

"The Origin of a Species: 1942–1957" originally appeared in the *Massachusetts Review* 7, no. 1 (Winter 1966): 121–35.

"Our Endless Plains" originally appeared in *Holiday* 24 (July 1958): 68–69,
138–43.

Plains Song: For Female Voices published by the University of Nebraska Press,
2000.

"The Question of Privacy" is from *Time Pieces: Photographs, Writing, and Memory* (New York: Aperture, 1989); it was originally published in a different form in *Magazine of Art* 44 (February, 1951): 51–55.

"The Ram in the Thicket" originally appeared in *Harper's Bazaar* 82 (May 1948): 133, 182–94.

"The Rites of Spring" originally appeared in *New World Writing* #1 (New York: New American Library, 1953), 140–45.

"The Safe Place" originally appeared in *Kenyon Review* 16 (Autumn 1954): 587–99.

"The Sound Tape" originally appeared in *Harper's Bazaar* 85 (May 1951): 125, 175–77.

"Technique and Raw Material" originally appeared in *The Territory Ahead* (New York: Harcourt, Brace, 1957).

"Wake Before Bomb" originally appeared in *Esquire* 52 (December 1959): 311–15.

Will's Boy: A Memoir was published by New York: Harper & Row in 1981.

A version of "The American Land, Character, and Dream in the Works of Wright Morris" by David Madden originally appeared in *Wright Morris* (New York: Twayne, 1964).

"'No Place to Hide': Biographical Backgrounds" by Joseph J. Wydeven originally appeared in a different form as "'No Place to Hide': Biographical and Critical Backgrounds" in *Wright Morris Revisited* (New York: Twayne, 1998).

Further Reading Suggestions

COMPILED BY JOSEPH J. WYDEVEN

Adams, Timothy Dow. "The Mirror without a Memory: Wright Morris." In *Light Writing & Life Writing: Photography in Autobiography*. Chapel Hill: University of North Carolina Press, 2000. Discussion of Wright Morris's "complicated intertextuality" and the autobiographical basis of much of his work.

Alinder, James. "Introduction." *Wright Morris: Photographs & Words*. Carmel CA: Friends of Photography, 1982, 7–11. Brief overview of Morris's career as a photographer. The book has sixty-one fine laser-scan reproductions of Morris's photographs.

Arnold, Marilyn. "Wright Morris's *Plains Song*: Woman's Search for Harmony." *South Dakota Review* 20 (Autumn 1982): 50–62. Fine close reading of Morris's final novel, focused on Sharon's reconciliation with Cora and the sexuality she rejected as a young woman.

Baumbach, Jonathan. "Wake Before Bomb: *Ceremony in Lone Tree* by Wright Morris." In *The Landscape of Nightmare: Studies in the Contemporary American Novel*. New York: New York University Press, 1965. Analysis of Morris's "comic despair," his use of acts of violence to indicate social impotence, and Boyd as "conscience."

Bird, Roy K. *Wright Morris: Memory and Imagination*. New York: Peter Lang, 1985. Revised dissertation, emphasizing Morris's deliberate intrusions into his photographs and texts, and his careful merging of memory and imagination, technique, and raw material.

Booth, Wayne C. "The Two Worlds in the Fiction of Wright Morris." *Sewanee Review* 65 (Summer 1957): 375–99. Early influential essay explaining

Morris as a Platonic dualist attempting in his novels to escape the mundane world through heroism, the imagination, and love.

Carlisle, Olga, and Jodie Ireland. "Wright Morris: The Art of Fiction CXXV." *Paris Review* 33 (Fall 1991): 52–94. Informative though long overdue interview with the novelist and photographer.

Crump, G. B. *The Novels of Wright Morris: A Critical Interpretation.* Lincoln: University of Nebraska Press, 1978. Crucial examination of Morris's themes of immanence and transcendence in the novels through *A Life*.

———. "Wright Morris: Author in Hiding." *Western American Literature* 25 (May 1990): 3–14. Focus on the "the hidden child" in Morris's novels and autobiographical works.

Halter, Peter. "Distance and Desire: Wright Morris' *The Home Place* as 'Photo-Text.'" *Etudes Textuelles* 4 (October–December 1990): 65–89. One of the best essays on *The Home Place*, and on the tension between "distance and desire, separation and identification" in Morris's and his protagonist's reaction to the rural environment.

Hicks, Granville. "Introduction." In *Wright Morris: A Reader.* New York: Harper and Row, 1970, ix–xxxiii. Appreciative introduction to Morris and to a judicious selection of some major moments in Morris's fiction. Hicks surveys Morris's life and fictional effects under the headings "Places," "People," "Things," "Shapes," "Words," and "Ideas."

———. "Wright Morris." In *Literary Horizons: A Quarter Century of American Fiction.* New York: New York University Press, 1970. 7–47. Ten reprinted appreciative reviews of Morris's books, from *The Works of Love* to *A Bill of Rites, A Bill of Wrongs, A Bill of Goods.*

Hollander, John. "The Figure on the Page: Words and Images in Wright Morris's *The Home Place.*" *Yale Journal of Criticism* 9 (Spring 1996): 93–108. Brief appreciation of Morris's photo-text practice in relation to his use of Henry James.

Howard, Leon. *Wright Morris.* University of Minnesota Pamphlets on American Writers 69. Minneapolis: University of Minnesota Press, 1968. Examination of Morris's search for meaning in American life. A professor of Morris's at Pomona College, Howard appreciates Morris's honesty and his sympathy for the comic human condition.

Knoll, Robert E., ed. *Conversations with Wright Morris: Critical Views and Responses.* Lincoln: University of Nebraska Press, 1977. Includes essays on and interviews with Morris by John W. Aldridge, Wayne C. Booth, Peter Bunnell, and David Madden when Morris was writer in residence at the University of Nebraska in 1975. Excellent bibliography through 1975, compiled by Robert L. Boyce.

Longmire, Stephen. "Picture a Life: The Photo-texts of Wright Morris." PhD dissertation, University of Chicago, 2010. Critical and biographical examination of all the photo-texts, from the perspective of a practicing photographer.

——. "Wright Morris: Reinventing a Photographer." *Afterimage: The Journal of Media Arts and Cultural Criticism* 30, no. 3–4 (Winter 2003): 10–12. Superb analytical review essay clarifying Morris's interest and practice of photography and photo-text. Thorough and reliable.

Madden, David. "Character as Revealed Cliché in Wright Morris's Fiction." *Midwest Quarterly* 22 (Summer 1981): 319–36. Examination of Morris's deliberate reinvigoration and transformation of clichés in his style and creation of character.

——. "Wright Morris's *In Orbit*: An Unbroken Series of Poetic Gestures." In *The Poetic Image in Six Genres*. Carbondale: Southern Illinois University Press, 1969. Superb essay, putting *In Orbit* into perspective in Morris's canon, appreciative of both the novel's "poetic immediacy" and Morris's comic but "frightening" commentary on American disorder.

——. *Wright Morris*. New York: Twayne, 1964. The first full-length study of Morris; still important for the work through *Cause for Wonder*.

Neinstein, Raymond I. "Wright Morris: The Metaphysics of Home." *Prairie Schooner* 53 (Summer 1979): 121–54. Probing analysis of most of the Nebraska works, including discussion of the photo-texts. Superb on the tensions between prose and photograph, author and character, nostalgia and nausea, and the expectations of viewer and reader.

Phillips, Sandra S. "Words & Pictures." In *Wright Morris: Origin of a Species*. San Francisco: Museum of Modern Art, 1992. 23–32. Rich biographical account focusing on Morris as a maker of photo-texts, "an indirect Midwestern way to tackle intimate emotion."

Rice, Rodney P. "Photographing the Ruins: Wright Morris and Midwestern Gothic." *MidAmerica* 25 (1998): 128–54. Connects Morris's photographs and photo-texts to "the larger romantic tradition."

——. "Wright Morris and the Poetics of Intimate Space: Photographing the Material Imagination." *Texas Review* 19 (Spring–Summer 1998): 45–62. Study of Morris's photography employing the phenomenology of Gaston Bachelard's poetics of space.

Szarkowski, John. "Wright Morris the Photographer." In *Wright Morris: Origin of a Species*. San Francisco Museum of Modern Art, 1992. 9–21. Appreciative analysis of Morris's subtleties, interests, and complexities, by an important champion of Morris's photography.

Trachtenberg, Alan. "Wright Morris: American Photographer." In *Distinctly American: The Photography of Wright Morris*. London: Merrell, in association with the Iris and B. Gerald Cantor Center for Visual Art at Stanford University, 2002. Important essay introducing the Morris collection at the Cantor Center and eighty fine photograph reproductions throughout the text.

———. "Home Place." *Raritan* 267 (Summer 2006): 64–87. Appreciative, accessible examination of Morris's photo-text novel, *The Home Place*.

———. "Wright Morris's 'Photo-Texts.'" *Yale Journal of Criticism* 9 (Spring 1996): 109–119. Perceptive appreciation and analysis of Morris's photographs as "endlessly generative" of narrative texts, in contrast to Walker Evans's more culturally "historical" approach.

Westerbeck, Colin S., Jr. "American Graphic: The Photography and Fiction of Wright Morris." In *Multiple Views: Logan Grant Essays on Photography, 1983–89*, edited by Daniel P. Younger, 271–302. Albuquerque: University of New Mexico Press, 1991. Excellent essay on Morris's photography in relation to his fiction, finding in *The Home Place*, for example, a strategy of deliberate counterpoint that relates "absence to presence" in both narrative and visual terms. Rich readings of several photographs.

Wright Morris: Structures and Artifacts, Photographs 1933–1954. Lincoln NE: Sheldon Memorial Art Gallery, 1975. Published in conjunction with the exhibition *Wright Morris: Structures and Artifacts, Photographs 1933–1954*, curated by James Alinder, at the Sheldon Memorial Art Gallery, University of Nebraska, October 21–November 16, 1975. Alinder also contributed an interview with Morris.

Wydeven, Joseph J. "Myth and Melancholy: Wright Morris's Stories of Old Age." *Weber Studies: An Interdisciplinary Humanities Journal* 12 (Winter 1995): 36–47. An exploration of Morris's later short stories, particularly "Glimpse into Another Country."

———. "'No Place to Hide': Wright Morris's Great Plains." *Great Plains Quarterly* 21 (Fall 2001): 287–308. Discussion of themes and motifs in Morris's Nebraska novels and photographs.

———. *Wright Morris Revisited*. New York: Twayne, 1998. The most recent book-length critical study of Morris's works and career, published shortly after Morris's death. Focuses on Morris's "dual artistic preoccupations" and includes a small portfolio of Morris's photographs.